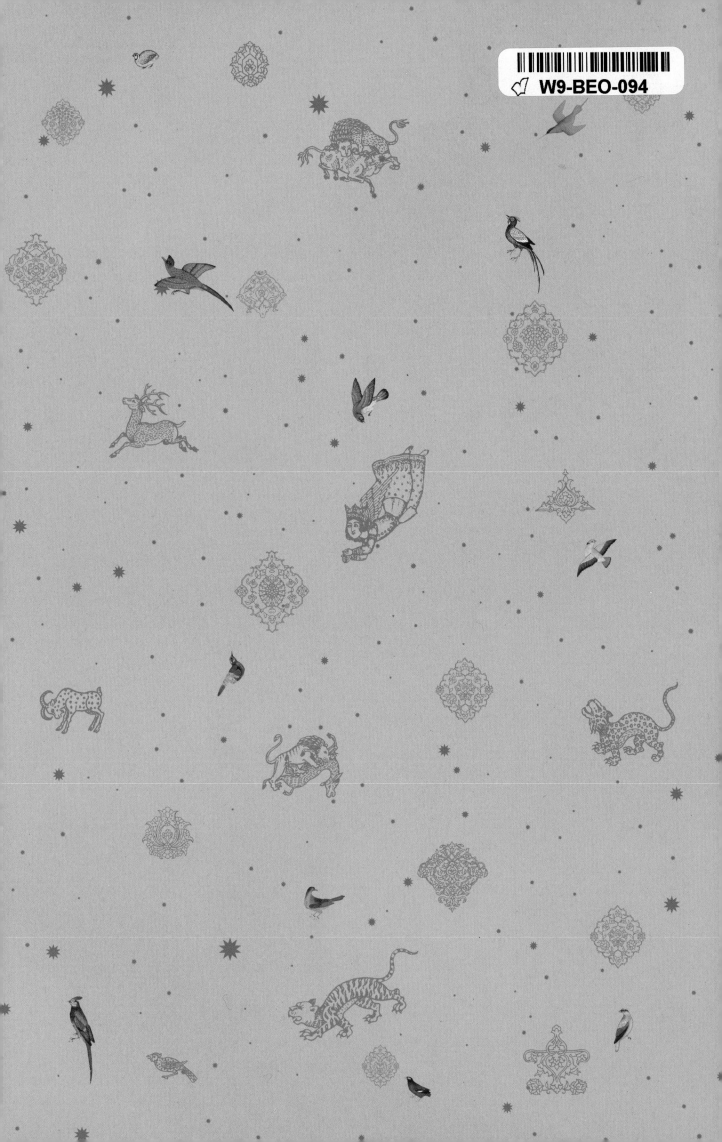

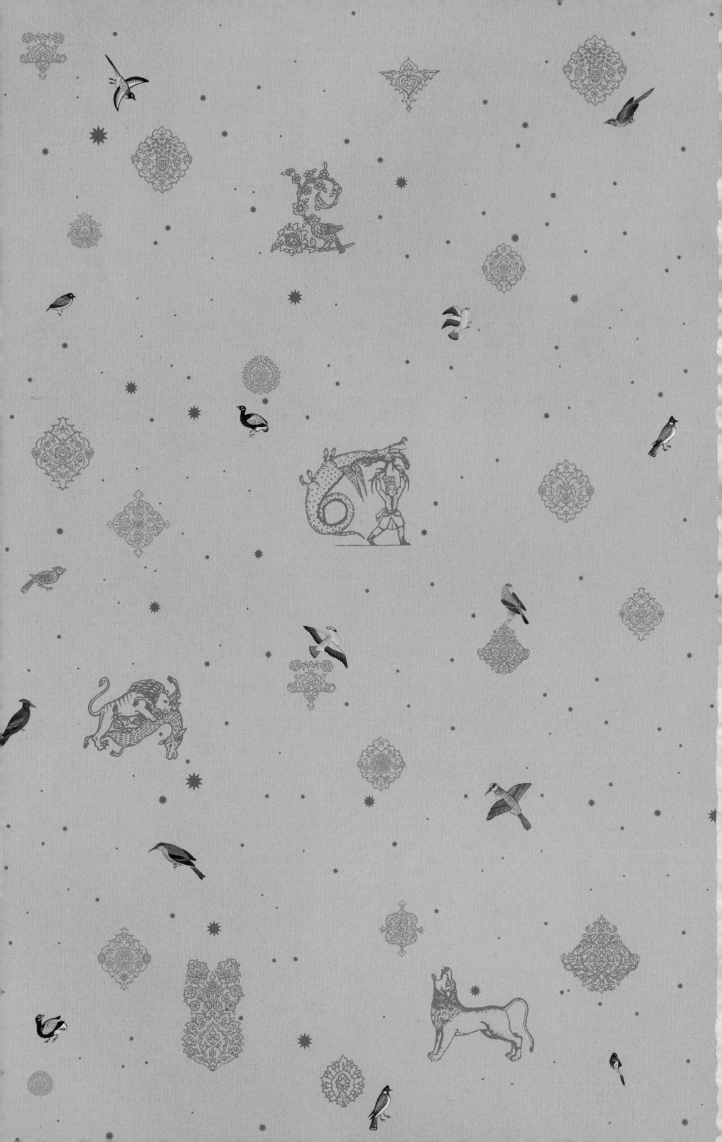

Shahnameh

The Epic of the Persian Kings

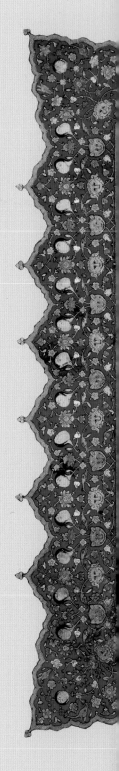

Shahnameh

THE EPIC OF THE PERSIAN KINGS

✦ Ferdowsi ✦

Illustrations & Design
Hamid Rahmanian

Translation & Adaptation
Ahmad Sadri

Editorial Director
Melissa Hibbard

Foreword by
Sheila Canby

THE QUANTUCK LANE PRESS
NEW YORK

Manufacturing through Asia-Pacific Offset
Printed in China

Library of Congress Cataloging-in-Publication Data
Sadri, Ahmad.
 Shahnameh : the epic of the Persian kings / Abolqasem Ferdowsi ;
illustrated by Hamid Rahmanian ; translated & adapted {to prose}
by Ahmad Sadri ; foreword by Sheila Canby.
   p. cm.
 ISBN 978-1-59372-051-3
 1. Firdawsi. Shahnamah—Adaptations. I. Firdawsi. Shahnamah.
II. Title.
 PK6562.29.A83S43 2013
 813'.6—dc23   2012034354

The Quantuck Lane Press, New York

www.quantucklanepress.com

Distributed by
W. W. Norton & Company
500 Fifth Avenue, New York, NY 10110
www.wwnorton.com

W. W. Norton & Company Ltd.
Castle House, 75/76 Wells Street
London, WIT 3QT

2 3 4 5 6 7 8 9

For those who seek beauty

and for Sophie

Contents

Acknowledgments

I would like to thank my partner, Melissa Hibbard, who was the inspiration and driving force behind this book.

My sincere gratitude goes to Dr. Ahmad Sadri for his masterful translation and adaptation of the poems. It was truly a pleasure working with him.

I also want to thank Mark Sloan at The Halsey Institute of Contemporary Art, who believed in this book from its beginning and who never left me alone, and Ram Devineni from Rattapallax, who helped me at every step. I would also like to thank Bita Shafipour and her parents, Hamid Shafipour and Fereshteh Amin, who are the flag holders of this *Shahnameh* and whose generous support helped me achieve the impossible.

I am grateful for the devotion of James Mairs and Austin O'Driscoll at The Quantuck Lane Press for believing in this endeavor and publishing this edition of the *Shahnameh*.

I would like to thank Milad Aramnia, Janet Byrne, Erica Ehrenberg, Majid Fadaeian, Sina Gudarzi, Mahsa Hakimi, Farhad Hakimzadeh, Koosha Hashemi, Don Kennison, Meredith Moore, Mani Nilchiani, Sourena Parham, and Jackie Zhu, whose contributions were invaluable, and the late Dr. Jafar Mahjoub, who taught me how to appreciate *Shahnameh*.

Special thanks go to Sudabeh Rahmanian and Mohammad Farshchi for emotional support and to my parents, Esmael and Akram, who are no longer here to see the completion of this project.

The production of this book was made possible with the generous support of the following individuals:

Hamid Shafipour & Fereshteh Amin
Mark Amin
Ali & Mojgan Amin
Michael & Shirin Amin
Farshid & Guila Zanjani
Farhad Mohit
Farhad Shamtoub
Saeed & Samira Amidi
Farid & Afsaneh Falsafi
Nasser David Havarim
Isaac & Angela Larian
Leon & Firoozeh J. Neman
Pouya & Pantea Shafipour

And with the support of the following organizations:

Aeen e Iran Society, Los Angeles
American Institute of Iranian Studies
Bijan & Soraya Amin Foundation
B. T. Manufacturing, Inc.
Primex International
Rattapallax, Inc.
World Unity Organization
Zero 1 Derfurl Trust

Additional help was provided by:

Farrokh Abolfathi, Ruben Abrams, Kourosh Aframian, Ali Reza Vatankhah & Farzaneh Amin, Nosrat Raji Amin, Ladan Behnia, Mahmoud Farahani, Shahrzad & Albert Hakimi, Marjaneh Halati, Stephanie McAndrew, David Mesri, Nahid Salim, Neman Brothers & Assoc., Inc., Kayhan S. Shakib, Ali Razi, Khashayar Hadipour & Negar Tabandeh, and Celeste Vardaman.

Foreword

Shahnameh: The Epic of the Persian Kings is the latest in a long tradition of illustrated texts of the Persian national epic. From the early fourteenth century, paintings of the most colorful and dramatic episodes in Ferdowsi's poem accompanied the written text. At first, the manuscripts were small and their illustrations appeared in bands across part of the written page. Even then artists did not hesitate to break through the frame and extend pictorial elements into the margins. By the 1330s royal and noble patrons were commissioning large-scale *Shahnameh* manuscripts with illustrations that were more complex in both their composition and the interaction of the figures than the earlier versions. In the fifteenth century the production of illustrated *Shahnamehs* increased, ranging from the most outstanding princely manuscript made for the grandson of Timur (Tamerlane) in Herat in 1430 to the numerous Turkmen-style manuscripts from Shiraz created to satisfy the growing market for such books. Illustrated *Shahnamehs* were not produced for Iranians alone, but were exported to the Ottoman Empire and India, where they inspired copies with paintings in the prevailing style of the region. The tradition of opulent royal *Shahnamehs* persisted in the sixteenth century, notably under Shah Tahmasp whose manuscript contained 258 remarkable illustrations. Although at times interest in illustrated *Shahnamehs* waned, the epic remained central to the poetic education of Persian-speakers. Even in the nineteenth century, when court artists were busy painting in oil on canvas or in lacquer on boxes and book covers, the new art of lithography was applied to illustrating the *Shahnameh*.

Hamid Rahmanian's new volume incorporates images that span the history of *Shahnameh* illustration, excerpting and weaving together figures familiar from many of the greatest manuscripts. Recognizing how broadly dispersed are the people in whose culture the *Shahnameh* plays a significant role,

Rahmanian has employed the modern technology of the filmmaker and graphic artist to produce images that will appeal to a modern audience. Anyone who has read the *Shahnameh* realizes that it is far from an iteration of battles; its stories involve love and luck, dreams and demons, prowess and political intrigue. In fact, the gamut of human emotion appears in the *Shahnameh*.

As in the *Shahnamehs* of past centuries, this book's many illustrations do more than translate the narrative episode into visual form. Rather, the illustrations and text enable a reader to contemplate the thoughts and actions of the protagonists while poring over the recombined details of a variety of earlier *Shahnameh* images. Many of the illustrations contain colors that recall those in Persian miniatures, but they have been intensified in keeping with a modern, cinematic sensibility. Likewise, the dynamic silhouetting of pictorial details mitigates the stylization of the earlier paintings that make up the compositions in this book. The varying scale of figures within individual illustrations breaks the conventions of earlier miniature painting, but for the modern viewer this corresponds to the distortions one finds, for example, in science fiction. In fact, the dreamscape of the real and imaginary worlds found in the illustrations of this *Shahnameh*, while totally dependent on the art of the past, most closely evokes the fantasy literature of today in visual form. Thanks to the dramatic dynamism of Ferdowsi's epic, its contemporary interpretation in images is a vibrant feast for the imagination, making this a *Shahnameh* for the digital age.

 Sheila Canby, Metropolitan Museum of Art

Preface

A little over a thousand years ago a Persian poet named Ferdowsi of Tous collected and put into heroic verse the millennium-old mythological and epic traditions of Iran. He called his sixty-thousand-verse tome *Shahnameh* (The Book of Kings). However, long before Ferdowsi's epic there existed a tradition of depicting the folklore of the Iranian plateau. This tradition grew with the *Shahnameh* and reached its zenith in the seventeenth century. The art form lost momentum over a century ago and has not been illustrated since, except in a few sporadic folios.

It is in this long tradition that I have created the illustrations for this new edition of *Shahnameh*. It is important to mention that I approached this work from a purely artistic perspective. It was my aim to revive this historic art form that sits at the center of Iranian visual culture. This effort has been made with the utmost respect to the master painters and illuminators whose names have been lost in the mist of history but whose pages still inspire awe. It was my desire to introduce this legacy to a new audience.

In this edition I have illustrated themes that have not been depicted before, not only nightmares and dreams but also plots such as the birth of Shaghad and the occultation of King Kay Khosrow.

Mixing old traditions and modern technology, I have tried to create a new *Shahnameh* in a dynamic way that would appeal to both those familiar with the stories as well as those unfamiliar with the mythology of Iran.

Hamid Rahmanian

Translator's Note

The ancient legends of the Persian Book of Kings (*Shahnameh*)[1] were versified by Abolqasem Ferdowsi (940–1020 CE), who was born to a family of small landowners near the city of Tus, in northeastern Iran. He dedicated thirty-three years of his life to *Shahnameh* and finished its second redaction one thousand and three years ago, in March 1010.

Shahnameh is of the essence of Iranian nationhood. Unlike the Egyptian, Syrian, and other North African populations of the Roman Empire that were thoroughly Arabized after their Islamic conquest in the seventh century, Persians were able to hold on to their language and calendar even after they converted to Islam. It has been argued that this was made possible because the Iranians' national identity was not fully invested in their pre-Islamic faith. Rather, it resided in a secular body of myth and legend that they preserved and which later would form the basis of Ferdowsi's great work. To this day men, women, and children in Persianate societies from Asia Minor to China are able to recite lines of *Shahnameh* by heart. The book continues to be read in family gatherings and performed by professional reciters in the teahouses of Tajikistan, Iran, and Afghanistan.

It was awareness of this living tradition of *Shahnameh* recitations that gave me and my colleagues Melissa Hibbard and Hamid Rahmanian the audacity to go where angels fear to tread. As we embarked on the journey to create a new edition of Iran's national epic with freshly narrated stories printed against a fully illustrated backdrop, we consoled ourselves that we were walking in the footsteps of generations of previous performers and illustrators.

I never forgot the first reciter of *Shahnameh* I saw at the age of seven somewhere near the city of Karaj. He wore a leather vest studded with shiny spikes and wielded a short cane that was his only prop. That lone cane turned into a sword, a mace, and even the neck of a neighing horse. The performer paced rapidly back and forth producing a range of sound effects for galloping horses, clashing swords, and collapsing rocks. He sonorously intoned the poems of *Shahnameh* in the middle of his prose narration as he played all of the parts from the last scenes of the battle of Rostam and Sohrab. What is remarkable is that I still remember not only the performance but also the pictures I made in my head as it went on. The session ended with a cliffhanger as the hero Rostam climbed a pile of rocks, put his neck in a self-made noose, and kicked the rocks from beneath him to commit suicide. Later I learned that this final scene was not in any of the known copies of *Shahnameh*. But the knowledge did not diminish the worth of that performance because I also knew that the stories existed and evolved both before and after the completion of Ferdowsi's magnum opus.

Editorial Philosophy

We are fortunate to live in the age of masterfully prepared critical editions of *Shahnameh*: the nine-volume Moscow edition and the eight-volume Khaleghi Motlagh edition have been the main sources of this rendition.[2] These editions relegate some parts of the *Shahnameh* to the category of "additional stories," that is, the parts that might have been added after the final redaction of *Shahnameh* in 1010. Of course, there is always a possibility that these stories might have been in the original copy given the fact that one sixth of the *Shahnameh* (ten thousand out of sixty thousand lines of poetry) is missing from all the extant copies.

In this rendition we have included some of these additional stories if they seemed to support the structure or the flow of the narrative. For instance, the adventures of Rostam as a young man (conquering an enemy castle and killing a rogue elephant) have been included in our version as they help set up the character of the hero before his first battle with Afrasiab. In a similar vein the character of Sohrab's maternal uncle (Zende Razm) and later the birth of Foroud in the story of Siavosh have been included because they appear to complement the structure of these stories. On a couple of occasions the sequence of events has been slightly altered for the sake of a smoother narrative.

The aim of this band of *Shahnameh* performers has been to tell an engaging and character-based story for a savvy generation that has read and seen movie renditions of such modern legends as *Star Wars* and *The Lord of the Rings*. This volume contains the first two thirds of the *Shahnameh*, that is, the brief mythological opening (the first chapter on Primordial Kings) and the epic body of the work that starts with the reign of King Feraydun and ends with the death of Rostam and the demise of his clan. The last third of the poem, which covers the history of the Sassanid dynasty and ends with the Arab conquest of Iran, is not included in this volume.

We agreed that the story should be told with relentless economy. Only persons with speaking lines have been named in this book but once a character is introduced we have followed him or her adding as much psychological depth and human interest as we could squeeze from the text. I should especially thank Melissa Hibbard for cracking her directorial whip whenever the academic in me would pause to longingly eye the textured pastures of the obscure. After all, we had a story to advance.

The Author's Voice, the Translator's Foregrounding

Unlike Homer, Ferdowsi does not claim to be possessed by a muse. Our author's sober voice brackets every story with moral and philosophical commentary and it occasionally breaks through the narrative, in the manner of a Greek chorus, to offer lessons that might be drawn from the action. Nor is Ferdowsi above using his authorial voice to complain of his poverty and the indignities of old age or to express his worries about finishing the *Shahnameh*. It is as if the poet is deliberately humanizing himself to counter the larger-than-life ideal image some would later build for him. To offer the reader a flavor of the original text I have included these interventions. Ferdowsi's own voice has been rendered in verse to set it apart from his narrative.

The translator of an ancient text cannot claim to be entirely objective about the task he undertakes. Changes of intellectual and historical horizons over the past millennium have been enormous. It is with the awareness of these differences that we read the text with our own questions of gender, race, and nationality. *Shahnameh* fares remarkably well for a thousand-year-old text on all these accounts.

Rudabeh, Tahmineh, and Manizheh, the heroines of the epic *Shahnameh*'s love stories, aggressively initiate romance and succeed in their sexual conquest of the enemy. The word "enemy" is chosen advisedly as all of these stories occur across national boundaries. Switching to the question of race and nationality it is noteworthy that the iconic hero of *Shahnameh*, Rostam, is not a blueblood Iranian. He is born to a mother descended from a hated Arab serpent king and a father who was born with white hair and was cast out on the suspicion that he was demonic. The man who committed this outrage was an exalted Iranian knight (Pahlavan) named Saum. He, like many others in his rank (e.g., Tous, Gorgin, and Rostam), is portrayed as a heroic if flawed character.[3]

Nor are all Iranian kings exalted in *Shahnameh*. Two kings lose their divine halo and their thrones to hubris and indolence. One king is so foolish and irascible that he is repeatedly excoriated by his knights and another is so corrupted by lust for power that he sends his crown prince to certain death to prolong his reign. Incidentally, the king who approaches the ideal of an excellent ruler is far from a full-blooded Iranian.

The nationalistic epic of Iran treats its archenemy, Turan, with surprising sensitivity and insight. To be sure there are some evil Turanians who deserve their vilification. King Afrasiab and his scheming brother Garsivaz top that list. Afrasiab's other brother, however, shields a group of Iranian captives from mass execution at the expense of his life. The Turanian field marshal Piran is portrayed as an impeccable soldier and a moral man who is respected by kings of both Iran and Turan. The touching scene of his demise and the eulogy offered at his funeral by the king of Iran make up one of the most beautiful passages of the *Shahnameh*.

The Vision

We have had a dream: to infuse the popular imagination of the English-speaking world with the legends of *Shahnameh*. We have labored with the hope to one day encounter someone who knows the intrepid heroines of the *Shahnameh*'s love stories through our work. All this labor will have been worthwhile should we hear one day that the four sweeping and increasingly human-centered tragedies of Sohrab, Siavosh, Forud, and Esfandiar have become as familiar to some as those of Oedipus, Hector, Hamlet, and Lear.

Ahmad Sadri

NOTES

1. These legends had been gathered in several volumes known as *Khoday Nameh* and Ferdowsi had access to the most complete of these volumes that had been commissioned by one of his contemporary kings. It is this volume that was Ferdowsi's main source.

2. *Shahnameh*, Abolqasem Ferdowsi, based on the Moscow edition, ed. Dr. Saeed Hamidian (Tehran: Nashr-e Ghatreh, 1997). *Shahnameh*, Abolqasem Ferdowsi, ed. Jalal Khaleghi Motlagh (Tehran: Center for the Islamic Encyclopedia, 2011).

3. In the current Persian usage Pahlavan refers to a man of prodigious size and power—most commonly a traditional wrestler. But in the world of *Shahnameh* Pahlavans were not just powerful warriors. They were knights who were given their own territories by the king, wore ceremonial golden boots, and sat on their regional thrones in their own torques and crowns. At the time of war these knights commandeered armies and came to fight for their king. Many scholars believe that most of the epic stories of the *Shahnameh* refer to the Arsacid dynasty (250 BC–224 CE) where central authority of the king was counterbalanced with a confederation of the lesser warlords. There are indeed two Arsacid kings who bear the name of Gutarzes (95–90 BC and 40–51 CE). This name is recorded as Gudarz who is one of the knights in the *Shahnameh*.

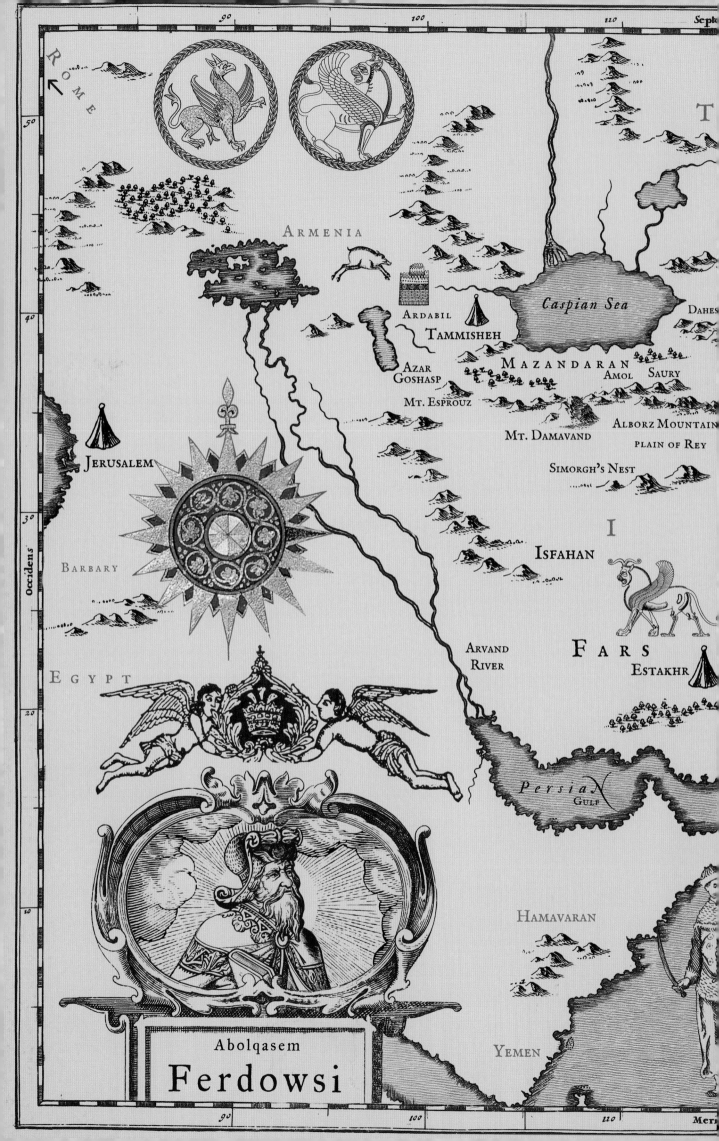

ROME

ARMENIA

Caspian Sea

DAHES

ARDABIL
TAMMISHEH

MAZANDARAN

AZAR
GOSHASP

AMOL   SAURY

MT. ESPROUZ

ALBORZ MOUNTAIN

MT. DAMAVAND

PLAIN OF REY

JERUSALEM

SIMORGH'S NEST

BARBARY

I

ISFAHAN

EGYPT

FARS

ARVAND
RIVER

ESTAKHR

Persian
GULF

HAMAVARAN

YEMEN

Occidens

Abolqasem
Ferdowsi

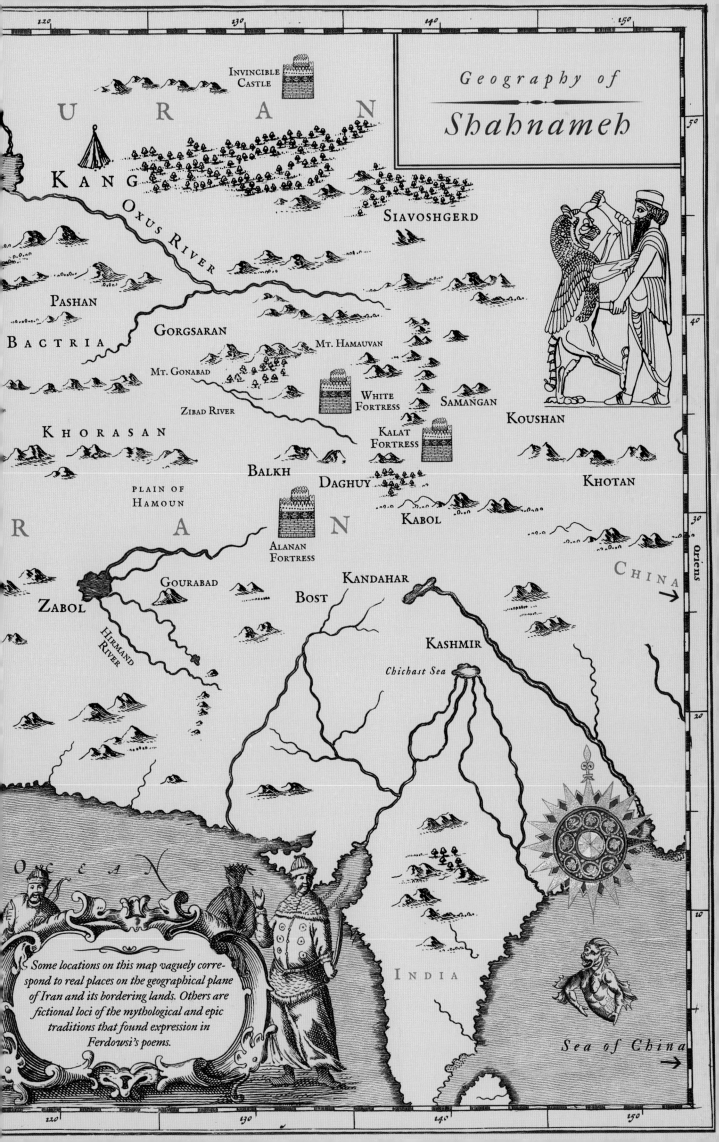

Geography of *Shahnameh*

URAN

KANG

INVINCIBLE CASTLE

OXUS RIVER

SIAVOSHGERD

PASHAN

BACTRIA

GORGSARAN

MT. HAMAUVAN

MT. GONABAD

WHITE FORTRESS

SAMANGAN

ZIBAD RIVER

KOUSHAN

KHORASAN

KALAT FORTRESS

BALKH

DAGHUY

KHOTAN

PLAIN OF HAMOUN

KABOL

IRAN

ALANAN FORTRESS

GOURABAD

KANDAHAR

CHINA

BOST

ZABOL

HIRMAND RIVER

KASHMIR

Chichast Sea

OCEAN

INDIA

Some locations on this map vaguely correspond to real places on the geographical plane of Iran and its bordering lands. Others are fictional loci of the mythological and epic traditions that found expression in Ferdowsi's poems.

Sea of China

Oriens

In the name of the God of life and wisdom, the sublime
Entity that conceived us but can't be conceived and in the name
Of the one who is beyond our ken and above our space and time.

In the name of the invisible maker of the moon, the sun
And the constellations who gave us wisdom to eschew evil
And enjoined us to acquire knowledge and pass it on.

Ponder these tales but don't call them fables or lies
Some of them conform to our reason while others
Are truths that come to us in disguise.

The Kings of Yore:
Kayumars to Zahhak

No one knows for sure how the first kingships began
Or who was the first man to wear the crown of sovereignty
But the forefathers have related the tales of one such man.

The First King, Kayumars

As the sun entered the constellation of Aries and the world rejoiced in the glory of spring, a man by the name of Kayumars ascended the throne of the world and started his rule. He took residence in the mountains with his companions, wore the skin of a leopard, and inaugurated the customs of

preparing food. He was tall as a cypress and his face shone with the halo of divine sanction like a full moon. Animals of the world, both carnivore and herbivore, humbled themselves at his threshold and pledged their obedience. He reigned for thirty years.

The king had no enemies in the world but for the archdevil, the source of all darkness in the universe, Ahriman. Rankled by envy of the new king, Ahriman hatched a plot with his son to crush Kayumars. Khazuran was the name of that son, and he resembled a fearsome wolf. Crowds of demons flocked to Khazuran.

Kayumars had a wise and handsome son named Siamak whom he adored. He cried with joy to see his son and dreaded being separated from him. The angel Sorush appeared to Siamak and told him that the forces of the devil were on the move. Siamak was stirred to anger and gathered an army to stand against Khazuran. The prince wore only a leopard skin, as armor did not exist yet. He went forth to wrestle with the fearsome son of Ahriman. But Khazuran threw Siamak on the ground and mauled him to death.

When Kayumars heard what had happened, he fell off his throne, lacerating his face and crying tears of blood. The army and all creatures, both man and beast, came to share in their king's sorrows. After a year of grief the angel Sorush appeared to the king and commanded him to stop mourning and prepare to avenge his son's death.

Kayumars was getting old and the world needed a new leader. He decided to entrust the command of the war of revenge to Siamak's son, a lad by the name of Hushang. King Kayumars stood at the heart of the army as Hushang

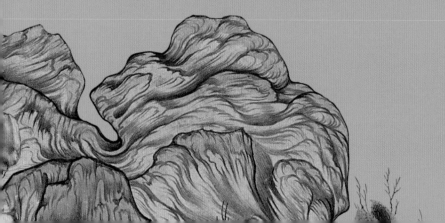

led the charge. His army consisted of men, fairies, and tame beasts as well as leopards and wolves. The black demon Khazuran fearlessly led his army, raising a great cloud of dust. The battle was joined. The two sides fought hard and at the end the demons were defeated. Hushang took Khazuran by the neck, ripped his hide, cut off his head, and threw his lifeless body on the ground. Having triumphed over his father's killers, Hushang went back to his grandfather and reported his victory. Kayumars was happy and, when he died, he was content that Siamak's death had been avenged.

Kayumars's reign ended but his reputation remained.
Sorrows and pleasures of this life vanish in time
Leaving behind only the good name one has gained.

The Second King, Hushang

Hushang ascended the throne after his grandfather and declared himself the king of the seven realms. During the forty years of his reign Hushang spread justice and enriched the world as he was commanded to do so by God. He melted iron and inaugurated the use of instruments such as hatchets, axes, saws, and maces. But all of these new inventions were made possible only after he accidentally discovered the secret of making fire.

During a hunting expedition Hushang saw a snake slithering in a cleavage of rocks. He took a piece of flint and threw it at the head of the snake. The missile missed its target, but the flint hit the rock face and a spark flew. Thus Hushang learned how to make a spark into a flame, and that night he made a bonfire and drank with his companions in celebration of his new discovery. He was the first to celebrate the Persian festival of Sadeh, which occurs on the fortieth day of winter.

Having mastered the element of fire, Hushang embarked on conquering the water by teaching people to irrigate their crops. It was Hushang who pioneered the art of making bread out of the harvested seeds. He also trained men to hunt wild beasts for their meat and pelts and to domesticate animals.

Hushang was a great king who avenged his father and made the world a better place, but he, too, succumbed to death, the common fate of all humans.

The Third King, Tahmures

After Hushang, his son Tahmures ascended the throne and ruled for forty years. At the outset of his reign Tahmures declared that he would disclose what was beneficial but hidden and that he would cleanse the world of evil. Tahmures taught people the secrets of breeding new and stronger animals as well as the arts of shearing, spinning, and weaving wool. It was by his skill that cheetahs and falcons were tamed to help man in hunting.

Above all, Tahmures subdued the demons, killing two-thirds of them and imprisoning the rest. That is how he earned the title of Demon Binder.

Some of the demons pleaded with Tahmures, saying that they would teach him an art with many benefits if he would let them live.

Tahmures gave them leave to reveal their secrets, and, lo, they taught him the art of writing in thirty languages, including Roman, Chinese, Arabic, and Persian.

For thirty years he lived and spread his knowledge of the arts, until it came time for him to die. Thus the demon binder king was succeeded by his son, the magnificent King Jamshid.

The Fourth King, Jamshid

Jamshid wore the crown of his father and declared himself both priest and king. The world took refuge in his protection and all submitted to him, including the birds of the sky, demons, and fairies. Jamshid charmed the iron and fashioned armor for both man and warhorses. He established the tradition whereby champions were encouraged to taunt their enemies and seek glory on the battlefield.

Among the important inventions of King Jamshid was his creation of social classes. He divided the people into four castes: the priests, the warriors, the farmers, and the artisans. Each profession was given its exclusive purpose. For fifty years the king allowed the four vocations to take root.

Jamshid allotted the next fifty years of his reign to building. He dragooned the demons to fashion mud into bricks and mix water with plaster in order to build palaces and bathhouses. They also carved blocks from boulders of granite in accordance with the rules of geometric design to erect magnificent buildings. Then the king mined gold, silver, and precious stones such as rubies and amber. He extracted and refined perfumes including camphor, musk, ambergris, and rosewater.

It was Jamshid who founded the field of medicine. And it was he who built ships and crossed watery passages that separate the realms of the world. These labors that contributed to human civilization consumed another fifty years of Jamshid's reign.

When all this was accomplished, the exalted Jamshid built a jewel-encrusted throne with the aid of his divine sanction. The throne was held aloft by demons and fairies whenever the king wished. When his throne was lifted to the heavens, Jamshid looked radiant upon the sky like the shining sun. The world gathered to behold the king in wonderment and rained on him a shower of gems. One such day coincided with the first day of spring. All praised Jamshid on his high throne. The day was given the name Nowruz, and it was made the eve of the Persian New Year.

The olden kings gave us the gift of a peaceful holiday.
Calling for wine and musicians at the onset of spring
They forgave, they forgot, and drank their worries away.

Thus for three hundred years Jamshid ruled in justice and triumph. People and demons obeyed the glorious king who was aglow with the halo of a divinely sanctioned monarch.

But Jamshid lost his way. He allowed himself to be seduced by the temptations of vanity. After all, insofar as he could see, he was the omnipotent sovereign of the world. Certain of his supremacy, Jamshid called together the elder noblemen and the clerics and declared: "I am the one who made the world good. I am the one who initiated the arts and transformed the earth. Everyone must recognize my ascendancy. Your satiety and safety, your garments and comforts, are all my gifts. I have banished sickness and death from the world. You are beholden to me for everything. I am the one with the crown of kingship, and none can challenge my preeminence in the world."

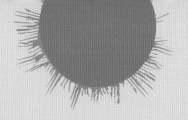

The noblemen and the clerics lowered their heads in silence. They dared not oppose the royal declaration. But the die was cast. Once Jamshid uttered these words, the divine halo of kingship scattered from around his face and his fortunes declined.

> It was an excellent piece of advice that a wise man gave
> To an ungracious ruler seduced by temptations of pride:
> "When you are made a king, adopt the humility of a slave."

The decline of the king took twenty-three years. Steadily the noblemen, the knights, and all worthy followers left the throne of Jamshid, appalled as they were with his hubris and conceit. As his authority eroded and the king further inclined to arrogance and iniquity, rebellion raged in the land. Eventually Jamshid was forced to abandon his palace and escape into obscurity.

In the meantime, another king was rising in a neighboring land.

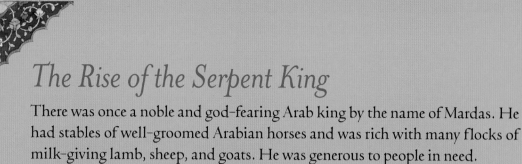

The Rise of the Serpent King

There was once a noble and god-fearing Arab king by the name of Mardas. He had stables of well-groomed Arabian horses and was rich with many flocks of milk-giving lamb, sheep, and goats. He was generous to people in need.

Mardas had a son by the name of Zahhak. Impetuous, petty, and ruthless, he was unlike his father in every respect. The wicked prince had a love of horses and spent most of his day in the saddle.

One day at dawn, the devil Iblis came to the prince disguised as a kindly adviser. Zahhak was mesmerized by his guest and asked for his guidance. The mysterious visitor agreed to offer his advice, but on one condition: Zahhak had to follow Iblis's directives and to keep their conversation a secret. Zahhak gave his consent. Then Iblis spoke: "Why should an old and decrepit father reign when he has a worthy son like you? The time has come for you to wrest power from him and rule the world."

Zahhak was tempted, but he did not wish to shed his father's blood. He said, "Give me a different piece of advice, for this cannot be done."

Iblis said, "If you refuse my advice, you have broken your promise to me. Your father will continue to rule over you as a king and you shall be nothing but an inferior subject."

Zahhak allowed himself to be seduced by the devil. He was complicit in the plot the devious stranger hatched to murder his father. He stood by and allowed Iblis to dig a pit on the way to a garden where his father went for his devotions. When Mardas rose at dawn to perform his prayers, he fell into the pit and broke his back. Iblis filled the pit with dirt and thus ended Mardas's reign.

Zahhak took the throne of his father, and soon after, Iblis returned in another disguise. This time he appeared as a young man adept in culinary arts and took over as the king's chef. Iblis was a sorcerer in the royal kitchen. He fed Zahhak a delectable diet of animal flesh to make him fearless as a lion. This did wonders for the new cook's reputation; people at that time were not used to exotic foods. Iblis flavored his cooking with spices and zests and brought such dishes as partridge, pheasant, and roasted sirloin of calf to Zahhak's table. Delighted by the talents of his capable and creative cook, Zahhak offered to grant Iblis a wish: "What is your pleasure? Ask and it shall be given."

Iblis said, "My heart is full of your love, my king. My only wish is to place kisses upon His Majesty's shoulders."

Zahhak granted the favor. Iblis kissed the shoulders of the king and magically dissolved into the ground. Suddenly, two black serpents sprouted on the king's shoulders. Zahhak screamed with horror. He tried everything to rid himself of the blight, but it was to no avail. Finally he ordered the serpents

severed at the root, but they grew back like the branches of a tree. Zahhak called on the physicians of the world to devise a cure, but none could rid him of his affliction.

Then Iblis appeared to Zahhak for a third time, in the guise of a skilled physician. He recommended that the serpents be fed the brains of young men so that they would not harm the king and eventually die of their own accord. Zahhak's henchmen sacrificed young men every day to feed their king's voracious serpents. Thus afflicted, the king of the Arabs inclined to evil and mastered the black arts of witchcraft.

Meanwhile, Jamshid's loss of divine charisma had plunged Iran into confusion. Since Jamshid had given up his sovereignty, pretenders to the throne had risen and fought each other for dominance. Iran needed a new mighty king to settle

disputes and restore order to the land. The Iranian noblemen and knights who were searching for a new sovereign finally settled on the fearsome serpent king of the Arabs. They went to Zahhak, swore their allegiance, and ushered him and his army to the palace that was known as the Throne of Jamshid.

Zahhak began his long, brutal rule over Iran. He immediately commanded his minions to search for the fugitive Jamshid. This search lasted one hundred years, until the deposed king was found hiding somewhere around the Sea of China. Zahhak had the doomed king sawed in half, filling the world with the terror of his brutality.

After seven centuries it was time for Jamshid's demise
In the blink of an eye he was swallowed by fate
As a speck of straw onto a lump of amber flies.

Zahhak dragged Jamshid's sisters Shahrnaz and Arnavaz out of their palace as they trembled with fear. He forced them to join his bed in wedlock and taught them witchcraft and the ways of iniquity. One can only teach what one knows, and Zahhak knew nothing but the evil trade of witchery, pillage, and slaughter. He was also in the habit of killing any soldier who had a beautiful daughter in order to possess the helpless maiden.

Time passed, and the snakes on Zahhak's shoulders continued to demand the lives of young men for their daily sustenance. Some of the victims were able to escape due to the mercy shown to them by a few good men who were in Zahhak's employ. Others perished as victims of the king's whims or to appease the appetite of his serpents. In this manner Zahhak tyrannized Iran for nearly a thousand years.

One night, as the king slept with the fair Arnavaz in his chambers, he had a terrible dream and woke up with a scream. In the vision he saw a young warrior who attacked him with an ox-headed mace, tied him up with leather cords, and dragged him to Mount Damavand for imprisonment.

Arnavaz said, "You have no cause to be frightened. You are the king of the seven realms and the sovereign to man and beast alike. Gather the soothsayers and prognosticators of the land and charge them with uncovering the name of the man who is destined to kill you. Once you know that name, it will be easy to find a solution to your problems."

Zahhak followed this advice. When the wise men had gathered, he said, "Tell me about my end. When is it written for me to leave this world? Who will inherit my throne? Reveal this to me or suffer great pain."

As the assembled wise men investigated the matter, their lips dried and their faces paled with fear. They stood to suffer whether they told the truth or withheld it. Finally a fearless and wise man rose and told Zahhak: "Stop the vain illusion that you will live forever. We are all destined to die. The name of the man who is prophesied to kill you is Feraydun. He is not born yet, but he will one day pummel your head with his ox-headed mace and drag you down from your throne."

Zahhak said, "But people don't act without reason. Why would this man assault and bind me?"

"Because you will have killed his father and butchered his beloved cow."

Zahhak lost consciousness and collapsed upon hearing this. When he recovered, he sent his deputies throughout the realm for signs of his nemesis.

The Rise of Feraydun

Feraydun was born to a woman named Faranak. He was luminous with the divine halo of kingship that had once adorned Jamshid.

Feraydun was still an infant when his father, Abtin, fell victim to Zahhak's henchmen who were on the prowl for young men in order to feed the voracious serpents of Zahhak. When Faranak heard that her husband had been murdered, she was grief-stricken and worried for her son's life. In desperation she took her newborn to a noble cowherd for protection. Feraydun was given for nursing to a cow named Barmayeh who was famous for her extraordinary beauty and dazzling colors. After three years Faranak had a premonition that Zahhak was closing in on her. In distress she went to the cowherd and said, "A divine fear has entered my heart. My life depends on this child and I am afraid for his safety. I shall take him away from this land of witchcraft. I will go toward the slopes of the Alborz range."

Soon after Faranak's escape, Zahhak learned about the farm where she had sought refuge. In great fury he descended on the farm with his men. Discovering that Barmayeh had nursed Feraydun, he killed the cow along with the entire herd. He also burned the farm and razed the houses.

Having narrowly escaped Zahhak's clutches, Faranak ascended to the heights of the Alborz Mountains and entrusted her child to a hermit who lived there, saying: "Oh, exalted man of the true religion, I am a bereaved widow from the land of Iran. This child of mine is destined to end the reign of Zahhak. A cowherd brought him up to this age on the milk of the noble cow Barmayeh. Now it falls upon you to accept his charge and lavish on him your fatherly care."

The good hermit took pity on Faranak and accepted the task of rearing Feraydun. He honorably discharged his duties until his ward reached the age of sixteen. Then Feraydun came down from the mountain and went to his mother to ask her about his lineage. Faranak said, "Your father was Abtin, a man of noble birth who was descended from King Tahmures. Zahhak's henchmen killed him by the order of the serpent king because Zahhak had heard that you would overthrow him one day, and that is why I had to separate you from myself. During this time a noble and magnificent cow, Barmayeh, nursed you. After our departure Zahhak came for you and, in his rage, killed the innocent and gentle Barmayeh."

Feraydun was furious. "The lion will gain his courage in action. It is time I wielded my blade and avenged my father. I shall rid the land of that sorcerer."

Faranak scolded her son: "This is not the way you will seek revenge. How can you fight Zahhak, who is able to rally a hundred thousand men from every corner of his realm? You are drunk on the wine of youth. Don't endanger your life on such a reckless adventure. The people will rise to your cause when the time comes."

The Story of Kaveh the Blacksmith

Zahhak was growing increasingly obsessed with Feraydun after Faranak's escape. The name alone stirred a great fear in his heart. One day he called the nobles and clerics of every realm to declare: "I have a fierce enemy, but he is in hiding. I am not in the habit of underestimating my foes, puny as they might be. It is my intention to gather a great army of men and demons to confront this foe when he rises. But first we must prepare a proclamation testifying that I am a just king. It must stress that I have eschewed falsehoods and iniquity."

Fearing the wrath of the king, the dignitaries endorsed the proclamation declaring Zahhak a just king. At this time a man appeared at the gates, loudly protesting his unjust treatment. Zahhak called on him to come forth and speak. He said, "I am Kaveh, a harmless blacksmith. But the king keeps pouring a torrent of fire on my head. You are the king of the seven realms, but it seems that our share of your great wealth and power is nothing but misery. Tell me, by what accounting is it my duty to sacrifice my son to feed your serpents?"

Zahhak ordered his men to release Kaveh's son, and in exchange for this favor, he asked the blacksmith to sign his proclamation of justice. Kaveh grew angry as he read the deed describing Zahhak's righteousness. He roared at the dignitaries who had endorsed it: "Hell is your abode, you minions of the devil. You are the admirers of an unjust king. Let it be known that Kaveh does not bear witness to this false proclamation. I am not afraid of this king!"

With this he tore the proclamation to shreds, threw it under his feet, and strode out, loudly voicing his defiance. Astonished at the boldness of Kaveh, the dignitaries turned to Zahhak and inquired why he had suffered a common man to publicly defy him and tear up the royal proclamation that they had signed. Zahhak was puzzled himself. "I don't know. As soon as I heard his voice it was as if I was paralyzed. I don't know what will come of this."

Kaveh left the palace calling the people to the cause of overthrowing Zahhak.
Great masses thronged to him. Hoisting his leather apron on a lance, Kaveh
walked through the crowd, chanting:

Let those who long for Feraydun

First lift the yoke of the cursed Zahhak

And walk with us in communion.

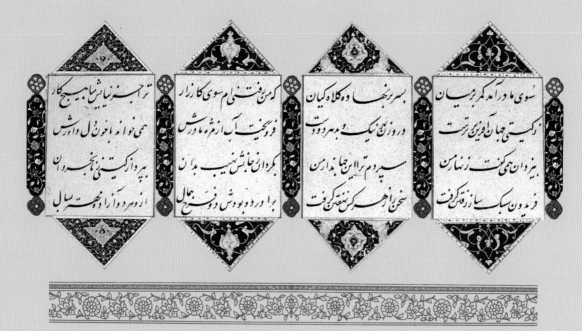

Kaveh knew where Feraydun lived and directed his rally toward his town. His followers grew as he marched, and soon he was leading a veritable army behind his makeshift banner. When the multitudes reached Feraydun's dwelling, a cry of astonishment went up from his household. Feraydun took Kaveh's banner as a good omen and adorned it with three silken strands of crimson, yellow, and purple. From then on, the blacksmith's apron became the symbol of the Iranian nation. Although each king adorned it with precious gems, the name of the leather banner remained the same: "The Standard of Kaveh."

The arrival of Kaveh was the sign that Feraydun had been waiting for. The time was ripe for his rebellion against the serpent king. He went to Faranak with these words: "The time has arrived for me to stand up and lead this uprising. I beg you for your fervent prayers. Don't worry for me, and put your trust in the creator of the world."

Faranak wept with joy as her valiant son went before the rebel army, flanked by his two elder brothers. They first went to the blacksmith's sector of the bazaar. Feraydun designed an ox-headed mace and charged the ironworkers to forge it in tempered steel.

The march toward the palace of the serpent king commenced. The destination was the city of Jerusalem, where Zahhak had erected his palace. The army stopped at an Arab oasis to rest. That night the divine messenger Sorush came to Feraydun and taught him the secrets of undoing magical spells, a skill that he would need in his fight against the witchcraft of Zahhak.

To reach Jerusalem, Feraydun needed to cross the river Arvand where the Tigris and the Euphrates merge. But the boatmen refused passage, as Zahhak had forbidden unauthorized movements across the water. Furious at hearing this, Feraydun boldly waded into the angry waves of the river. His companions followed suit, and in one magnificent movement the army crossed the formidable Arvand. The march continued, and before long the army of Feraydun was in Jerusalem.

The fearsome edifice of Zahhak's palace was
visible from a great distance. It was obvious that
the soaring vault of the palace could not have
been made by ordinary means. Realizing that
the castle was enchanted, Feraydun decided
to act swiftly. Wielding his ox-headed mace he
stormed the gates, slew all of its sentries, and rode
into the courtyard. There, with the help of what
he had learned from the angel Sorush, Feraydun
undid the magic and brought down the canopy that
crowned the castle.

Having removed the magical spell from the palace, he reclined
on Zahhak's throne and called for Shahrnaz and Arnavaz,
the exquisite sisters of King Jamshid, who in their ageless beauty
rivaled rosebuds and narcissus petals. He had them purified and
cleansed with water. After their spells had been broken, the
princesses emerged from the inner quarters, staggering as if they had
been awakened from a trance. Gradually they regained their composure and

addressed Feraydun. Arnavaz said, "Who are you and what is your name? What is your noble origin? It took great courage and prodigious fortune to challenge the witchcraft of the mighty sorcerer Zahhak. We cannot begin to tell you of the suffering we have endured in this palace."

Feraydun replied: "I am Feraydun, the son of Abtin, who was killed by Zahhak. A noble and beautiful cow named Barmayeh was my nursemaid. Zahhak killed the poor, innocent animal for having nourished me. Now I have girded my loins to repay him for his cruelty and injustice."

Arnavaz recognized Feraydun as the man prophesied to end the reign of Zahhak and said, "The serpent king is not in his palace. He has gone to India in search of potent spells in order to prolong his rule. As if it weren't enough for him to shed young men's blood to feed his serpents, now he has taken to more ghoulish practices that include bathing in the blood of young people in order to enhance his magical powers."

Feraydun in Zahhak's Palace

Zahhak had a caretaker, Kondrow, who looked after the affairs of the court in his absence. He lived some distance away from the palace, and when he heard the news that the castle had been conquered, Kondrow rushed to see what was happening. He was surprised to find a stranger reclining on the royal throne, flanked by Zahhak's wives. But he kept his composure and pretended that nothing unusual had transpired.

Kondrow stood at the foot of the throne and admired Feraydun's royal halo and wished him long dominion over the world. Feraydun issued orders for a feast, complete with musicians and good wine. Kondrow obeyed his new master's command and prepared the banquet. While festivities were in progress he snuck away and rode off to inform Zahhak of what had happened.

"Exalted king! A young lad has scorned you, riding into your castle on horseback and undoing your spells. He is reclining on your throne as we speak."

Zahhak did not want to lose face by appearing surprised. He said, "No matter. He is a guest in our palace."

"But, Your Majesty, what manner of guest wields a deadly mace? He is killing your demons and wearing your crown and torque?"

"Don't whine about this man. It is said that an insolent guest is a good omen!"

"Well, then, I am sure the great Zahhak will explain what this guest wants with His Majesty's queens. He sits on your throne caressing the lovely face of Shahrnaz while allowing Arnavaz of the ruby lips to nibble his other hand. And he does all this in broad daylight. When the night casts its darkness upon the world, this guest takes more liberties with the musk-haired queens of His Majesty."

At long last Zahhak lost his composure. Cursing Kondrow, he declared: "You will never work in my court again!"

Kondrow replied: "Frankly, I doubt you will ever see your throne again. Nor are you in a position to confirm or deny me my office. You will do well to take care of your own business as you are cast out of your palace the way a strand of hair is pulled out of dough."

Zahhak quickly gathered an army of demons to storm his palace. The army of Feraydun came forth and engaged the forces of Zahhak in the narrow alleyways around the palace. The people of the city helped the army of Feraydun by throwing bricks and stones at the minions of Zahhak from their rooftops, chanting:

> We detest this dragon who stole our throne
>
> And hail Feraydun as our new righteous king.
>
> We shall fight until Zahhak is overthrown

As the battle raged around the palace, Zahhak disguised himself in full body armor and climbed to the roof of the palace using his lariat. From this vantage point, he saw Shahrnaz holding an intimate discourse with Feraydun, speaking harshly of the former master of the palace, the evil serpent king. Blinded by jealousy, Zahhak lowered himself into the courtyard and drew his dagger to kill Shahrnaz. But Feraydun rushed him with his mace and lowered him to the ground with one mighty blow. Zahhak's helmet cracked. One more blow would have finished him off.

At that moment, the angel Sorush reappeared to Feraydun and warned him that it was not decreed that Zahhak be killed at his hand. He was to be taken to Mount Damavand and imprisoned. Feraydun tied Zahhak's hands to the saddle of a camel and dragged him to a deep cave under the dome of Damavand and chained him to the ground.

Feraydun avenged his father and put Zahhak in chains
Crushing the unjust and selecting noble men for rule
He settled the affairs of the land and staked his claims.

Feraydun was not made of ambergris and musk
Nor was he a celestial angel although he was righteous
He attained greatness by practicing virtue from dawn to dusk.

By such deeds did the king secure his legendary fame.
Practice justice and generosity and you, too, shall be
A latter-day Feraydun by a different name.

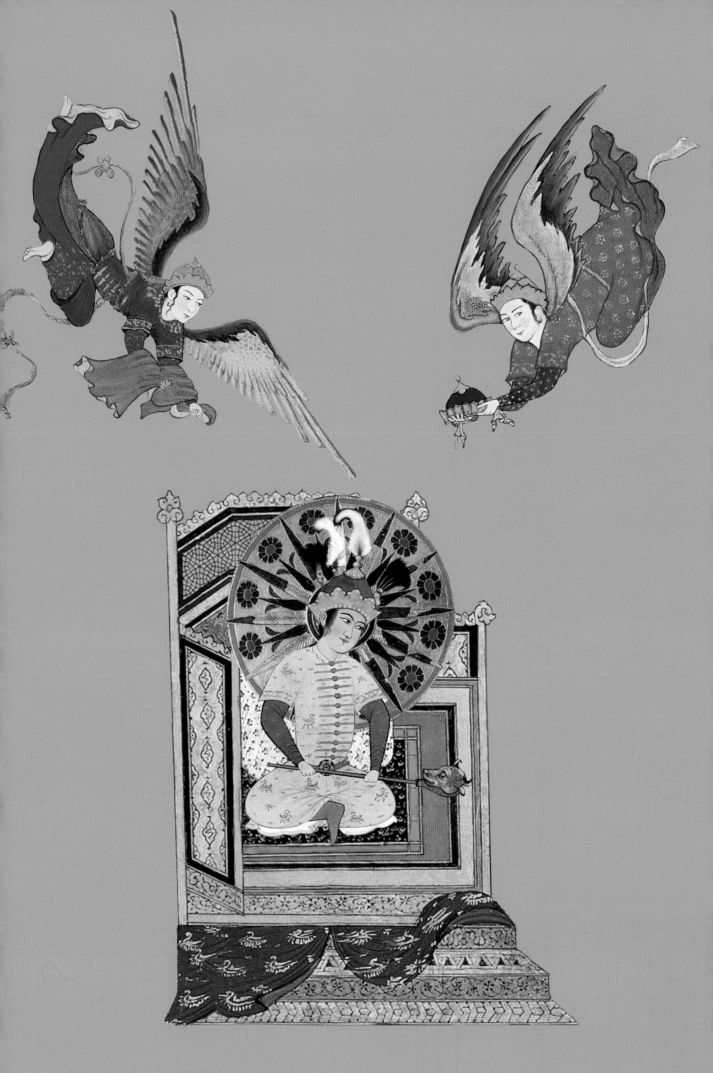

A World Divided:
Sons of Feraydun

Feraydun ascended the throne when the season of autumn arrived
He named the day "Mehregan," a holiday of joyous bonfires
As people forgot their sorrows, avoided judgments, and contrived

To burn ambergris and saffron and imbibe the ruby wine.
And thus commenced the five centuries of an unimpeachable reign
And the tenure of a king no one could in fairness malign.

Feraydun Wears the Crown

Feraydun ascended the throne of Iran after a millennium of its usurption by the serpent king. He disbanded his popular armies, allowing only the cast of warriors to carry weapons. Faranak rejoiced to hear that her son had overcome the serpent king and ascended the Persian throne. She bathed and purified herself and humbly offered abundant thanks to God. She discreetly gave a bounty to the poor and held a public banquet at which she enriched her friends with gifts. Then she loaded precious jewels, garments, and weapons on a convoy of golden bridled Arabian horses and sent them as a present to her royal son. Feraydun kissed the ground in thanks and accepted his mother's gifts. The nobility also displayed their joy at the crowning ceremonies by showering the new king with pieces of gold and gems.

When the festivities ended, the new king made a voyage around the world, built up all that had fallen into disrepair, and eradicated injustice everywhere. As the royal voyage approached its completion, the world resembled a garden of paradise. Feraydun established the Persian capital at Tammisheh near the city of Amol and began his reign.

At the age of fifty the king had three sons, all tall, handsome, and deserving of the crown. The first two had been born to Shahrnaz and a third to Arnavaz, the sisters of Jamshid. Feraydun had not named his sons, as he wanted them to prove their mettle in life before they received their proper names.

As time came for the princes to marry, the king charged a wise nobleman by the name of Jandal with finding three brides born to the same parents for his sons. Jandal searched the world for girls worthy of the royal house of Iran until he heard that Sarv, the king of Yemen, had three lovely daughters. Jandal traveled to the court of Sarv, kissed the ground, and said, "I am a humble messenger from the mighty Feraydun. He sends his greetings and wishes you perpetual tenure on the Arab throne. My king desires that your daughters be betrothed to his royal sons. There is no doubt that the princesses of Yemen would be suitable matches for the princes of Iran."

The king of Yemen wilted like jasmine plucked from the branch, as he was devoted to his daughters and did not wish to part with them. But he knew that he could not refuse the king of Iran as the fate of Zahhak was still fresh in his mind. Sarv consulted his allies in the land of the lance-bearing Arab tribesmen. They pledged their allegiance in war should their king decide to defy Feraydun. But Sarv chose the wiser path, telling Jandal: "I am ready to follow the directives of the great King Feraydun, although my daughters are dearer to me than the throne of Yemen. At least allow me to see Feraydun's sons. I want to be sure that I am entrusting my daughters to men who have justice in their hearts."

When Feraydun heard what Sarv had required, he summoned his sons and advised them: "I have asked for the hands of the three daughters of the king of the Arabs as your brides. Now he wants to see you in person. Go to him and be truthful in answering his questions. He is a discerning man."

The three princes of Iran each took a band of their loyal warriors and went to Yemen. King Sarv plied his future sons-in-law with riddles and trials, but they proved equal to all of his challenges. Finally, Sarv consented to the marriage of his daughters to the sons of Feraydun and called for a celebration. But he did so with a divided mind and a troubled soul. To be fair, Feraydun was not the one who had wronged him. Providence had decreed that he would have daughters instead of sons. He had lost the chance to pass on his name and kingdom to a male successor. Now he was losing his daughters, too.

When the festivities began, however, the king found himself in better spirits. He was now singing a different tune. "One must honor a child who is refined and respectful. It is virtue, not the gender of a child, that matters."

When the lavish ceremonies ended, Sarv bid his daughters farewell and sent them off with a caravan of camels, loaded with their rich dowry, toward the capital city of Iran.

Feraydun heard the news of the departure of his sons from Yemen and decided to try their mettle before giving them suitable names that would fit their characters. To this end, he transformed himself into a fire-breathing dragon and stood on the road. As the caravan of the princess brides and their husbands approached, the dragon roared and blocked their way. The king's eldest son was stricken with fear. He turned tail and fled the scene, saying, "A man of good sense never picks a battle with a dragon." The second son notched an arrow in his bow and went forth, declaring, "I shall fight when I am challenged. Neither lions nor dragons scare me." The third son, however, spoke to the dragon with these words: "Remove yourself from the road if you have heard of the name King Feraydun. We are three warlike sons of that king and you block our way at your own peril."

Feraydun, who had heard enough, stopped the trial and vanished. The caravan continued its journey and reached the capital city of Tammisheh. The king welcomed his sons on a war elephant wielding his ox-headed mace. He said, "The dragon that you saw was me and what you went through was a trial. My elder son, who sought the way of prudence, will be called Salm, meaning peace. He shall not be blamed for escaping the dragon, because recklessness is closer to madness than courage.

"My middle son, who was ferocious in confronting the dragon, will be known by the name of Tur. And my youngest, who combined courage and prudence, will be named Iraj."

Then the king had his astrologers cast the horoscopes of his sons. They were all born under the signs of fire. The cunning Salm's planet was Saturn, in the constellation of Sagittarius. The headstrong Tur's planet was the bloody Mars, in the constellation of Leo. And the courageous and trusting Iraj's planet was the moon in the constellation of Aries. The stars silently portended the conflict that would come.

Dividing the World

Feraydun had spent a long time in consultation with astrologers and seers to determine the proper division of his kingdom. Having named his sons, the king was now prepared to divide his vast kingdom among them. Salm was given Rome and the lands to the western horizon, and Tur was allotted the kingdom of the eastern provinces, where the Turks and the Chinese resided. After this declaration, Salm and Tur left for their kingdoms, to rule as sovereigns.

Then it was time for Iraj to receive his share of Feraydun's empire: the middle kingdom of Iran, along with its Arabian provinces.

And thus the prosperous and peaceful reign of Feraydun continued until the flush of the king's youth was painted over by the pallor of old age. His sons, by contrast, continued to grow in strength. But all was not well among the brothers.

Salm had long begrudged his younger brother Iraj for inheriting the best part of Feraydun's kingdom. One day he sent a message to Tur: "We were sons of a great king, all deserving of the crown. I was the eldest and the most deserving

of us. After me, you were the one to get the lion's share of our father's kingdom. But the unjust king gave the best of his kingdom to Iraj, banishing us to the outer reaches of the world. We must not be blamed if we should resent this unfairness."

Salm sent forth a silver-tongued emissary to deliver this missive to Tur in the eastern kingdom. The impetuous Tur felt a wave of rage rising in him as he listened to his brother's message. He sent back this response: "What you said is true. Remember how our father deceived us when we were young? He is the one who planted this blood-soaked tree that has borne bitter fruit. Let us speak in person. This matter has festered long enough."

When the two brothers met, they agreed to send a clever priest to their father with this impudent message: "Greetings from your two sons. You are old and it is time for you to depart this world. Only a misguided man clings to life after his time has come. God gave you the world but you have been derelict in your duties toward the Creator. You did not divide your kingdom in justice. You gave your youngest the kingdom of Iran and relegated your elder sons to the ends of the earth.

"Now take the crown from the worthless head of Iraj and banish him to a desolate corner of the world. We will bring upon you the armies of Rome, China, and Turkistan if you refuse. Beware, a mace-wielding horde is on the move to lay low Iraj and his kingdom."

The messenger arrived at the glorious palace of Feraydun. Its tall ramparts scraped the clouds. He passed through a wondrous avenue where lions and leopards were tied on one side and war elephants stood on the other. Magnificent warriors who wore fine garments and carried glittering weapons crowded the halls of the palace. Mesmerized by the splendor of the court of Feraydun, the envoy offered his abject apologies for the severe message he was about to deliver.

"Fear not," Feraydun said. "I don't fault the messenger for the message."

When the recitation of the letter was complete, the king said, "Those unclean souls have ceded themselves to the devil."

He charged the messenger to tell his sons the following: "You have spurned my teachings and become malevolent creatures with no shame before God and man. I, too, was once young. My hair was pitch-black and my back was straight as a tall cypress. The same world that bent my back is still at work. It will bend your backs and it will not stop at that. Know that I did not divide my land on a whim. Nor did I play favorites. I consulted the wise men who know the ways of the stars on this grave matter.

"My time has arrived to leave this world, but heed these words of advice. The dragon of greed has overcome your reason. Why else would you choose worthless soil over your own brother? The world has seen the likes of you. It has not kept faith with them and it will not be kind to you, either. Remember that you will one day face divine judgment."

When the envoy left with the king's message, Feraydun turned to Iraj with these words of advice: "My sons were wicked, and they have become even more so since they were sent to rule over fierce peoples. They are bringing great armies against us. A brother is a brother only as long as he acts the part. Be wise and do not open your arms to embrace a drawn sword. Eat their breakfast before they devour your dinner. And seek no confederates in the world, for righteousness is your only true ally."

Iraj responded: "I shall not fight my brothers. Let them have my crown, for I have no abiding love for this office. Nor will I fight my own brothers over worldly possessions. I will tell them that this world is an unfaithful lover. It was false even to the great King Jamshid. With the king's permission I will go unarmed to Salm and Tur and calm their anger."

Feraydun was taken aback. He said, "Shining is in the nature of the moon. Your brothers seek to shed your blood and you speak of making peace. You love those who hate you. But it is unwise to place one's head in the mouth of a serpent. At least take along this royal writ to ensure your safe return."

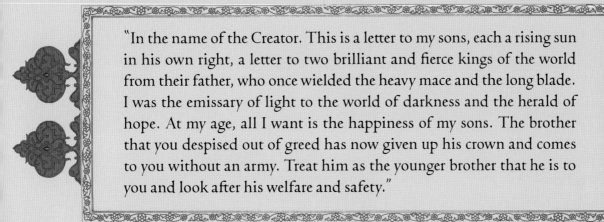

"In the name of the Creator. This is a letter to my sons, each a rising sun in his own right, a letter to two brilliant and fierce kings of the world from their father, who once wielded the heavy mace and the long blade. I was the emissary of light to the world of darkness and the herald of hope. At my age, all I want is the happiness of my sons. The brother that you despised out of greed has now given up his crown and comes to you without an army. Treat him as the younger brother that he is to you and look after his welfare and safety."

Iraj took the king's sealed letter and set off to meet his brothers. Salm and Tur brought their armies forth to greet their younger sibling. They glared at Iraj and seemed to resent his serene countenance. The armies that witnessed the encounter were charmed by the nobility of the prince of Iran. All the talk in the camp revolved around the young prince who had come in peace. Warriors paired off, telling each other that Iraj deserved to be the king of the world.

Salm heard these rumors and went to Tur in great agitation, saying: "Did you see that our soldiers did not take their admiring eyes off Iraj? It is obvious that they want him for their king. We begrudged him the rule of Iran, but now he is laying claim to our kingdoms."

The evil brothers spent the entire night conspiring against Iraj. In the morning they rushed to his tent. Tur said, "You are younger than both of us. How is it that you lay claim to the throne of Iran as we are banished to inferior and inhospitable provinces? I will not stand for this. I shall destroy you and your kingdom."

Iraj replied. "Be calm, my elder brother, and you shall receive what you want. I don't wish to rule over the East or the West. Nor do I want the kingship of Iran. Power that is gained in hatred will bear only bitter fruit. On the day of our death we will all have only a brick for our pillow. I have given up the throne of Iran. It is yours. I shall not fight you over it."

Tur flew into a rage over Iraj's composed manner. He jumped to his feet and hurled his golden dais at Iraj's head, grievously injuring him. Iraj pleaded for his life: "Do you have no shame before God and our father? How can you wantonly take a life? One must not needlessly kill even an ant, as life is sweet for all living creatures. You need not make a murderer of yourself. I assure you that I will disappear into obscurity. You will never see me again."

Tur did not respond. Instead, he pulled a dagger from his boot and beheaded Iraj.

> Why did fate indulge the prince in luxury and ease
> Only to abandon him at the hands of his cruel slayers?
> The wise know there is no justice in this vale of tears.

Tur sent the severed head of Iraj to Feraydun with this message: "Here is the head that you raised above us. Put the crown of our ancestors on it if you wish."

After murdering their brother, Salm and Tur went back to their own Western and Eastern realms.

In preparation for Iraj's return from his mission of peace, Feraydun had arranged a lavish reception. The throne was adorned with turquoise, and the crown glittered with added jewels. War elephants marched under the city's decorated gates, driven by drummers in festive garments. In the palace a lavish feast was arranged, with wine and skilled musicians.

To the dismay of the expectant crowds, however, a camel appeared on the horizon, shrouded in a cloud of dust. At the gates of the city the camel stopped and a gloomy rider dismounted, tears streaming down his sallow face. Holding a strange golden chest, he approached Feraydun. Attendants rushed forth and lifted the lid of the ominous case. Under a sheet of perfumed silk lay the severed head of Iraj.

Feraydun lost consciousness and fell off his horse. The throngs that had gathered at the gates merged into a mourning procession that moved toward the palace of Iraj. Disconsolate at the injustice of his beloved son's demise, Feraydun set fire to the young prince's palace and prayed that he would live to see his son's death avenged.

The king's dark night of despair persisted for months until he learned that one of Iraj's consorts, Mahafarid, had given birth to a beautiful daughter. Feraydun embraced the infant, who resembled her father, and reared her in the royal court until she came of age and married the king's nephew. In due time a son was born to the young couple. A nurse rushed the baby to Feraydun, saying, "Behold, a second Iraj!"

The king rejoiced. He had a sense that his dear son had been reborn. He named the boy Manuchehr and saw to his proper education. Iraj's great-grandson was a prodigious student of the royal arts, and in a short time he earned the admiration of the king and the respect of the army. Feraydun gave Manuchehr the keys to his treasure houses and called upon the commanders of his army to pay their respects to the crown prince. In the celebrations that ensued, great heroes such as Gharan, the son of Kaveh the blacksmith, and Shiruy and Saum rained a shower of emeralds on the young man who would avenge Iraj.

The new, hopeful disposition at the court of Feraydun was not hidden from Salm and Tur. They knew about the rise of Manuchehr and feared that the day of their reckoning was upon them. To mollify their father and prevent the coming war of revenge, Salm and Tur sent a rich caravan loaded with precious gifts to the court of Feraydun. They also sent an eloquent envoy who brought a letter to their father:

May the divine halo of King Feraydun shine forever. This is a letter from two unjust men whose eyes are full of tears and whose hearts are branded with the indelible guilt of their wickedness. Their shame is so great that they dare not look upon the countenance of their father. Hence these lowly slaves have sent an envoy rather than coming to beg for mercy themselves. The wisdom of the learned sages is now confirmed: evil deeds are surely punished.

But what could we do when our fate was written in this way? Even ferocious lions and formidable dragons cannot escape the cunning of fate. The unclean devil is also at fault for deceiving us. We were possessed and our judgment was corrupted.

Now we hope that our crowned father will forgive us. Our guilt is indeed great, but we believe that our father's forgiveness is greater. Now we request that Manuchehr honor us by his presence. Send him to us so we can wash the old hatreds with the tears from our repentant eyes and soothe his aching heart with our rich treasures.

Feraydun sat in state upon his throne joined by Manuchehr, on his right side, wearing the crown, the torque, and the earrings of the crown prince. The heroes of the army stood at attention, displaying their golden shields and maces. The envoy of Salm and Tur was ushered in and seated on a golden dais. The emissary of the guilty brothers gave a moving performance in submitting their apologies and extending their offer to host Manuchehr. Feraydun heard the message in silence and then uttered these words: "The evil heart of those men is on display like the sun upon the sky. I have heard all that you said, envoy. Now take your blood money and your empty words and go back to those shameless rogues and tell them: 'You sent me the head of Iraj in a golden chest and left his body to the beasts of prey. Now you profess to love Manuchehr and express a wish to see him? You will see him soon enough, in full battle gear and at the head of an avenging army. You will answer to him and his commanders, Gharan, Sarv, Shiruy, and Saum.' "I wanted to avenge Iraj myself, but the rules of filial piety forbid a war between a father and his sons. Now Manuchehr has grown, a branch from that mighty tree. He will wage war, refusing your insincere pleas and bribes."

The envoy trembled with fear as he took his leave. He traveled back and delivered Feraydun's message to Salm and Tur. Upon hearing their father's rebuke, the guilty brothers knew that war was inescapable. Salm said, "We must kill that lion cub before he sprouts teeth."

With this they gathered a great army in the plain of Hamoon and prepared for war. Feraydun charged Manuchehr to go forth and take the battle to the enemy: "Salm and Tur have brought their forces to Hamoon. It is the sign of a hunter's good fortune when the antelope wanders into his range."

Manuchehr said, "I shall gird my loins to avenge Iraj. I don't have high regard for the armies of Salm and Tur. I don't see a worthy opponent among them."

The army of Iran left Tammisheh, marching behind the standard of Kaveh until they rested at the elm forest that bordered the plain of Hamoon. Manuchehr and his lieutenant Gharan came out of the forest to review the flanks. King Sarv of Yemen stayed at the heart of the army.

Tur came forth and said to one of Manuchehr's scouts who had been sent to appraise the strength of the enemy: "Remind this upstart king that Iraj had a daughter and no son to avenge him. Tell him that he has no claim to the throne of Iran."

The scout replied, "I will take your message to Manuchehr. But it would behoove you to think of your own predicament before sending such messages. This army is massive and your men are sure to lose their nerve if they see the glint of the naked blades behind the standard of Kaveh."

Manuchehr laughed when the scout related the foolish words of Tur regarding his lineage. Everyone, and above all King Feraydun, knew the legitimacy of his descent from Iraj. Manuchehr urged his troops to fight to the death in the righteous cause of avenging their martyred prince's death. The battle was joined. The Iranian combatants dominated for the first two days. As the sun set on the second day of battle, Salm and Tur conspired to ambush the Iranians under cover of darkness.

Manuchehr, who had received the intelligence regarding the surprise attack, appointed Gharan to lie in wait for the raiders with thirty thousand men. Tur arrived at the Iranian camps with one hundred thousand troops, only to find an army ready to fight. The advantage of surprise was lost, and the army of Tur would be fighting in the dark and on unfamiliar ground. But withdrawing from the confrontation was not possible. Tur desperately hurled his army at the Iranian forces. The din of the battle was deafening, as blades struck shields and lances broke on the armor of horses. At long last, the armies of Tur were routed.

Manuchehr scanned the field for Tur. He found him in the process of escaping the front lines and gave chase, striking him with his javelin. Tur fell off his horse. Manuchehr dismounted and swiftly beheaded him. He sent Tur's head, along with a letter, to Feraydun:

"In the name of the God of nobility, purity, and justice, I greet the rightly crowned Feraydun, the wielder of the ox-headed mace. I came to avenge the death of Iraj and fought three battles in two days under the sun and the moon. Tur conspired to ambush us by night, but I set a trap for him. He tried to escape, but I gave chase and forced him to dismount. He had sent you Iraj's head as a trophy. Now that you receive his head, the scores are nearly settled. I am off to pursue Salm, whose chastisement is long overdue."

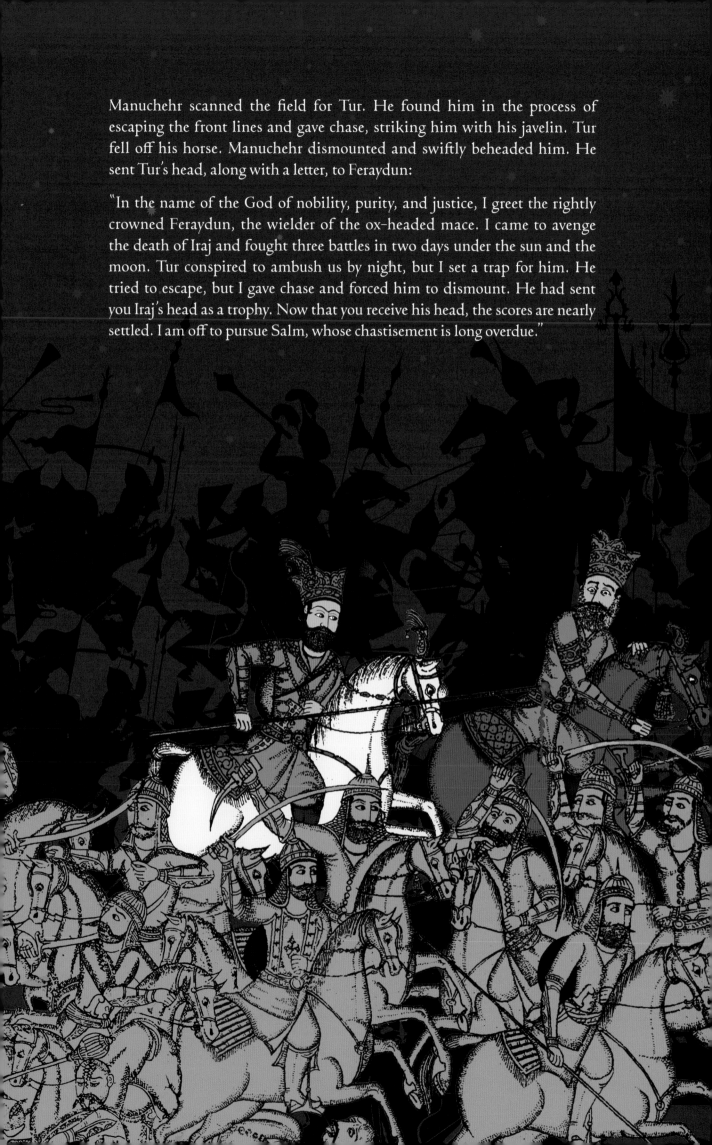

The Batle with Salm and Kakouy

Salm was alarmed by the fate of his brother. But he knew that in the event of danger he could always retreat to the impregnable granite castle of Alanan, which was surrounded by the sea. Wishing to block this avenue of escape, Gharan asked Manuchehr for a contingent of warriors in order to deprive Salm of his last refuge.

For the success of his plan, Gharan needed the royal standard and the signet of Tur. Manuchehr approved the plan and sent Shiruy along to assist Gharan. Gharan kept Shiruy's forces back in the vicinity of the castle and went up to the gate with his own men. He gained entry on the strength of Tur's signet, convincing the gullible gatemaster that he and his troops had been sent by their king to help defend the castle. Once safely in the fortress, however, Gharan went up to the ramparts and unfurled the royal standard. Shiruy knew that this was his cue to storm the gates of the castle. The defenders were caught between the invading forces outside and the troops of Gharan inside. By sunrise, the castle of Alanan was conquered and torched. Gharan went to Manuchehr and reported the success of his mission.

Manuchehr told Gharan that there was new trouble brewing, as one of the grandsons of Zahhak, Kakouy, had come to the aid of Salm with one hundred thousand troops. "He has the reputation of a fearsome warrior. I have not tried his mettle myself, but I am sure to examine his strength in battle soon."

Gharan said, "Kakouy will never be a worthy opponent for my prince. But let us ferret him out and see if he is equal to his reputation."

The army of Manuchehr stormed the gates of Kakouy's castle where Salm's forces had camped, and the blood began to flow. Kakouy came out shouting his war cry and struck Manuchehr with his lance. The blow undid Manuchehr's chain mail. In response, the Iranian prince struck Kakouy's neckpiece, causing his entire armor to fall. Finally Manuchehr took Kakouy off the saddle, threw him on the ground, and slashed at him until he was dead. With the death of their commander, the confederated forces of Salm and Kakouy ran from the battlefield.

Manuchehr removed his horse's armor to lighten the animal's burden. He searched the field for Salm, until he spotted him. Salm took off and Manuchehr gave chase, cutting the distance between them by leaps and bounds. As his horse came close to the escaping Salm, Manuchehr taunted his treacherous great-uncle: "Why are you running away? Did you not murder your own brother for the sake of a crown? Well, then, I am coming to bring you the crown you coveted. The sapling that you planted has borne fruit. You have only yourself to blame if the fruit is bitter."

Manuchehr continued his taunts until his steed ran side by side with Salm's horse. Then he unsheathed his sword and slashed at Salm's neck. This feat of swordsmanship astonished the onlookers as Salm's head went flying.

With the demise of Salm, the armies of the enemy asked for quarter. Their envoy came to Manuchehr and said, "We are farmers and husbandmen forced into this war. We have no hatred toward Manuchehr. Now we are at his mercy. If he wants to kill us, we are ready for the gallows. But if he will let us live, we will bring him our leaders for punishment."

Manuchehr said, "I prefer a good name to garnering worldly advantages. Your love or hate is immaterial to me. When victory is achieved, the victor must refrain from bloodshed. Now drop your arms and return to your homes in peace."

The surrendering men approached the king and dropped their weapons, forming a mound of armor, shields, and swords. Manuchehr sent another letter to Feraydun, apprising him of the completion of the mission to avenge Iraj. Then he returned to Tammisheh by the way of the Caspian Sea. At the region of Saury the standard of Feraydun, who had come to welcome the triumphant prince, was sighted.

Manuchehr dismounted and kissed the ground to greet King Feraydun. The king took him by hand, honoring him, and motioned for him to step up and recline on the throne of kingship. Feraydun prayed to the heavens: "You said that you are a just God and that you are on the side of the oppressed. I bear witness that you have fulfilled your promise, bringing me justice and perpetuating my progeny on the throne."

King Feraydun passed away and Manuchehr was enthroned. The new king saw to the construction of a worthy crypt for Feraydun and laid him to rest on a bed of ivory. The crown of Feraydun hung above his body.

Iraj was avenged when Feraydun's demise was at hand.
Then the leaf of that royal tree withered on the branch and fell.
Death carried off a king whose good name became legend.

A Love that Triumphed:
Zaul and Rudabeh

Manuchehr mourned his grandfather for a week and then reclined
On the ivory throne, declaring himself a divinely sanctioned king.
He pledged to follow the example of Feraydun who was inclined

To comfort the poor, humble the proud
And to treat oppressors as rebels against the Almighty.
Then Saum rose on behalf of the knights and bowed.

Saum, who was the first among the knights and bore the title of Champion of the World, spoke on behalf of the assembly at King Manuchehr's coronation with these words: "You are the king of justice and generosity, a lion on the battlefield, and a shining sun at any banquet. If I am a knight it is because of the honor your ancestors bestowed upon my clan."

Saum shone on that day but his tale of woes
Had just begun, as he was misled
By fate and the wrong path he chose.

Zaul in the Wilderness

Saum, the son of the famous heroic knight Narimon, was the most prominent knight of Iran, but he was unhappy, for he did not have an heir. All this changed when a musk-haired consort whose face was fresher than the petals of a flower bore him a son. The newborn was fine and healthy, but his hair was white. The nurses called him Zaul, meaning old. For a week none dared break the news to Saum. Finally a brave attendant went to him and said, "May this day be auspicious for the great knight, and may his ill-wishers be cursed. You are blessed with a boy who is perfect in every respect. He has only one flaw: his hair is white. Such is your fate, oh great warrior."

Saum rushed to the women's quarters to see the newborn. His spirits sank when he looked upon the face of the infant. In his despair he turned to the heavens and said, "My God, you are above wrongdoing. Accept my contrition for my sins. But it was my hope that you would punish me in private for my infractions. How am I to face my fellow knights if they ask me about this demon boy? They are sure to mock me in public and speak evil words behind my back. How am I to live in this land with the shame of a son who is born old?"

Saum weighed his options. He could not bear the shame of having such a child. Thus he ordered his attendants to expose the helpless infant on a high mountain, spurning human ethics and natural law all at once.

A lioness once suckled her cub to satiety and said,
You're not obliged to me for this milk nor would you be
If you bled me for your own sustenance instead.

The attendants left the helpless infant on the high rocks and returned home. Zaul lay there on the cold dirt for a while, not knowing that he had been forsaken. Then he started crying from thirst, hunger, and discomfort.

That part of the Alborz Mountains was home to a magical bird, the Simorgh. The magnificent bird flew over and saw the helpless naked baby who was

kicking up the dust and crying. She had taken wing from her nest to fetch food for her hungry hatchlings. But when she picked up Zaul and brought him to her nest, the chicks looked on the human infant with kindness and shared their food with him. From that day on the Simorgh loved Zaul as her own and sustained him into adulthood.

In time, travelers in the caravans that passed by would tell stories about an agile, silver-headed young boy who roamed the impossible heights of the Alborz Mountains.

Zaul Is Found

When Zaul had grown into a strong young lad, Saum had a dream of a man riding a horse. The rider brought Saum the good tidings that his son was alive. Upon waking, Saum called the wise men who could interpret dreams and asked their opinion of his vision. They were unanimous, and one of them expressed all their feelings: "Beasts of the wild and fish of the sea care for their young. You alone have cast out your innocent child in breach of the rules of morality. Now repent to God, for he is our guide to what is good and bad."

The next night Saum had another dream. Again, a handsome young man galloped from the mountains, flanked by a priest and a sage. He berated Saum: "You are a shameless man of impure thoughts. How can you call yourself a knight while a bird rears your child? If you consider white hair to be a defect, then look upon your own white hair. Do you fault God for this, too?

"The Almighty has appointed one of his wild creatures to foster your son. You need not worry, for she is kinder to him than you were."

Saum roared like a lion caught in a trap as he woke from that dream. Unable to delay any longer, he rushed to the mountains with some of his lieutenants. They reached the foot of the mountains, overgrown with a thick blanket of intertwined trees. High above the valley, on the soaring rocks, was the nest of the mighty Simorgh. In vain Saum attempted to scale the cliff. Finally he knelt down and asked for divine assistance.

The Simorgh in her high nest saw the commotion below and knew that the visitors had come for Zaul and that it was time to bid farewell to her ward. "Your father has come to seek you," she said. "Allow me to take you to your true family."

Zaul was not eager to join his father. "Are you tired of me? This nest is my home, and I am proud to wear your plumes in my cap."

The Simorgh replied: "Soon you will be at the royal court of Iran. Soon you will have forgotten this nest. But do not worry. I have taken you under my wing, and I will never deny you my protection. Take this feather of mine and burn it if you need my assistance. I shall come to your aid like a black cloud and bring you back whenever you wish."

The Simorgh took Zaul on her shoulders, flew off the nest, and alighted on the ground. Saum bowed in front of the magnificent bird and offered her his prayerful thanks. Then father and son embraced. Zaul was given garments to cover his nakedness and a horse to ride. The company was flushed with excitement and sang joyful songs as they returned home.

The saga of the abandonment and the discovery of Zaul was the talk of the town. King Manuchehr was very happy when he heard that Saum had a son and that he had been found after being exposed and given up for lost. The king sent his crown prince, Nowzar, to invite Saum and Zaul to the capital city.

On the appointed day, King Manuchehr sat in state, flanked by his knights
Saum and Gharan as Zaul was ushered in wearing a golden helmet and
holding a javelin of glittering gold. He was breathtaking in his looks and
presence. The courtiers were astounded. The king was duly impressed as
well. He turned to Saum with these words of advice: "Take good care of this
lad and delight in his presence. He possesses the heart of a wise man and the
quiet swagger of a lion. He has a halo of divine sanction around his face."

Then the king called on his astrologers to cast the horoscope of Zaul. They informed the king that the stars were kind to the young man of the mountains. He would be a great knight and a prodigious hero. Manuchehr delighted in the news and called on the scribes to write a charter of endowment for the realm of Zabol and its vast territories, from Kabul to the Sea of China. He donated all of that land to the clan of Saum.

Father and son kissed the royal throne and traveled to Zabol, loaded as they were with the lavish gifts of the king. After a short stay with his newly found son, Saum was summoned by the king. He was commanded to return to Bactria to crush an insurrection. Saum called the noblemen of Zabol and said, "As a young man I made a reckless decision to abandon my own son. But the noble Simorgh found and reared the son that I had rejected. I thank God, who forgave my sin and restored my child to me. Now that I am commanded to leave, I entrust him to your care. Hold him dear and offer him your good counsel."

Zaul addressed his father: "If anyone was ever born under an ill star, I am that person. There are many flowers in the world. But my share of these flowers is only their thorns. I grew up on a bed of dirt, drinking blood with the hatchlings of a bird as my father lived in comfort. Now I am being abandoned again."

Saum replied: "It is just to give vent to your complaints, for I have been derelict in my duties toward you. But the astrologers have determined that this is the realm where you shall thrive. Stay here, and gather learned men about you. Let them instruct you in every field of knowledge. This is your realm. Rule and serve and learn and be merry."

Zaul went along with Saum's departing army for two milestones. Then they bid farewell. Zaul embraced his father and wept with bitter abandon. From there he returned to his palace, donned his golden torque and belt, and sat on his turquoise throne. Zaul invited equestrian and martial arts trainers as well as diviners and scholars of all nations to his court. He studied day and night and absorbed the knowledge and the arts of his teachers until he was unrivaled in knowledge and a shining star among the learned men of the world.

Zaul and Rudabeh

One day Zaul decided to tour his eastern provinces along with some of his companions. Mehrab, the vassal king of Kabul, who had descended from Zahhak, came forward to welcome the famous knight of Zabol. Zaul hosted a lavish banquet in honor of Mehrab. During the course of the night the host was impressed by his guest's heroic build, handsome features, sartorial splendor, and refined manners.

It was at this gathering that an attendant told Zaul about Mehrab's luminous daughter, Rudabeh. She was said to be possessed of skin whiter than ivory and hair blacker than musk. Her cheeks were soft and her lips were redder than pomegranate seeds. Her dazzling eyes were framed by eyelashes that competed in blackness with the feathers of a crow, and her eyebrows were shaped like a long bow at rest. Her breasts were the image of unripe pomegranates breaking through a smooth, silvery surface. The princess of Kabul was also refined and possessed of great wealth. The description ended here, but the image of the lovely daughter of Mehrab was so seared in Zaul's mind that he was unable to sleep that night.

The next day Mehrab came to pay his respects. Zaul asked if there was anything he desired, adding that his request would be granted regardless of its magnitude. Mehrab replied, "My only wish is to host you in my palace so that you can shed your light upon my domicile."

This was the only request that Zaul could not grant. He said, "But this cannot be done. Saum and the king would frown on my going to the house of an idol worshipper to drink and get drunk with him! Ask me something else and your wish will be granted."

Mehrab said he had no other wishes and took his leave. Zaul watched his guest leave in disappointment and found himself compelled to praise Mehrab to his companions. The company first thought Zaul had lost his mind in flattering the king of Kabul after that exchange. But when they realized that he was serious, they too praised his many talents, manly stature, and quiet dignity.

Meanwhile, the love Zaul felt for Mehrab's daughter had caused turmoil in his soul. Of course, he knew that marriage to the house of Mehrab, which followed a different religion and whose members traced their lineage back to Zahhak, would cause a scandal. He did not wish to get embroiled in such a difficult affair, damage his reputation, and become the laughingstock of the world. But his heart was set on the beautiful maiden. Love had conquered reason.

The next morning, Mehrab went to his inner quarters and was dazzled by the resplendent beauty of his wife, Sindokht, and his daughter, Rudabeh. The fair Sindokht asked him to share what manner of man this new knight of Iran was. She had heard that he had been reared by a wild bird. Did he appear human? Was he more suited for the throne or for the lair of a wild beast? Mehrab said, "Zaul is peerless among the knights of the world. Blessed with the strength of an elephant and the heart of a lion, he is generous at the royal court and courageous on the battlefield. He is a sprightly young fellow, with a complexion that puts the flowers of a redbud tree to shame. His only flaw, if one might call it that, is that his hair is white."

That was all the description Rudabeh needed to fall in love with Zaul. Her face was instantly flushed with excitement, and a sweet melancholy filled her heart. All desires, save the wish to be with her beloved, vanished from her mind. Rudabeh felt like she was transformed into an entirely new person.

Later she would trust her five attendants with her secret love: "You are my confidantes. I confess to you my consuming love for the knight of Zabol. Now tell me if you are my allies in this affair of the heart."

The attendants were confounded. One of them spoke up. "Your beauty is admired from India to China. You can bring down suitors from the fourth sphere of the heavens, if you wish. Why then fall for a man who was spurned by his own father and brought up by a bird? To make the matter worse, he has white hair, like an old man."

Rudabeh was enraged. "Your unworthy opinions don't concern me. Nor do I want the emperor of China or the czar of Rome for my husband. I want Zaul and I don't care if you call him old."

The attendants saw Rudabeh's determination and pledged their loyalty to her. "Forgive us," one of them said. "We are your servants. Command us and we will fly with the birds, roam with the deer, learn sorcery, and go down the wells of the world to bring you the man you love."

Rudabeh smiled, and her sallow cheeks regained their rosy color. She accepted their pledge and charged them to use all their wiles to find Zaul and bring him to her. The attendants happily dressed themselves in Roman silk, wore blossoms in their hair, and set off on a jaunt to collect flowers. It was March, when wildflowers bloomed along the riverbed.

Zaul noticed the group of girls strolling near his camp and asked his young squire about them. They were attendants from the court of Mehrab and had come to pick flowers, he replied. Zaul was intrigued. He picked up his bow, jumped on his horse, and rode out to the riverbank where the girls were. As luck would have it, a flock of ducks was gliding along the river. Zaul quickly notched an arrow in his bow and shot a duck as it attempted to soar.

The attendants were enchanted by the young man who had performed this feat. One of the girls turned to the squire and asked, "Who is this charming young man? We have never seen such a splendid hunter."

The squire chided them for not observing proper decorum when they spoke of his master. "Don't speak of him in such familiar terms, for he is Zaul, of the house of Saum and Narimon. He is no ordinary hunter but a knight who is unrivaled in the world."

The attendants teased him. "You think so highly of this Zaul," one of them said, "but that is only because you don't know our mistress, who is far superior to your master. She is the daughter of the king of Kabul. Her name is Rudabeh, and she is tall, with beautiful ivory skin, and possessed of eyes so sad and sleepy that they rival a pair of narcissus flowers. Rudabeh's ruby red lips burn in expectation of a kiss from Zaul. What do you think your master would say to that?"

The squire demurred and indicated that he would never convey such a crass message. Then he rushed to his master with laughter on his lips and related the entire conversation. Zaul's heart leapt with joy when he learned that his secret love had been reciprocated. He prepared a small package of precious jewels wrapped in embroidered Roman silk as a gift for his beloved.

The squire took the package to the attendants so they could deliver it to Rudabeh. He also swore them to secrecy, despite the old wisdom that so many people could never keep a secret:

Cut the numbers to two to keep a secret down
For at three it becomes a rumor
And at four, it's the talk of the town.

Rudabeh's attendants giggled, and one of them said, "The lion is caught in the trap. Soon Rudabeh's hopes will be realized."

Zaul was so excited that he could not let them go. He rushed out and interrogated them about the attributes of his beloved, and with every description his love grew. Finally he said, "Meeting her is my one and only desire. Tell me, can you arrange an assignation?"

An attendant replied: "Your wish is our command, sire. We shall stoop to every lie and deception so as to help you snare our lovely mistress in your noose."

They returned, and the lovelorn Zaul went back to his camp to spend another sleepless night, a night that seemed longer than an entire year.

Rudabeh's attendants returned to the castle of Mehrab with their flowers. The gatekeeper chided them for staying out so late when strangers were camping so close to the castle. But the girls teased him and laughed the matter off. They went to their mistress to bring her their good tidings. Rudabeh asked: "So, how was your encounter with the son of Saum? Tell me every detail. Is he handsome? Do his looks and manners match his reputation?"

The attendants responded by singing Zaul's praises. One of them gushed: "Built like a lion with charming white curls, he has the complexion of a crimson flower, the heart of a mage, and the charisma of a king. We promised to arrange a tryst. Now make haste and prepare to receive him. And tell us what message to take back, for he is awaiting your reply with bated breath."

Rudabeh laughed and chided them. "Suddenly the wild, feral boy turns into a winsome prince with white curls and the complexion of a redbud tree! You

surely have changed your estimation of my Zaul. I bet you promised to deliver me into his hands for a handsome reward, haven't you?"

They all laughed and went to work preparing a room for the meeting of Zaul and Rudabeh. They brought golden vessels filled with wine, musk, ambergris, and rosewater and arranged them on a spread of Chinese silk. Heaps of violet, hyacinth, and jasmine were brought in to freshen the air. The evening of the next day, an attendant brought word to Zaul that all was ready. Rudabeh went out on the battlements to wait for her beloved. At long last Zaul appeared, and Rudabeh watched him come to the walls of the castle. Then she addressed him. "Welcome, my gallant knight! You are as striking as my attendants described. I thank you for crossing the long, arduous road on foot to come here."

Zaul looked up at the beautiful Rudabeh on the high ramparts and thought she was like a rising sun peeking from an eastern mountain range. He said, "I have spent many nights praying to be united with you. I have watched the moon go through its stations in the sky dreaming about you. Now, at long last, I am hearing your sweet voice. But what good does it do us if I am down here and you are high on the ramparts? Come and let us find a way to be close. We have waited long enough for this tryst."

Rudabeh untangled the dark coils of her hair and dangled one of her long braids off the wall, commanding Zaul to climb. Not dreaming of hurting his beloved in this manner, Zaul looped his lariat around one of the teeth of the ramparts and scaled the forbidding, sixty-fathom-high wall with ease. At the top, Rudabeh kissed the ground and led her secret caller down the stairs to the room she had prepared for their visit. Zaul was as stunned by the beauty of Rudabeh as she was by his kingly radiance. They drank wine together and kissed and caressed. They spent the night in this manner but remained chaste.

At the approach of dawn Zaul said, "I know that neither Saum nor King Manuchehr will approve of our union. But I pledge my life to your love. I will get my father and my king to consent to our marriage."

Rudabeh replied, "I, too, take God as my witness that you will be my one and only king."

They said good-bye at dawn with tears in their eyes before the dashing knight rappelled down the wall. Back at his pavilion, Zaul called the magi and reminded them that every young man must marry and procreate. Then he entrusted them with the secret of his love for Rudabeh and asked for their opinion. Knowing that Mehrab was descended from the demon king Zahhak, the magi were afraid to approve of the marital connection to the clan of Mehrab. Instead they suggested that Zaul write Saum to solicit his approval for marrying Rudabeh.

Zaul Pleads with Saum

Following the advice of the magi, Zaul wrote to his father:

In the name of the God of Venus, Saturn, and the Sun, the Creator of all that exists.

This is a letter from Zaul, a devoted and humble servant to Saum, who wields the mace and the blade. In court the great Saum is a kingmaker and on the battlefield he sustains the scavenging birds that feed on carrion that he leaves behind.

You know well that I was born in adversity. Such was my fate, and I shall not complain of it. Now I have a problem of a different sort: I have become enthralled by the daughter of Mehrab. But love has not made me insolent. First let me remind you that you swore an oath before the king to grant my every wish. Now, command me and I shall follow.

Zaul sent this letter with a messenger, providing him with two additional horses lest his own steed prove unable to withstand the rigors of the journey. The messenger rode day and night until he reached the mountains of Bactria, where Saum was hunting, using cheetahs and falcons. Zaul's envoy came forth, kissed the ground, and submitted the letter. Saum descended from the

hunting ground to his pavilion to read Zaul's dispatch. Then he sighed and muttered, "What is one to expect of a boy raised by a wild bird?"

Saum brooded on this quandary. If he were to oppose Zaul's choice, he would be blamed for breaking his oath. But he could not agree to the marriage of Zaul and Rudabeh, either, as he was wary of what would result from the marriage of a man reared by a bird and a woman descended from a serpent king.

He slept on this matter and the next day called the magi and said, "I am uneasy about the union of Zaul and Rudabeh. Water and fire don't mix. How could Feraydun not fight Zahhak? Go forth and look into the future of this marriage."

The wise men took their astrological tables and charted the stars for the proposed marriage. After a day and night they returned, smiling. One of them said, "Good tidings, our lord. The daughter of Mehrab and your son will produce a hero who shall humble the enemies of Iran. Happy is the king to have your grandson among his knights."

Saum rewarded his wise men and entrusted the envoy of Zaul with this message: "Tell my son that yours is indeed an odd whim. But since I have pledged to grant all your wishes, I shall see what I can do. Let me go to the king to disentangle this knot."

Crisis in the Kabul Palace

Happy to receive his father's approval, Zaul sent a courier to Rudabeh apprising her of the positive development. The courier delivered her message but she was stopped by Sindokht on her way out. The queen interrogated her with some severity. "I keep seeing you around the palace, but you deliberately hurry past my chambers. Who are you, and what is your business here?"

Upon further questioning of the courier, Sindokht suspected that Rudabeh was having an affair. She ordered the gates of the palace closed and called on Rudabeh to come forth and explain the matter. Rudabeh appeared with her head hung low. Sindokht said, "I have not denied you a single thing throughout your life. So why have you chosen the path of wickedness? Who is this courier, and who is the man who has stolen your heart? The crown of the Arabs has been a mixed blessing for us, but there is no blemish on our reputation. You are throwing all that to the wind. Woe is me with a daughter like you."

Rudabeh stared at the ground and said faintly: "The truth is that I am in love. I adore Zaul with all my heart and consider as expendable everything that does not pertain to him. Zaul and I have a covenant of loyalty. He has sent word to the great Saum and convinced him to give his blessing to this union. The woman you just abused was bearing Saum's letter."

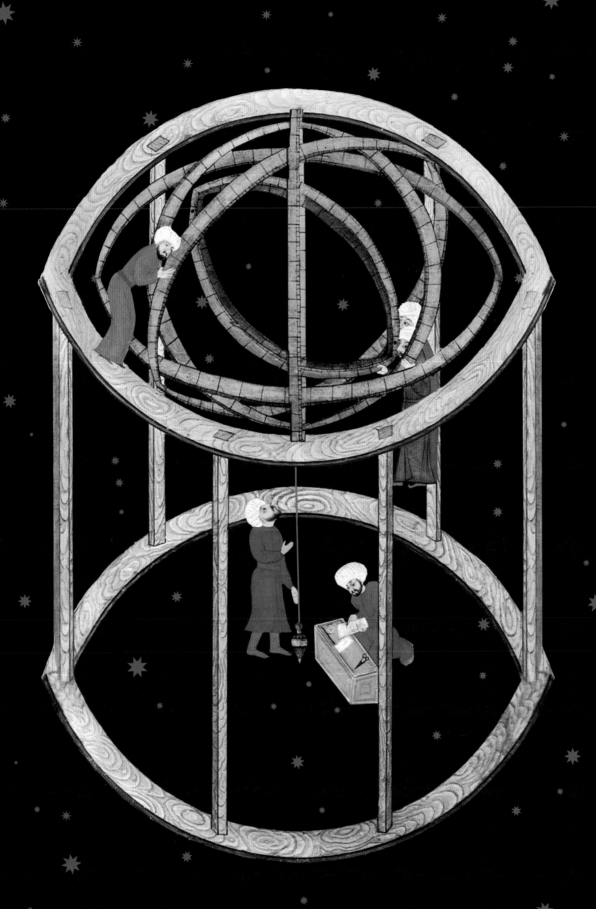

Sindokht fell silent. She approved of Zaul, of course, but she knew that this union would enrage the king of Iran and imperil the kingdom of Kabul. Sindokht allowed her daughter to retire to her chambers. Then she went to her quarters in great anxiety and stayed there until her husband returned.

Mehrab asked what was wrong and Sindokht replied: "I was thinking of the ways of the world. Everything appears so untrustworthy. Powers wane, people get old and die, and this palace of ours, along with all our precious possessions, is destined to decay and disappear."

Mehrab dismissed Sindokht's concerns. "But this has been the way of the world since time immemorial."

Sindokht replied that her musings were meant to prepare him for some news. The truth was that Zaul had seduced their pure daughter. Rudabeh was pale with the misery of love and deaf to the voice of reason.

Mehrab jumped to his feet, trembling with rage. Grasping the hilt of his sword, he shouted, "I shall make a river of blood flow from the veins of Rudabeh."

Sindokht put her arms around her husband and implored him to calm down and hear the rest of the story. But Mehrab slipped from her grasp and threw her down, saying: "I should have killed her at birth, as my ancestors used to do. I took pity on her, and this is how she repays me! If Saum and King Manuchehr hear of this, they will lay waste to our land and sack our city."

Sindokht enjoined her husband to rein in his anger and listen to her. She said that Saum not only knew of the matter but indeed had approved of it, and the king was likely to be persuaded as well. But Mehrab was not convinced.

"Why are you lying to me, woman? It is not that I resent the idea of such a marriage. Who wouldn't want to be related to Saum? The point is that such a marriage is inconceivable. Saum and Manuchehr would never stand for it."

Sindokht argued that it all made sense. Hadn't Feraydun sought the daughters of Sarv, the king of Yemen, as brides for his sons? Nature combined opposites all the time. Marriage with strangers would make a clan strong.

Mehrab was not moved. He listened to Sindokht's words in silence and then commanded her to produce Rudabeh.

Fearful for her daughter's safety, Sindokht made Mehrab swear an oath not to harm her. She went to Rudabeh and instructed her to put on her finest clothes and go to her father. Rudabeh protested that she was unable to dress up in her misery. But she obeyed her mother nonetheless and went to her father, radiant as the rising sun. Mehrab was silenced by his daughter's splendor and praised her in his heart. Then he proceeded to berate her for intending to marry a man so utterly unsuitable.

King Manuchehr's Decree

At the Persian capital, the story of the love of Zaul and Rudabeh reached King Manuchehr before Saum could intercede on his son's behalf. He called a counsil of priests and decreed that this connection would spell disaster. "I did not rid Iran of the talons of the lions and leopards to lose it again to a silly love affair. If the son of Zaul and Rudabeh inclined to his mother's side, he would attempt to reclaim the throne for the house of Zahhak."

The counsil concurred and urged the king to take the appropriate measures. The king then commanded the crown prince Nowzar to go to Bactria and summon Saum to court.

Saum warmly welcomed Nowzar, and they spent a night in drinking and merrymaking. The next morning they took off for the capital and passed through many cities until the glittering weapons and colorful standard of Manuchehr's sentries were in sight.

Saum entered the court, kissed the ground, and gave a report of his pacification of Bactria. King Manuchehr was pleased. He replied: "You have nearly finished off the rebels of the North. Now go south to the land of Kabul and burn it to the ground. Bring me the head of Mehrab and kill his entire clan. Cleanse the land of the spawn of Zahhak."

Saum was troubled by his new charge, but he had no choice but to carry out the command of the king. The next day, he gathered his army and set off for Kabul.

Zaul in Action

When this intelligence reached Zaul, he jumped on his horse and set off in a cloud of gloom to confront his father, saying: "The raging dragon Saum must first separate my head from my body if he wants to set fire to my world."

When the standard of Zaul appeared on the horizon, a company of the elders from Saum's camp went forth to greet him. They paid their respects, and one of them said, "Your father is angry at your insubordination. Offer your apologies and don't be stubborn."

Zaul replied: "Then let him not start a quarrel if he is a man of reason. Let him not speak to me in anger or I will shame him into tears."

At the camp, Zaul dismounted, kissed the ground, and addressed his father with tears in his eyes. "May the heroic Saum be content. May his mind be disposed to justice. The world submits to your blade when you charge your gray horse. An army that feels the wrath of your mace does not last long.

"The whole world benefits from your justice. I alone seem to have no share of this blessing. I have committed no sin that I am aware of, unless being the son of Saum is a sin. You abandoned me at birth and denied me your fatherly love. I did not suckle the breast of my sad mother, nor did I rest in a cradle. You should have taken up your quarrel with God, for he created me the way I am.

"And yet the Creator saw to my care, restored me to the world, gave me my own kingdom as well as a beloved soul mate in Kabul. I stood in the eastern frontier of Zabol and kept faith with you in hopes of one day being of use to you.

"Now you bring me this gift. You come here with a ruthless army to wreck my house and home. Is this the way you repay me for all my suffering? Now, look at me. Here I stand, exposed to your rage. Cut me in half if you want. But I will not allow you to invade Kabul while I live."

Saum hung his head and said, "Yes. You are right. Everything I did was unjust. But don't be hasty in your judgment. Allow me to remedy the situation. I will send you to the king with a letter. If the Creator helps us, everything will work out."

Saum's letter started with a list of his heroic labors. He had slain the legendary dragon of the Kashaf River with one blow of his mace, earning the title of One-Blow-Saum. And he had crushed the rebellions of Bactria and Mazandaran. Then Saum pleaded with the king to be kind to his son and ended his letter lightly: "My son has come to me now saying that he would rather be

hanged than witness the invasion of Kabul. Well, what can we do? The lad is in love. Is it any wonder that a boy who grew up in the wilderness is smitten by a girl who happens to be the daughter of Mehrab? I hope that the king will understand his state and forgive his youthful indiscretion.

"Your Majesty, the ward of the bird has fallen in love and he is shedding tears enough to turn the dirt at his feet into a patch of mud. He is so miserable that ordinary folks take pity on him. Now he comes to you as a supplicant. Treat him with the benevolence that befits a king."

Zaul took the letter and set off to King Manuchehr's capital.

A company of dignitaries went out to welcome the young knight and ushered him into the royal court. Zaul prostrated himself before the king and remained in that position. Manuchehr ordered his attendants to raise the young man and perfume his face. Zaul bowed and presented Saum's letter. As the king read the letter, his demeanor changed to one of joviality. He laughed and said, "I was deeply concerned about this marriage, but this pleasant letter from old Saum has moved me. So despite my misgivings I am prepared to grant you this favor. Go forth and marry your beloved."

Manuchehr engaged the royal astrologers to determine the fate of Zaul and Rudabeh's union. After three days the prognosticators returned with the good news that a peerless warrior would be born to them. The king charged the magi to test the young man's intelligence with their difficult riddles, and Zaul proved equal to this challenge. Then he asked for leave in order to return to Saum. The king playfully retorted: "What is this talk of missing your father? We all know the one you miss is the fair daughter of Mehrab. I am sure you can spare us one more day."

The next day, the sound of drums, trumpets, and cymbals announced elaborate games arranged by the king. Zaul shined as a hero in contests of shooting and fighting, and he bested all his challengers. At the conclusion of the games the king sent Zaul off along with a letter addressed to Saum: "You are my dear companion in fighting and in feasting. You are pleasant in looks and wise in consultations. I have examined your son and found him courageous and wise. I have granted all his wishes."

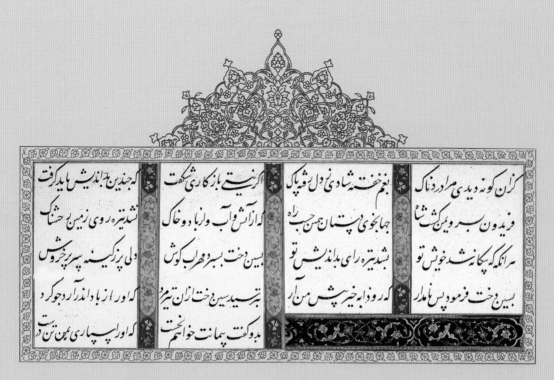

Panic in Kabul

Mehrab's reaction to the news of Saum's approaching troops was even more frenzied than Zaul's. Rumors of an army on the move had caused panic in Kabul. Mehrab contemplated slaying Sindokht and Rudabeh in order to appease the king and thus save the people of Kabul. But Sindokht had a better idea. She said, "Be patient, for this dark night shall pass. The dawn is about to break."

Mehrab retorted: "Don't ply me with old platitudes. Show me a solution, or prepare to pay with your life and that of your daughter for this scandal."

Sindokht said, "Shedding my blood would hardly solve your problems. I suggest that you open your treasure houses instead and allow me to go on a mission of reconciliation to Saum, but first give me your word that you will not harm Rudabeh in my absence."

Having secured Mehrab's promise, Sindokht got to work donning an extravagant jewel-encrusted silk gown. Then she collected the lavish offerings that she intended to bring to Saum. Ten golden bridled horses carrying thirty thousand dinars as well as a crown, a torque, bracelets, and a pair of earrings led the caravan of gifts. Fifty slaves in golden belts walked behind the horses. Following them came thirty more Persian and Arabian horses, each flanked by two slaves carrying golden chalices full of musk, camphor, sugar, and rubies. Then walked a line of one hundred red-haired she-camels and one hundred hinnies carrying forty bolts of gold-embroidered silk and two hundred Indian swords, thirty of which were laced with a deadly poison. At the end of the convoy, four war elephants carried the disassembled pieces of an enormous golden throne. When all was prepared, Sindokht led the procession to Saum's camp riding on the back of a swift horse. She had disguised herself and told the heralds not to reveal her identity.

Saum was surprised to see a beautiful woman as the ambassador of the king of Kabul. He was also astonished by the lavish gifts she had brought along. The enchanting Sindokht went to Saum with three of her most beautiful attendants each carrying a goblet of gems and said, "You are a legendary knight, and your fame for valor and justice precedes you. If Mehrab is guilty, why should the people of Kabul pay for his sins?"

Saum replied: "First tell me who you are. Then speak to me of how Zaul got to meet Mehrab's daughter. And don't forget to describe the looks and the wisdom of this Rudabeh."

Sindokht asked for immunity so she could speak freely and then said, "I am the wife of Mehrab and mother to Rudabeh. It is true that we have descended from Zahhak, but we are loyal vassals of King Manuchehr. Now I have come to see what you intend to do with Kabul. And I come to you in humility. Kill me if you wish, or bind me. But spare the people of Kabul. If we have erred, let them remain unharmed, for they are your loyal subjects."

Saum was impressed by the elegance of Sindokht. He held her hand and comforted her. "Rest assured that you and the people of Kabul are safe. I have already given my consent to this marriage. You are our equals, although you have descended from a different race. This is the way of the world. One cannot quarrel with God for creating different races of people. And I have sent a letter to the king by the hands of Zaul. I am sure the king will smile when he reads the letter, and all will be fine.

"Now, show me the face of this angel descended from the demon king, and receive a king's ransom!"

Sindokht was all smiles. "We would be honored to host you at our palace."

Then she sent a swift messenger to her husband apprising him of the success of her mission. The next day she asked leave to join her husband in Kabul.

Shortly after Sindokht's departure, Zaul arrived at Saum's camp, unannounced, from the court of King Manuchehr. He had galloped so fast that Saum's scouts had not been able to precede him to the camp. He brought the good tidings that his marriage to Rudabeh had been approved. Saum was delighted, but Zaul was so flushed with excitement that he was unable to sleep that night. The next day he sent a missive to Mehrab, saying that the king no longer opposed his marriage to Rudabeh and they should prepare for the wedding festivities.

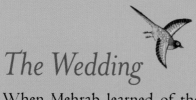

The Wedding

When Mehrab learned of the success of Sindokht's mission to Saum, he showered his wife with praises and rich gifts. A few hours later his happiness was complete as he received word from Zaul that the king, too, had approved of the proposed marriage.

The happy queen of Kabul went to Rudabeh and said, "You sought to be united with your beloved and did not vacillate in your determination. Rise and rejoice, for all your dreams have come true."

Sindokht attended to the details of the upcoming royal wedding and issued orders to decorate the city of Kabul for the festivities. Mehrab went out to welcome Saum and Zaul. When the father and son came through the decorated gates of Kabul, Sindokht came forth, ahead of three hundred slaves each holding golden chalices of wine and goblets of jewels. They rested and drank. Then Saum addressed Sindokht: "For how long do you intend to hide the fair Rudabeh from us?"

Sindokht rejoined: "And where is the king's ransom that you promised to offer for a glimpse of the sun?"

All were merry as they went to the palace. Saum was stunned and speech-less when he saw the heavenly beauty of Rudabeh. The wedding services commenced and all were gay for three weeks. Then Saum and Zaul returned to Zabol as Rudabeh followed them in her splendid litter. The newly married couple remained in Zabol, but Saum, who had unfinished business in the battle against the insurgents of Bactria, bid them farewell and set off in a northerly direction.

> Zaul crowned his consort with a golden crest
> And his heart brimmed over with the joys of love
> He called for a great feast, as he felt utterly blessed.

A Hero Is Born:
Rostam

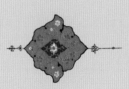

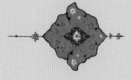 *The young sapling of love took root.*
As time passed the young
Proud poplar was laden with fruit.

The Simorgh's Gift

Not long after the wedding of Rudabeh and Zaul, the fair Rudabeh became heavy with child. She felt as if she were carrying a mass of iron or a boulder in her belly. Rudabeh's complexion turned from rose to saffron, and she despaired of surviving her pregnancy. In vain did Sindokht try to comfort her. With the first pangs of labor, Rudabeh lost consciousness. Sindokht clawed at her face in grief, and the disconsolate Zaul stayed at her bedside, tears streaming through his silver beard.

In the depths of his desolation, Zaul recalled the carefree days he had spent in the nest of the magnificent Simorgh, the bird that had raised him from a foundling. Suddenly a ray of hope shot across the clouds of his despondency. He remembered the solemn promise of the Simorgh at the moment of their farewell. Zaul only needed to burn one of her feathers and she would come to the rescue. The silver-headed knight of Zabol set to work fetching the feather and called for a brazier. Then he sent word to Sindokht that perhaps all was not lost. A fire was kindled, and Zaul extended the long, multicolored plume to the flames.

The feather was not fully singed when the sky grew dark with a massive cloud gleaming with coral rainbows. The sight of those familiar colors brought great comfort to Zaul's unhappy soul. The Simorgh wheeled and landed. The wondrous bird gathered her wings and approached with delicate steps, lowering her head in deference to the great knight. Zaul humbled himself to his benefactor and praised the incomparable Simorgh in a tremulous voice. Then the Simorgh spoke: "Why this sorrow, why these tears in the eyes of my brave knight? Your beautiful wife is blessed with an auspicious child that will humble the beasts of the wild and the kings of the world. Tall as a cypress and powerful as an elephant, your child will inherit the wisdom of his grandfather Saum.

"But this birth is not destined to be an ordinary one. Call a skilled mage ready with a sharp dagger. Induce the mother into a stupor with wine and instruct the able practitioner to slice open her side and deliver the baby. Once he has sutured her, mix this medicinal plant with musk and milk and apply the balm to the mother's wound. To complete the cure, pass a feather of mine over the scar, for its magical shadow shall heal her. Now be content and praise God, for your happiness is of divine origin."

With these words, the Simorgh shed a feather from her wing and took to the skies.

Those who witnessed the scene were awed by this spectacle. And yet Sindokht
had reason to feel uneasy. None had ever heard of a baby born in the manner
described by the Simorgh, but they followed the advice of the enchanted bird
and all went well. At the conclusion of the ministrations of the skilled mage,
an astonishing baby was born, with a face radiant as the sun. Within one day
he was as big as a one-year-old child.

It took a long time for Rudabeh to wake, but upon coming to consciousness, she rejoiced to see her son, who was healthy, vigorous, and as full of color as a heap of lilies and roses. Rudabeh called him Rostam. Ten wet nurses could hardly keep up with the appetite of the extraordinary infant. When he had been weaned, he consumed the rations of five men in bread and meat.

Zaul and Sindokht were proud, and to indicate the prodigious size of the baby, they had a silken likeness of Rostam made and sent to his grandfather Saum, the noble knight of Bactria. Saum's delight was boundless. He could hardly contain his desire to see his grandson. When Rostam had grown as tall as his father's belt, he was said to resemble his grandfather in appearance, grace, and intelligence. At this time Saum embarked on a journey back to Zabol.

Zaul and Mehrab, Rostam's maternal grandfather, went out to greet the elder knight. The hosts dismounted and prostrated themselves. The child Rostam was presented to his grandfather on top of a war elephant. Saum praised Rostam as one praises a grown man—nay, a great knight worthy of a crown. Rostam dismounted and said, "I am your servant, great ancestor. I shall seek my own steed and armor. I shall take a quiver of arrows to the battlefield and send forth my own greetings to our foes. I pledge to humble the enemy with the blessings of the king and God. It is said that my countenance is like yours. My only wish is that I will be your equal in courage."

Saum took him by the hand and kissed his face and head. Then they all retired to the terraces of Zaul's palace, and a month was spent in merrymaking, eating, and drinking upon daises of gold.

One day, as Saum admired Rostam's broad shoulders, slender waist, and muscular build, he thought about the child's magical birth and the intercession of

the Simorgh. He declared: "No one is the equal of this child, nor has there been one born like him in one hundred generations. So let us drink in his honor, for this fleeting world does not last, and the habit of the world is to bring forth the new and carry off the old."

Mehrab drained many chalices of wine. Then he made an outlandish jest: "I will no longer fear Zaul, Saum, or even their hallowed king. When I ride with Rostam on a worthy steed, holding a well-honed blade, not even the clouds will dare cast a shadow on us. We will revive the ways of our common ancestor, the serpent king Zahhak."

Saum, the old knight of Bactria, laughed with abandon, recalling the false misgivings that he and King Manuchehr had harbored for this good-natured and loyal vassal.

The next day Saum prepared to return to Bactria. At the moment of departure he left his son with these words of advice: "Walk only in the path of righteousness, and obey the commands of your king and the edicts of reason. Hold your hand from doing evil, and follow the path of God, for no one lives forever. I know I don't have much longer in this world."

Zaul and Rostam escorted the old knight for three milestones and returned to Zabol, where Zaul saw to the comfort and education of his son. The world was suffused with hope from the surface of the earth to the constellation of Aries.

A Hero's First Adventures

After much merrymaking one night, the young Rostam heeded the advice of his father and presented his companions with gifts of gold, garments, and horses. All retired to their quarters drunk with wine and heavy with abundant riches. They had not rested for long when their sweet slumber was marred by the din of Zaul's war elephant, which had broken its chains and was running amok.

Not one among the warriors dared approach the fuming beast. Suddenly Rostam roared into the melee. Some of the attendants tried to prevent him from confronting the rampaging elephant, but Rostam pushed aside his well-meaning minders and stood in front of the beast wielding a large mace. The furious elephant rushed the hero like a moving mountain. Rostam held his ground, swung the mace, and killed the vicious elephant. Then, as if he had performed a simple chore, the young hero turned around and went back to bed. The next morning Zaul heard of his son's daring feat. The silver-headed knight of Zabol was proud of his son, although he had lost a good war elephant. Now he knew that he could set his son on the path of glory.

Rostam's first mission was to conquer the impregnable Arab castle on Sepand Mountain. Zaul's grandfather Narimon had lost his life laying siege to that stronghold. Unlike his ancestor's direct approach, Rostam's path to breaching the castle involved subterfuge. He was to disguise himself as a merchant leading a salt caravan. The castle of Sepand was sufficient unto itself for all things except salt.

Rostam took a few brave warriors with him. They hid their weapons in the loads of salt and easily gained access to the castle. Rostam gave two loads of salt to the lord of the fortress as a gift and sold the rest to its denizens. When night fell, Rostam and his warriors attacked the guards, and by morning they had taken the castle.

Upon inspecting the premises, Rostam came across a curious and well-hidden room made of solid granite. He smashed the iron gate of the room with his hefty mace. The room was filled to the dome with gold coins and precious gems. It was as if the mines of the world and the bottoms of the oceans had been scraped clean to fill the chamber.

Rostam sent a missive to his father reporting that he had avenged their ancestor and garnered untold treasures. Zaul shed tears of joy, sent the good tidings to Saum, and dispatched thousands of camels to carry off the treasures. Indian trumpets blared in Zabol, and the town's enormous drums boomed to announce the return of the triumphant Rostam. The young hero dismounted and prostrated himself before his father. Then he went to his mother's chambers and rubbed his forehead in the dust at the threshold. The fair Rudabeh kissed the shoulders of her victorious son and praised him. The young Rostam was now prepared to serve his king.

The New King

Astrologers had foretold the day of King Manuchehr's passing. As it did not befit a wise king to be ambushed by death, he called the noblemen, the high clergy, and his firstborn to a final audience. The king turned to the crown prince and spoke: "Heed my words, Nowzar. Don't let this throne bewitch you, nor be seduced by its comforts and glory. Like wayfarers resting at an inn before setting off on the road, we all linger for a spell in this caravanserai. Let not the love of this fleeting world run deep in your heart. All that remains from us is our deeds, so deviate not from the path of righteousness. I have suffered much, fought great battles, crushed enemies, and avenged my father on his evil brothers. For sixscore years have I served the throne of our fore-father Feraydun. I cleansed the land and erected entire cities of abundance.

"I have to leave all of this to you now. Meditate on this lesson and know besides that great evil awaits you from Turan, the land ruled by the children of Tur. Be wise weathering the storms. Attack and parry, now as a wolf and then as a ram. Seek the support of your knights Saum and Zaul in this hardship. And know that a mighty scion has been born to Zaul, a hero at whose assault the Turanians shall drop their shields. Rely on him, for he is the one to avenge you."

With these words the king's eyelids fell for the last time and he passed into legend.

An auspicious day was chosen for the crowning ceremony of Nowzar, the new king of Iran. All were merry as the king sat on the throne. Gifts were bestowed upon the army and knights pledged their allegiance. At the end of the ceremonies, the king disappeared into the opulent corridors of his palace and did not emerge for two months. He gave in to sloth, gluttony, and avarice away from the public eye. Nowzar had abandoned his father's ways all too soon. He burdened the farmers with taxes until they took up arms and rose up in rebellion. External threats menaced Iran as enemies detected that the sovereign power was weak. God had withdrawn his sanction from Nowzar, and the divine halo had left his face. He had lost his way and his kingdom was in shambles.

In great fear the king sent an urgent dispatch to Saum, reminding him of Manuchehr's final words and asking for his help to restore calm and order to the land.

Saum was swift in obliging his king. As he approached the palace, an assembly of Iranian knights went ahead to welcome him. They were unsatisfied with Nowzar's reign and proposed a plan to raise Saum, who was the first among them, to the throne. But the noble Saum would not brook rebellion against his king. Instead he persuaded the assembly to return to court and plead with His Majesty to mend his ways. They all went to the royal court and registered their dissatisfaction with the reign of Nowzar. The king, who was aware of his lapses, listened to their counsel. He was contrite and pledged to be just from that day forward.

The Invasion from Turan

Indeed King Nowzar did attempt to restore order to his land, but it was too late. Tidings of disarray had reached far and wide. King Pashang of Turan called his knights to assembly, refreshed the old grievances, and lamented that the blood of his grandfather Tur had been spilled by Manuchehr. His son the gallant Afrasiab stood up in the gathering and girded his loins in a pledge to exact revenge on Iran for the defeat and execution of the mighty Tur. Proud of his spirited son, Pashang opened the treasure houses and decreed that an army be assembled for the invasion of Iran. In his desire to expand his realm, the king of Turan turned a deaf ear to the sage advice of his other son, Prince Aghrirath, who said, "Weak as it has grown, Iran still has many courageous defenders, not the least of whom is the noble Saum."

Not long after this pronouncement, the great warrior Saum passed away. When the news reached Afrasiab, he knew that Zaul and Saum's entire clan would be distracted by his funerary rites. He surmised that the whole of Iran was ripe for conquest.

With the coming of spring, the armies of Turan gathered. One glorious morning, Afrasiab's drums of war sounded from atop armored war elephants, and his mighty army crossed the Oxus River, which had separated Iran and Turan since the times of Feraydun.

Afrasiab sent one prong of his army toward Zabol, as he was sure of a swift victory against the bereaved clan of Saum, and led a second prong toward the Persian capital. Nowzar, too, brought out an army to stand against the Turanian flanks, and the two sides met at the battlefield of Dahastan.

In the grim battles that ensued on both fronts, Afrasiab lost some of his best warriors. He fought fearlessly, but several of his deeds were ignoble. His greatest victory was the defeat and capture of King Nowzar. When news arrived that some of Afrasiab's kinsmen were slain at the battle of Zabol, he bellowed with rage and ordered Nowzar to be hauled in rags to his presence. Afrasiab reminded his royal captive of the vendetta between their ancestors, asked for a sword to settle the feud, and decapitated King Nowzar.

This regicide did not sate Afrasiab's fury, so he called for the massacre of all the Iranian captives. The monstrosity of this edict dismayed Afrasiab's brother, the righteous Prince Aghrirath. He asked for a stay in mass executions and took the prisoners into his own custody. Later Aghrirath would allow them to escape, as he feared for their lives. Such was the anger of Afrasiab at learning this intelligence that he rushed his own brother and cleaved him in half with one blow of his sword.

With the death of King Nowzar, the throne of Iran belonged to Afrasiab, but he yearned to possess and control the entire nation from the Oxus River in the east to the deserts of Arabia to the west. His campaign in Zabol had not succeeded in dislodging the clan of Saum and Zaul from their stronghold. Pashang, the king of Turan, issued fresh orders for Iran to be subdued in its entirety. Afrasiab launched new waves of invasion, leaving the Iranians vulnerable and terrified.

Neither of King Nowzar's sons, Tous or Gostaham, was deemed worthy of ascending the throne of Iran. It was assumed that the divine sanction had been withdrawn from the line of Nowzar. The knights then appointed a very old man named Zav, and then his son, Garshasp, to the throne, but they, too, proved ineffective. After Garshasp's death Iran was utterly helpless in the face of the ferocious armies of Afrasiab.

Iranian knights who had been disheartened by invasions and insecurity went to Zaul and bitterly lamented the impending demise of Iran. The kings were incompetent, the enemies were at the gates, and Zaul was too old to lead the knights and save the day.

Rostam Finds His Steed

The ancient land needed a new hero, and the adolescent Rostam had proven himself in battle against beast and man. Keenly aware of his duty, the young champion came to his father shortly after his victory at Sepand Mountain and asked permission to confront Afrasiab. The idea had occurred to Zaul, but he was torn between paternal love and patriotic duty. On the one hand, his brave son, his prodigious strength and agility notwithstanding, was still too young to face a mighty opponent like Afrasiab. On the other, Rostam was an exceptional hero. He could be the savior of his homeland despite his tender age.

The decision was made easy for Zaul when Rostam came to him again, declaring that he wished for the life of a hero, not the comforts and trivial games of his peers. The boy was consumed with the desire to win glory in combat. Zaul finally relented, and, to solemnize his approval, he honored his son with the gift of the ox-headed mace of the great Saum. Rostam's joy upon receiving the legendary weapon was boundless. He proudly accepted it and then asked his father, "Now, where is the steed to carry my stout body wielding the mace of Saum?"

Zaul smiled and called on his aides to send forth the herds of Zabol and Kabul. On the appointed day, the herdsmen rustled the horses. Rostam searched for a long time but could not find a horse with the strength to carry him. They all buckled under the pressure of his right arm as he pushed down

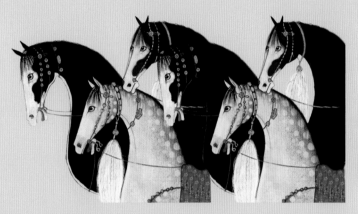

on their backs. Finally, he looked upon a brawny colt the color of rose petals dappled in saffron. The colt was following a feisty mare. He was a splendid specimen, keen enough to track a distant ant on the blackest night. Seeing that it was not branded, Rostam prepared to capture it, but the herdsman protested, "It is not right to steal a horse that belongs to another."

"But I don't see a brand on that horse!"

"True. This recalcitrant fiend goes by the name of The Bright One, or Rakhsh. None has been able to ride it although it has been long ready for saddling. We have heard of a legendary hero, a giant by the name of Rostam. We call this wild stallion the Rakhsh of Rostam. Beware of him and his fire-breathing mother."

Rostam was delighted to hear the description but in order to capture the colt he had to frighten away the aggressive mother with a mighty scream. Then he approached Rakhsh and pushed down on its back with all his might, but the horse stood its ground. Rostam knew that he had finally found his mount. Here was the worthy steed that he would ride into war, the companion that would share the many labors that awaited them both. Rostam asked the herdsman, "What is the price of this horse?"

"If you are Rostam, then the horse is yours. Ride him well and defend the land, for the price of this horse is the safekeeping of Iran."

The young hero saddled Rakhsh and, giving in to fantasies of combat, brought him to a full gallop. Yes, this horse was capable of carrying him in full battle gear. This was a magical gift—a strong, clever stallion with round haunches and an elegant gait. Beautiful as a deer and pleasant to touch, Rakhsh had a neck softer than a thick layer of goose feathers. Rostam burned clouds of incense for Rakhsh to ward off the evil eye.

Zaul's heart bloomed like fields of spring when he saw his gallant son riding a steed that resembled a dragon. As was the custom, he generously gave a fortune to the company of the attending noblemen to celebrate Rostam's new stature. Then he sounded the bell from atop his war elephant to initiate the march toward the forces of Turan.

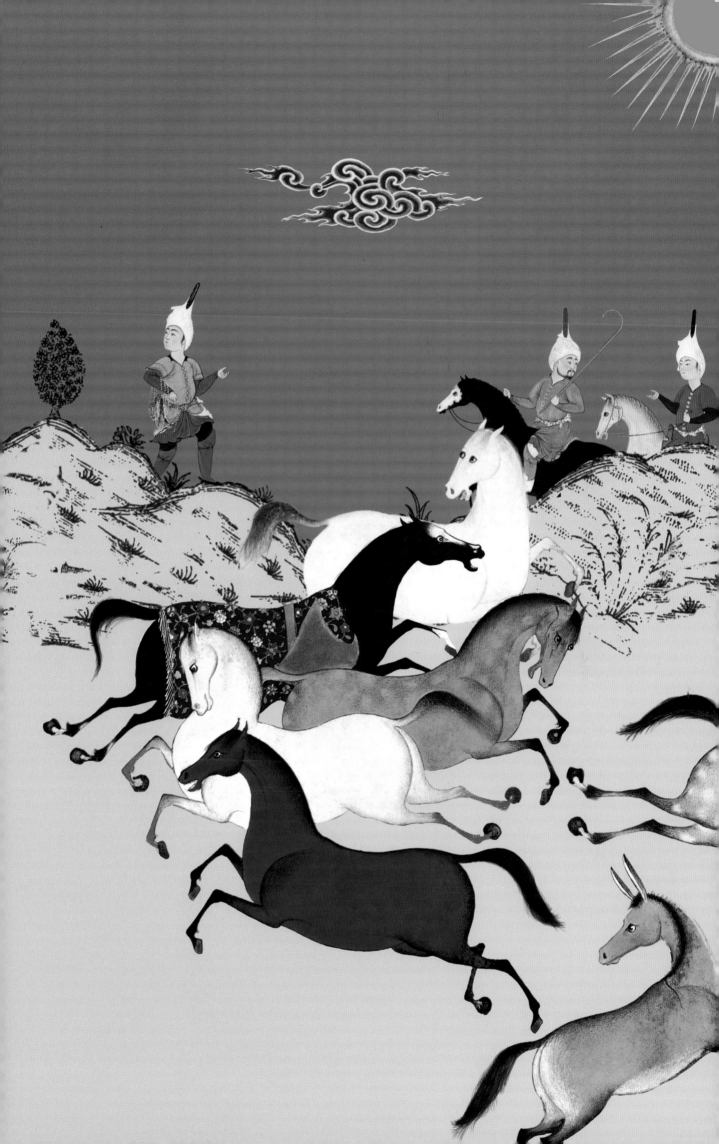

The army of Zabol moved forward until it reached the Turanian front lines at the plain of Rey. Afrasiab lost all desire for food and was struck by insomnia when he heard of the gathering of the Iranian troops under the command of Zaul two miles south of his front lines.

Rostam Fights Afrasiab

On the Iranian side, all appeared ready for the battle. But Zaul knew that something was amiss. Rostam and his troops needed a royal commander, and Iran needed a monarch hallowed by divine grace. Zaul consulted with his advisers, who informed him that a young descendant of the magnificent Feraydun named Kay Qobad lived in obscurity in the Alborz Mountains. Without delay Zaul dispatched Rostam to fetch the man who would assume the empty throne of Iran. Swift as the wind, Rostam rode his stallion into the heart of the forbidding mountain range. Fighting fatigue and Turanian foes, he did not rest until he came back with the royal master whom he would obey and serve.

According to tradition, Zaul convened a gathering of the high clergy and noblemen to name Kay Qobad the new king of Iran. They hailed the young king as sovereign and rejoiced for seven days and nights. On the eighth day he sat on the throne and admitted the assembly of knights. They pledged their loyalty and called on Kay Qobad to cleanse the homeland of foreign hordes. The new king promised to reward bravery on the battlefield, and unfurled the crimson, yellow, and purple standard of Kaveh. He then charged the knights to take the battle to the marauders of Turan.

As the armies approached the decisive hour, Rostam asked his father to point out the standard of Afrasiab. Zaul warned that the commander of the Turanian forces was no easy prey for an inexperienced warrior like him. The ambitious Rostam knew that Afrasiab would be a worthy opponent, and it was for that exact reason that he sought to vanquish him first. Spotting the black flag of Afrasiab, the hero cued Rakhsh to a charge, thundering his battle cry. Afrasiab turned to his advisers and asked, "Who is that ferocious lad?"

An attendant replied: "This is the new warrior Rostam, the son of Zaul. Do you not see that he has come wielding the mace of Saum? Do you not see that he has come to seek glory?"

Locking gazes, Rostam and Afrasiab spurred their horses into a furious gallop. The Iranian hero gripped Rakhsh against his thighs and lifted his mace. Afrasiab unsheathed his sword and the combatants grappled. Rostam returned his mace to its holder and grabbed on to Afrasiab's belt, lifting him off his saddle with ease. He wanted to carry his royal captive straight to the throne of King Kay Qobad. But Afrasiab's belt gave way, and he was saved by the ignominy of falling on the ground. A few soldiers rushed in to help him regain his composure. Afrasiab added to his humiliation by running from the field and leaving his troops to their own fate.

Distraught that he had lost his captive, Rostam snatched the crown off the dishonored commander of Turan as he fled. King Kay Qobad was pleased with Rostam's victory and ordered the Iranian troops to charge. Rostam went back to the battlefield wielding his ox-headed mace, and wherever he turned, heads fell to the ground as the leaves of autumn fall from the trees. The battle went to the Iranians, and what remained of the crushed Turanian throngs retreated behind the Oxus River in dishonor and disarray. The knights of Iran returned to their capital weighed down with booty. King Kay Qobad sat upon the throne flanked by Rostam and Zaul, the father and son who had made him king and saved Iran.

Suing for Peace After the Defeat

Afrasiab left the defeated army at the banks of the Oxus River, went to the court of his father, Pashang, and harangued him for breaching his covenant of peace with Iran. He heaped blame on his father for coveting the land given to the children of Iraj and said, "You relied on wild rumors instead of investigating the facts of the strength of your enemy. Iran's throne did not remain empty for long. The worthy Kay Qobad rules in Iran now. Nor was Iran ever devoid of courageous defenders. One among them is Rostam, a wonder of nature who humbled me with one blow of his hefty mace and lifted me off my horse as if I weighed no more than a mosquito. My belt broke and I escaped the grip of that gigantic man. You know my courage and cunning in war. But in his hand I was like a weed about to be pulled out of the ground, root and branch.

"You thought of war as sport and caused the best of our knights along with ten thousand soldiers to fall in battle. Worst of all, we have to live with the ignominy of a defeat that shall never be forgotten.

"I, too, erred in slaying my own brother, Aghrirath. I lived to learn a hard lesson about the wages of injustice. I was ambushed by legions of knights, each flying a different standard. I regret my evil deed, and I, too, hope to be forgiven by you. But let us forget the past, for the only way forward is to sue for peace. This powerful enemy will no doubt vanquish us if war continues."

Pashang listened with tears in his eyes, staggered by the sudden wisdom of his once impetuous son. Then he called for a scribe and dictated a solicitous letter. It started by praising God and the divinely inspired Feraydun, who apportioned the world among his three sons. If Iraj met treachery at Tur's hand, Pashang contended, he was rightly avenged by his son, Manuchehr. Feuds should have ended there. Pashang pledged that the rulers of Turan would forget the old vendettas. They would not dream of crossing the Oxus River again unless in peace and brotherhood.

The letter was sealed and entrusted to the wise Viseh, the king's brother. A great offering was sent along with the message of peace from Turan. Heaps of jewels were among these gifts, and gold was the essence of crowns and daises as well as the belts of beautiful slaves. There were also many Arabian horses caparisoned with golden bridles, and silver scabbards hung from their saddles.

King Kay Qobad graciously responded to Pashang's offer. "You must know well that we did not preempt you in this conflict. Tur was the one who betrayed and murdered his own brother, Iraj. And it was Afrasiab who initiated this war and slayed our King Nowzar in captivity, an act so egregious as to offend even the wild beasts. Nor did he spare his own brother, the wise Prince Aghrirath.

"But if the children of Tur are inclined to peace, I will not deny them this wish. I shall not hold a grudge, for I have withdrawn my passions from this ephemeral world. Let the Oxus River remain the border between us, as it was decreed from the olden times."

Rostam protested that the proposed peace was disingenuous; that it rose not from a sudden Turanian thirst for justice but from the impact of his mace on the battlefield. King Kay Qobad's magnanimity was greater than Rostam's worldly reckonings.

When peace was established, Rostam and Zaul went back to their domain in Zabol, and King Kay Qobad retired to his winter palace in Fars, from where he ruled Iran in peace, prosperity, and justice for a century. As time came for the king to pass on, he called his firstborn, Kay Kavous, and advised him to be just and generous.

"Time has come for me to leave this world and for you to inherit the throne. Be mindful of the fickleness of this world. It is as if it was yesterday that I arrived from the slopes of the Alborz Mountains to become king. Only the unwise pass their time without reflection. If you rule with justice you shall be rewarded in this world and the next. If you unsheathe the sword of injustice, you shall be slain by it."

With these words the king traded his palace for a wooden chest.
A coffin became his home when he left this world behind.
We came from dirt and that is where fate will put us to rest.

The Follies of a King:
Kay Kavous

When a crooked branch grows out of a tree
The root does not take the blame, nor should
A father's name be sullied if a son betrays his legacy.

A truant child who spurns his teacher goes
Unprepared into a life of hard lessons
And a farmer only reaps what he sows.

The Mazandaran Expedition

After Kay Qobad, his son, Kay Kavous, sat on the throne wearing the bejeweled golden crown of his father. He was adorned in lustrous earrings and the torque of royalty. His treasure houses were full, and his stables were teeming with Arabian horses. The domain of the earth submitted to the new sovereign's command.

One day, as the king sat in his pleasure gardens drinking with his knights, he was approached by a devil in the guise of a skilled musician. The devil wished to turn him from the path of righteousness, so he sang a bewitching ballad about the ever-blooming orchards and the majestic green slopes of the enchanted land of the demons.

> Now I shall sing the praises of Mazandaran for my king
> Where mountains bloom with hyacinth and tulips
> And a confusion of warblers serenade the eternal spring.
>
> The lords of that land spend their days
> In hunting and falconry as they are served
> By lovely slaves worthy of a king's praise.

The devil enthralled Kay Kavous with his song, and the king burned with the desire to possess the riches of Mazandaran. His craving for that land was evident as he turned to his warriors and said, "We are growing soft with merrymaking. I surpass Zahhak, Jamshid, and Kay Qobad in fortune, divine grace, and justice. I ought to exceed them in conquests as well."

The knights were silent. Their faces were ashen and their foreheads were furrowed. Not one among them relished the thought of waging war on the powerful demons of Mazandaran. But they dared not oppose their sovereign's new ambition. Instead, they intoned their humble submission and retired for the night.

Later they gathered and one of the knights said, "A great misfortune has befallen us. Was it the wine, or does the king really plan to invade Mazandaran? Jamshid, Feraydun, and Manuchehr were mighty kings who knew how to subdue demons, but even they did not set out to conquer Mazandaran. Now this conceited king who has inherited the windfall riches of his predecessors intends to squander the royal treasure houses and forfeit our lives in this misadventure of his.

"Only one person can save us from this calamity, and that is Zaul. He and his son, the young Rostam, saved this land from the disaster caused by Nowzar. All those efforts will have been in vain if this king gets his way."

A swift messenger was dispatched to bring the old knight to court without delay. Zaul shuddered with fear when he learned that the novice king had chosen the path of recklessness. He knew that Kay Kavous would probably ignore his counsel, but he was bound by duty to speak the truth to the king.

The knights came forth to welcome Zaul and ushered him into the palace. The old knight of Zabol humbly bowed his head and advised Kay Kavous against stumbling into a war with the demons. He warned that it would be a bloody and bitter conflict, one that had been avoided by previous kings. Kay Kavous turned a deaf ear to these warnings and boasted that he was superior to all past kings. Then he solemnly thanked Zaul for his concern and commanded him to stay behind and protect the land in his absence.

Zaul, who had said his piece, pledged his submission and expressed his hope that the venture would be successful and that the king would never have the occasion to regret his decision. With these words he left the royal court with downcast eyes, bid farewell to the knights, and traveled back to Zabol.

Soon the drums of Kay Kavous's war sounded, and an army gathered under the leadership of two prominent knights: Tous, who was the son of King Nowzar, and Gudarz, who was the great-grandson of Kaveh, the black-smith. The forces of Kay Kavous marched out of the gates of the capital and did not rest until they came to the slopes of Mount Esprouz, on the border of Mazandaran. They set up the royal camp in a beautiful meadow and prepared for the invasion. The next morning Kay Kavous commanded Geav, the gallant son of Gudarz, to select two thousand warriors skilled in wielding the mace and the blade.

"Raid them. Exterminate man, woman, and child, and don't spare the old reclining on canes, either. Burn every domicile, and turn medicine into poison and day into night. Let the archdemons who protect this land hear of our might."

Geav unsheathed his sword and carried out the king's orders. The rampage went on for seven days. Great treasures were found, and dazzling cities were plundered. Kay Kavous was thrilled by his success and extolled the musician who had sung the praises of Mazandaran.

On the eighth day, intelligence of the Iranian invasion reached the king of Mazandaran. In great anguish, he called on the chief guardian of his realm, the White Demon, to rid the land of the invaders. The White Demon swiftly engulfed the Iranian soldiers in a noxious, pitch-black cloud that blinded them. For a week, arrows and javelins rained down from the poisonous cloud onto the warriors. Helpless and wounded, the Persian army staggered about, cursing their king.

The White Demon appeared in the midst of the dark cloud and taunted Kay Kavous:

"You are to the kings what the willow is to the fruit trees. You followed the path of pride and coveted the throne of Mazandaran. Like an elephant run amok, you only saw your own power. Now you have lost your throne and earned this captivity and the death that will come soon enough."

The White Demon appointed twelve thousand of his minions to guard Kay Kavous and his troops. They were kept in darkness, and their rations were meager. The king sat in the company of his defeated knights Tous, Gudarz, and Geav. He recalled Zaul's sage advice and ruefully muttered, "A good adviser is better than a full treasure house."

The king recovered from his apathy long enough to secretly dispatch a message to Zaul confessing the utter foolishness of his endeavor and asking for the help of Rostam. Zaul was saddened that his vision of disaster for Iran had come to pass. Not for one second did he gloat over the misfortune of the arrogant Kay Kavous. Rather, he urged his son to ride out to the rescue of the captive king. As Rostam mounted his steed, the fair Rudabeh came out with tears streaming from her eyes, worried for her son's safety. Rostam addressed his mother. "A wise man does not willingly go to the gates of hell or offer his flesh to a raging lion. But it is my destiny and duty to slay the White Demon and rescue my king. Pray for me, Mother, and grant me your blessings, for this is a grave undertaking."

With these words the young Rostam set off on his mission. There were two ways to Mazandaran: a long and safe road and a shorter but far more dangerous path. Due to the urgency of his mission, Rostam took the shorter path.

The Seven Trials of Rostam

Rostam rode out of Zabol in such high spirits that he did not pause for two days. Finally, he stopped at a thicket, hunted a wild ass for his supper, and allowed Rakhsh to graze. Then he lay down to rest. Unbeknownst to the hero, the thicket was the lair of a ferocious lion, which returned while Rostam was fast asleep. Thinking Rostam's horse easy prey, the lion decided to make a quick meal of him. But Rakhsh soared in the air and brought down the lion by blows with his front hooves. When Rostam woke up and saw the carcass of the dead lion, he chided Rakhsh for risking his life. If the lion had gotten the better of the horse, Rostam would have been lost without a mount to carry his heavy weapons. "In the future," Rostam commanded Rakhsh, "wake me up when danger approaches." The next day, when the sun rose above the mountains, Rostam rubbed down and saddled his horse and continued on his way.

In front of Rostam and Rakhsh lay a seemingly endless desert, devoid of water and vegetation. They rode on until Rakhsh could not go any further for want of water. Rostam dismounted and staggered ahead, leaning on his lance. Parched and exhausted, he finally collapsed and prayed for divine succor. Suddenly a beautiful ram leaped into his range of vision. Rostam found new hope at the unlikely sight and crawled after the ram, using his sword for support. At the end of this pursuit the hero came upon a lovely spring and found the ram drinking from it. Surely this was a divine sign.

Rostam thanked God and praised the ram that had saved his life. "May grass grow on your field aplenty, my ram of well-formed haunches. May cheetahs never be sated on your flesh. May the bow that aims at you snap. May arrows coming at you miss their mark. For the formidable knight of Iran would be lost and dead without you."

Rostam drank deeply and washed himself. He saw to the needs of his horse, hunted an onager to sate his hunger, and then made his bed, warning Rakhsh once again not to needlessly endanger himself.

This time the place that Rostam had chosen for rest was the den of a dragon that returned while Rostam slept. The dragon was amazed that a man had dared to venture into his territory, let alone fall asleep in his den without a care. The dragon rushed Rakhsh with great ferocity. Fearing to disobey his master, Rakhsh retreated and stomped the ground to wake Rostam. But when Rostam awoke, the magical dragon disappeared from view. Rostam scolded Rakhsh for interrupting his rest and went back to sleep. The dragon reappeared and attacked once more. Rakhsh neighed and raised a cloud of dust to wake his master, whereupon the dragon vanished again. This time Rostam sternly warned Rakhsh against disturbing his sleep. When the dragon attacked for the third time, Rakhsh was torn. He feared the dragon's claws, but he also feared Rostam's wrath. Finally he decided to awaken his master, but this time fortune smiled on him, as a divine light flashed and the dragon was revealed as a huge shadow against the sky.

Rostam beheld the beast and drew his sword. He asked his opponent's name. The dragon breathed out a dark cloud, flickering with sparks, and replied: "What is your name, and who shall cry over your lifeless body?"

"My name is Rostam, the son of Zaul, the son of Saum, the son of Narimon. I am the destroyer of armies and the master of Rakhsh."

At this they rushed each other and wrestled with all their might for a long time. Then Rakhsh joined the battle and tore at the shoulder of the dragon with his teeth. Rostam used this respite to swing his sword and behead the creature. A river of the dragon's blood turned the dry earth into a field of mud. The hero washed the blood off his garments in the nearby stream, thanked God for his victory, and rode out of the dragon's den.

The journey to Mazandaran was long and arduous, but our knight pressed on until the sun started to descend from the zenith of the sky. Then the landscape changed and Rostam found himself at a pleasant spring in the middle of a lush garden. A delectable meal of lamb and bread along with garnishes, desserts, and cups of wine was set upon a spread. There was also a lute next to a golden chalice. Unbeknownst to Rostam, this was a gathering of witches who had scattered at the approach of the stranger. In great astonishment the hero dismounted, filled a cup, and picked up the lute and sang:

"This is the song of a vagrant hero branded
By a life that offers him grief and sorrows
And a fate that leaves him stranded

In strange lands parched and hurt.
Bare crags and wastelands are his abode
And his pleasure gardens are fields of dirt.

Lions and dragons tackle him in each labor.
Beset by the demons of the desert he stands
His ground wielding his glittering saber.

Fate doesn't grant him friends, or wine.
His portion of the pleasures of this life
Is a barren desert, an ocean of brine.

Rostam ever wrestles the whales of the sea
Or else find him in a forest, grappling
With leopards one, two, and three."

One of the witches was attracted by Rostam's song. She transformed herself into a lovely maiden and came forth. Rostam offered her a cup of wine and bid her to drink it in the name of God. The witch, who could not bear the divine name, lost her spell and relapsed to the shape of the hag that she really was. Rostam quickly slayed the witch and set off on the road again.

The hero trekked on and on, through an ominous realm that was dark as night. He dared not stop while he was enveloped in this interminable world of shadows. When finally he emerged into the sunshine, Rostam stopped at a wheat field, lifted Rakhsh's bridle, and allowed him to graze.

As the hero slept, a man who had been charged with caring for the crops rushed in and struck Rostam's feet with his stick. Insulted, Rostam rose and meted out a swift and rough punishment to the rude man who had awakened him. The anguished guard ran away to inform his master, Oulad, about the fierce trespasser in the fields. The master gathered an armed posse and gave chase, but in the battle that ensued, Rostam slaughtered the armed gang and captured their leader.

Oulad pleaded for his life. Rostam relented and said that he would allow his captive to live if he acted as his scout and lead the hero to the Iranian army and then to the den of the White Demon. Rostam promised Oulad the kingship of Mazandaran if he acted in good faith. The choice between certain death and the promise of becoming the king of his realm was not a difficult one. Oulad agreed to accompany Rostam on the rest of his trials and set the course for Mount Esprouz, the camp of Kay Kavous that had become his prison.

Once they arrived at the edge of the encampment, Rostam bound Oulad to a tree and asked him for the name and a description of the head demon guarding Mount Esprouz. Oulad revealed that the name of the commander of the demons was Arzhang. Rostam packed his ox-headed mace in his saddle as his heart raced with the excitement of the battle. He brought Rakhsh to full gallop, shouted his terrible war cry, and waded into the army of demons who scattered from his path, stepping on each other. In the pandemonium, fathers trampled their own sons to escape. Arzhang was frightened by the commotion and by Rostam's battle cry. He rushed out to see what calamity was descending on his troops. Rostam grabbed him, tore off his head, and flung it at the throngs of demons. Now the demons were routed as they saw this spectacle. Rakhsh was neighing as he rode through a sea of demons, causing a great commotion.

King Kay Kavous recognized Rakhsh's neighing and with great delight said, "Our sorrows are at an end, my worthy knights. I have heard Rakhsh, and soon we will see Rostam, who has come to our rescue. I remember this sound from the wars Rostam fought under my crowned father, Kay Qobad."

Soon the captive king and his warriors Tous, Gudarz, and Geav were greeting the hero in gratitude and humility. Kay Kavous embraced Rostam, shed tears of joy, and asked about Zaul's well-being. Then he heard a brief account of Rostam's feats and urged him not to waste time.

"Once the White Demon hears of the slaying of Arzhang, he will bring an army against us. You must go to his lair, beyond the seven mountains. There you will find a great pit, where he resides. As you can see, we are all struck with the curse of this blindness caused by the White Demon's sorcery. Slay him and bring back a vat of his blood, for it is said that it is the only cure for our blindness."

Rostam untied Oulad and the two set off once again.

At the pit of the White Demon, Rostam asked Oulad for the secret of overcoming the demons. Oulad said that it was best to attack them at noon, for the demons were nocturnal and weakest at midday. Rostam rested for a while, preparing to attack as the sun rose high in the sky. Then he yelled his battle cry and rode into the camp. Only a few sentries were posted, and they were sluggish and disoriented from the bright sun. Rostam had no trouble fighting his way to the opening of the dark pit of the White Demon. He was

forced to stop at the entrance of the cave until his eyes were used to the dark. Gradually he was able to make out the massive form of the White Demon filling the enormous cavern.

Suddenly the beast awoke and rushed at Rostam who quickly drew his sword and lopped off the beast's leg. The monster threw himself on the hero, and they wrestled for a long time. It was with supreme effort that Rostam was finally able to sink his dagger in the White Demon's heart. Suddenly the massive body of the monster went limp, and the cave filled with a torrent of blood.

The Final Battles and the Triumphant Return

Rostam came back from the cave, carrying the enormous, bloody liver of the monster to cure the blindness of the prisoners. He untied Oulad for the last time, and they headed back to Mount Esprouz. Oulad ran beside Rakhsh, holding the liver of the White Demon and reminding Rostam of his promise to grant him the kingship of Mazandaran. He told Rostam that it would be unseemly if such a gallant hero as himself failed to honor his word.

Once they arrived at Mount Esprouz, they cured the multitudes of Iranians by dripping the White Demon's blood into their eyes. Then Kay Kavous drafted a letter to the king of Mazandaran, urging him to humbly come to court and pay tribute. After all, without the White Demon and Arzhang, he had little hope of fighting off the armies of Iran.

The king of Mazandaran refused to pay tribute and prepared for war instead. Gudarz, Geav, and Rostam commanded the right, left, and center of the Iranian troops, and a great battle ensued. The victory went to Kay Kavous, while the king of Mazandaran lost his land and his life. Rostam interceded with Kay Kavous to grant the kingship of Mazandaran to Oulad, who had been loyal to him in his labors. The king called the noblemen of Mazandaran together and asked for their endorsement of Oulad before naming him their new king. With this the hostilities came to an end, and the Iranian troops returned home from their adventures in the land of demons.

After the triumphant procession, Kay Kavous sat on the throne and called Rostam to his presence in order to reward him for his heroic deeds and his great service to the crown. Rostam was honored with a gem-encrusted crown, and he was seated on a turquoise throne next to Kay Kavous. The king lavished on the hero garments, bracelets, a magnificent torque, and a hundred purses of gold. He was given a hundred mares and a hundred Arabian horses loaded with Roman fabric and festooned in golden bridles. Rostam's caravan included a hundred beautiful slaves wearing golden belts. The king wrote a new deed renewing the command of Zabol to Rostam and his clan.

It was known throughout the world that Kay Kavous had subdued Mazandaran. The earth was like a paradise once more, filled with riches and justice.

Kay Kavous and Sudabeh

To celebrate his victory over the demons of Mazandaran, Kay Kavous went on an expedition to the territories that lay between Iran and its powerful neighbors to the east and west. Everywhere rulers greeted him with lavish gifts and tribute. The news of the conquest of Mazandaran had awed the lesser kings, and they were keen to show their respect to the victorious Kay Kavous. Only the defiant ruler of Barbary was unimpressed. He came forth with a massive army whose lances resembled a dense thicket. Offended by this show of disrespect, Kay Kavous charged Gudarz to subdue the rebellious king. With the backing of one thousand brave soldiers, Gudarz savaged the heart of the army of Barbary and routed them. As the king entered the defeated city, the elders of the town greeted him in humility and pledged to pay tribute far in excess of what he had demanded. The king forgave them the impudence of their ruler and returned to Zabol for a month of rest.

Kay Kavous's sojourn was interrupted when word of a new revolt in the provinces of Egypt and Hamavaran arrived. The rebellious Barbars joined this coalition despite their previous pledge of loyalty to the king of Iran.

Kay Kavous launched a massive land and sea expedition to quell the new insurgency. On the battlefield, the Iranian knights found the troops of Barbary and Egypt on their right and left. The army of Hamavaran occupied the center of the arena. The war started in full force as the Iranian knights kissed their saddles and rushed the allied armies of the three kingdoms, wading into a sea of blood. The din of clashing lances and battleaxes was deafening. The Persian army was unstoppable. The first to drop his sword in surrender was the king of Hamavaran. He asked for quarter and pledged to pay a heavy tribute in horses, arms, gold, and jewels. Kay Kavous accepted the terms of his surrender, and when the two remaining rebellious armies fell, the Persian king took all three kingdoms into his protection.

After the provinces were pacified, Kay Kavous set up camp near the battlefield and took a respite to celebrate his victories. During an evening of merrymaking, an attendant told Kay Kavous about the daughter of the king of Hamavaran, Sudabeh. She was said to be exquisitely beautiful and possessed of the elegance of a queen. Tall as a cypress, Sudabeh was graced with a magnificent crown of musk-black hair that set off lips sweeter than sugar. Kay Kavous burned with desire and sent a messenger to the king of Hamavaran to ask for the hand of Sudabeh.

The king loved his favorite daughter, and, having lost the battle to Kay Kavous, he was reluctant to give Sudabeh in marriage to the victor. Of course, he knew that he had little choice in the matter. In desperation, he asked for his daughter's opinion and was surprised to learn that Sudabeh was agreeable to the proposal of marriage.

"It is true, Father, that we have no choice in the matter. Indeed, a king is entitled to whatever he has conquered. But why would one spurn good fortune? This connection is indeed cause for joy."

For a week, the king of Hamavaran prepared his daughter's wedding procession. After the requisite ceremonies, he reluctantly sent Sudabeh to Kay Kavous along with a magnificent train of slaves in golden belts and many royal gifts.

Sudabeh was happy with the union, and as time passed she grew to love the king and her position as the queen of Iran. When her father invited the royal couple back to Hamavaran to celebrate a festival, Sudabeh advised the king against going as she suspected foul play. She knew that her father resented Kay Kavous for breaking down his resistance and for taking away his favorite daughter. But Kay Kavous, who was not disposed to listen to wise counsel, ignored this warning and went to Hamavaran anyway, accompanied by his queen and his knights Gudarz, Geav, and Tous.

The king of Hamavaran hosted Kay Kavous and his retinue, while secretly plotting with the kings of Barbary and Egypt. On the eighth day of festivities, the king's soldiers filled the streets, and the royal guests were taken prisoner. Sudabeh was furious with the treachery of her father and refused to leave her husband's side. As a result, she was thrown into the dungeon of an impenetrable mountain fortress along with the king of Iran and his knights.

With Kay Kavous nowhere to be found, chaos descended on Iran. Enemies breached the borders on all sides and often fought each other for the spoils of their raids. Afrasiab, sensing an easy victory, also crossed the borders of Turan, laying waste to Iran and taking its inhabitants as slaves. He won a three-month battle against the Arabs, who had also invaded Iran in the king's absence.

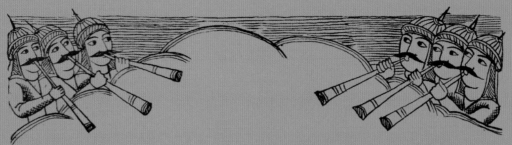

Iran had become a battleground for foreign marauders. Fugitives from these wars fled to Zabol and pleaded for help. It was at this time that King Kay Kavous managed to send a secret missive appealing to Rostam from his prison.

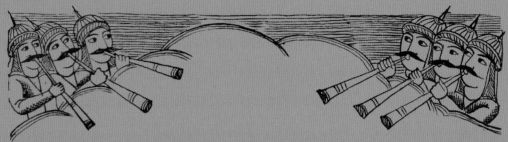

The hero gathered an army, and after many hard battles he succeeded in routing the forces of the three defiant kings. Having once liberated the king from captivity in Mazandaran, this was the second time that Rostam had reinstated the king to his royal seat. Kay Kavous returned to Iran, hauling the treasures and tributes of the three defeated kingdoms. Queen Sudabeh, who had defied her father and remained loyal to Kay Kavous, traveled back with her husband in a dazzling litter to the capital of Iran.

Once Kay Kavous was back in Iran, it was time to expel Afrasiab from the land. Kay Kavous sent him a letter, advising that it would be best if he withdrew his troops to avoid war. But Afrasiab refused, citing flimsy arguments that his grandfather Tur was a descendant of King Feraydun and that he had a right to the Iranian land. He also claimed that he had not taken the territories from the Iranians. Rather, he had fairly won them from the Arab invaders. It was obvious that dislodging Afrasiab would not be possible without another conflict.

Rostam went to subdue the army of Turan. In the great battle that ensued, Afrasiab found himself on the losing side once again. In desperation, he promised to marry his daughter to anyone who would kill Rostam. But his efforts came to naught, and he was forced to redeploy back to his ancestral land, beyond the Oxus River.

Kay Kavous lavished praise on Rostam once more and appointed him the Champion of the World. He reasserted his sovereignty and built a castle in the Alborz Mountains. Many nations came to pay tribute to the triumphant and just king Kay Kavous.

Kay Kavous Reaches for the Heavens

Iblis, the highest of all the devils, was not pleased that Kay Kavous was starting to lean toward righteousness. So he dispatched another devil disguised as a young boy holding a bouquet of flowers to tempt the king. The lad kissed the ground in front of Kay Kavous and said, "A king with your divine halo deserves to ascend to the heavens. You have conquered the world. You are the shepherd, and all the potentates of the world are your herd. Only one thing remains. What secret is the sun hiding from you about its zenith and nadir? What manner of thing is the moon? Wherefore is this day and night? Who oversees the revolution of the stars?"

Not recognizing God's dominion over the heavens, Kay Kavous gave in to the temptations of ascending to the skies. He devised a contrivance whereby eagles attached to the four corners of a dais would lift him up into the sky. At each corner of the platform, a piece of lamb dangled, tempting the eagles to fly up higher to reach the meat. The idea worked. The throne of Kay Kavous was lifted into the air, and the king was elevated to the clouds. But the eagles eventually grew tired, and the ill-conceived flying machine crashed in a thicket near Amol.

After the failure of this pretentious scheme, the king was contrite. He was also lost and in need of rescue.

The royal retinue that had kept track of Kay Kavous from the ground reported that the flying machine had crashed. Gudarz and Rostam went to find and rescue their king. As they went, Gudarz grumbled to Rostam: "Among all the kings I have seen, not one has been so bereft of judgment and wisdom. Kay Kavous has no sense or intelligence."

When the knights found the humiliated king they were furious. Gudarz reprimanded him: "The insane asylum is more suitable for you than the royal palace. You go off on your own, endangering your life and the safety of the country. Three times have you done this, and you don't seem to learn from your mistakes. Do you remember what disasters ensued following your foray into Mazandaran? Then you decided to be a guest in your enemy's house. Only God was not harangued by you. And now, having finished with the earth, you have got it in your head to set the affairs of the heavens in order! People will deride you as the king who wanted to manhandle the sun and the moon and to count the stars. You ought to follow the way of the good kings of the past and be humble."

Kay Kavous meekly accepted the rebuke. He locked himself in prayer for forty days to ask forgiveness for his impudent adventure into the heavens. God forgave the king, and once more Kay Kavous reigned over the land in justice.

I've spoken of the way this king behaved.
He tried to be just, but a truly just king
Has no need of being so frequently saved.

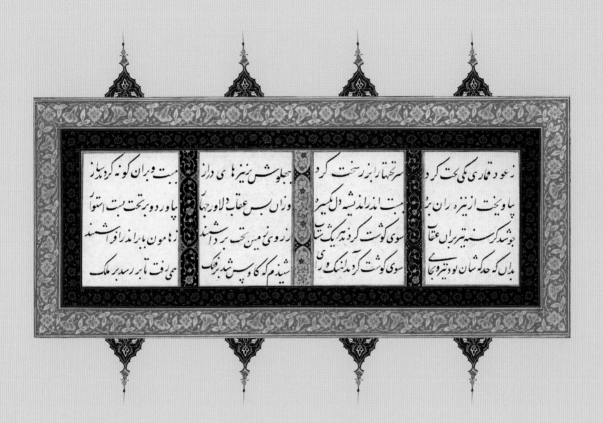

زعود قماری یکی تخت کرد | سرتخمار ابه برشخت کرد | بجلوشش سنیزها یی دراز | سبت وبران کونه کرده بساز

پاویخت از نیزه ران بزا | سبت اندر اندشیه دلکند | وزان بس عقاب دلاورجها | پاور دوبرتخت سبت استوا

جوشد کرسنه تیربراں عقا | سوی کوشت کرد دریک تا | دروی یمین تخت بردشند | زامون بابرا اندر اوشمند

بدان که حدکشان لو دتیزوجا | سوی کوشت کرد مدانک و ری | شندم که کاوپس شد برلنگ | سحی رفت تابه رسد بر ملک

A Tragedy of Errors:
Rostam and Sohrab

When a wind rips an orange off the branch
Before it has had time to ripen and grow
In its own corner of the ranch

Or when a young life is snuffed
Before its time, unfulfilled,
What do we call these without being rebuffed?

If we claim by some contrivance of the mind
That these are acts of justice, then what would we
Call injustice, a hard example indeed to find.

Rostam Meets Tahmineh

Rostam packed his quiver full of arrows one day and went hunting on the border of Turan. Soon a spitted onager was roasting in a great fire, and Rakhsh was happily grazing in the fields. Rostam sated himself and reclined to rest. While he slept, a band of horse rustlers captured his steed after a great struggle and led him away. The hero woke and saw that Rakhsh had vanished. He was troubled; it was a disgrace for a knight to allow his horse to be stolen.

Rostam took his saddle and followed the tracks of Rakhsh until they faded near the city of Samangan, within the borders of Turan. The local king, who had learned of the arrival of Rostam, came out on foot to welcome the hero and allay his worries. He said that a prominent stallion like Rakhsh would not remain hidden for long and invited the famous Iranian knight to his palace for a night of rest and merrymaking. Rostam accepted the invitation, as there was nothing to be done about his predicament that evening. After the festivities, when the hero had drunk his fill of wine, he was led away to his own quarters, where a fragrant bed awaited him.

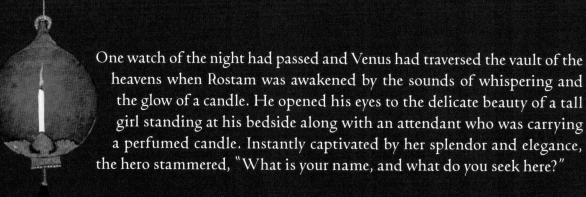

One watch of the night had passed and Venus had traversed the vault of the heavens when Rostam was awakened by the sounds of whispering and the glow of a candle. He opened his eyes to the delicate beauty of a tall girl standing at his bedside along with an attendant who was carrying a perfumed candle. Instantly captivated by her splendor and elegance, the hero stammered, "What is your name, and what do you seek here?"

"I am Tahmineh, the daughter of the king of Samangan, the offspring of leopards and lions. There is none like me under the dome of the heavens. No one has ever seen my beauty, nor will anyone see it after this night. I have heard the legends of your heroic deeds and bitten my lips in longing. Now I stand before you, having traded reason for desire. I want to have a son from your seed. And in return I promise that your horse will be found."

Rostam was charmed by Tahmineh's ethereal beauty. He opened his arms and they spent the long and dark night in the glow of their passion. At dawn he bestowed on her a badge that he wore on his arm.

"If our child is a daughter, she must tie this in her braids as an amulet of good fortune. But if we have a son, suffer him to wear it on his arm as a sign of his father, for he will be noble, tall, and generous, like my ancestors Saum and Narimon."

In the morning the local king greeted Rostam with the good news that Rakhsh had been found. Happy to be reunited with his loyal companion, the hero quickly saddled his steed and said farewell to the King of Samangan. His consort of the night, the angelic Tahmineh, looked upon the scene of her beloved's departure with tears in her eyes. When Rostam disappeared over the horizon she returned to her chambers with an aching heart.

Sohrab Comes of Age

After nine months a son, bright as the full moon, was born to Tahmineh. She named him Sohrab. The infant had the large frame of Rostam but resembled Saum in countenance. At one month he was bigger than a one-year-old child. As he grew, Sohrab excelled at polo and hunting, and at ten no one could match him in wrestling. Noticing that he was different in appearance from his peers, and far superior to them, Sohrab went to his mother and asked. "From whose seed am I? What shall I say when I am asked about my father? It is best that you tell me the truth right away."

Tahmineh replied: "Don't be severe with me but rather rejoice. You are the son of the gallant Rostam, who descended from the illustrious Zaul, the son of Saum, the son of Narimon. Hold your head higher than the clouds. You are from an exalted lineage."

As proof she showed Sohrab a letter written by Rostam and three gold-encrusted rubies that he had sent along. Sohrab was pleased to learn of his noble pedigree. Tahmineh had two requests of her son. First, Sohrab was to hide the secret of his paternity from Afrasiab, for this would expose him to certain peril. Second, he would have to keep the secret of his precocious maturity from his father as well. If Rostam found out that Sohrab had already surpassed his peers in size and strength, thought Tahmineh, he would surely take him away and break her heart. Sohrab granted the first wish but he thought it absurd to hide from his father.

The ambitious young Sohrab started to chart his future plans. He would raise an army of Turanian warriors, wrest the crown from Kay Kavous, and bestow it upon his father, Rostam. Then he would throw Afrasiab off his throne and unite the two kingdoms. With a father and son like Rostam and Sohrab, it would not behoove anyone else to rule as king. After all, would the stars dare sparkle in the sky while the sun and the moon dominated the heavens? When Tahmineh learned of her son's plans, she consented on the condition that she send her brother, Zende Razm, along. He had seen Rostam in battle and could point him out. With this, Sohrab made known his plans for an invasion of Iran, and soon an army gathered around him.

Afrasiab's informers had learned of Sohrab's noble lineage and his plans to invade Iran. As the new king of Turan after the passing of Pashang, Afrasiab was delighted by this intelligence. With some deceitful planning, he could do away with Rostam by the hands of his own son. Afrasiab quickly dispatched an auxiliary army of twelve thousand warriors to Samangan under the leadership of his trusted knight Houman. Afrasiab had entrusted Houman with the secret of Sohrab's lineage as well. It was his task to misdirect the young champion and prevent him from identifying his father on the battlefield. This way, Sohrab was sure to challenge his father to a duel and kill him. After Rostam was killed, it would be easy to dispatch the young hero by some intrigue.

Sohrab was emboldened at the approach of the forces of Afrasiab. And he was delighted to read the king's letter, which promised him the crown of Iran. He marched his vastly augmented forces toward

Iran until they came to the first Iranian outpost, known as the White Fortress. Hojir, the guardian of the fortress and one of the sons of the Iranian knight Gudarz, rode out of the castle to confront the young champion who was leading the forces of Turan.

Sohrab Fights Gordafarid

Hojir and Sohrab met and exchanged lengthy taunts. Sohrab wondered why Hojir had been so foolhardy as to come to the arena alone and predicted that his poor mother would mourn him that night. Hojir said that no Turanian was his match and that he had plans to send Sohrab's severed head as a trophy to King Kay Kavous. When the combat got under way, however, it went badly for Hojir. Sohrab easily threw his Iranian foe off his horse with a thrust of his lance and swiftly dismounted to sever his head. Hojir dodged Sohrab's blow and asked for mercy. His plea was granted. Instead of killing him, Sohrab tied Hojir's arms and sent him staggering toward the ranks of Turan.

Those who watched from the ramparts of the White Fortress were appalled by the quick and rather shameful course of the duel. But none was more dismayed by the scandal of Hojir's easy defeat and captivity than Gordafarid, the daughter of the lord of the fortress, Gazhdaham. She was a formidable equestrian and worthy warrior in her own right. Enraged by the insult meted

out to Hojir, she hastily donned a coat of chain mail, hid her long, flowing hair under a helmet, and rode out of the castle like a prowling lioness. When she reached the ranks of the enemy, Gordafarid called on the warriors of Turan to come forth and defend their honor.

Sohrab chuckled and said to himself, "Another victim walks into the hunter's ambush." But as he put on his helmet, Gordafarid showered him with such a torrent of arrows that he could not move. It was only fear of disgrace that pushed Sohrab forward as he held his shield aloft against the barrage of arrows. When he came closer, Gordafarid slung her bow on her shoulder. She brought her horse to stand on its hind legs and hurled her lance. Sohrab turned aside to evade the missile and simultaneously hit the disguised warrior with his lance, causing her coat of chain mail to come unfastened. Gordafarid broke the lance with her sword and turned to flee, but the young hero gave chase and lifted her helmet to reveal a cascade of lovely hair.

Sohrab was astounded that the able warrior who had been fighting him was indeed a woman. Quickly he caught her in his noose and said, "Why would a lovely creature like you come to the battlefield? Now that you are here, don't dream of escaping my noose. I never caught game lovelier than you. So give up your struggle, because I shall never let you go."

Gordafarid knew that she was in a difficult spot and sought to escape by deception. She turned her lovely face to Sohrab and suggested that they should keep her identity a secret because Sohrab would be disgraced if his peers realized that he had been fighting a woman. "Besides," she said, "I am at your mercy, and if you let me go I will open the gates of the White Fortress to you."

As she said this, Gordafarid appeared like a blossom about to open up into a flower. She allowed her hair to fall onto her face, and looked upon Sohrab with the soulful eyes of a captured elk. Enamored by her beauty, Sohrab boasted that he would not need her help to win the castle. Pointing disdainfully at the fortress, he said that he could bring down the entire edifice on his own. Gordafarid used this moment of distraction to loosen the noose that bound her. Having freed herself, she turned around and galloped toward the gates of the castle. Gazhdaham, alert to his daughter's actions, quickly opened the gates and then closed them behind her. Sohrab went after her but was left alone at the entrance. Gordafarid appeared on the ramparts and taunted Sohrab. "It is time for you to return to your land, my dear commander. Don't regret losing me, for fate did not decree that you find a companion from among the women of Iran. If you remain here the news will reach our king

and then he will dispatch Rostam. It would be a pity for him to kill you and rout your army."

Sohrab was ashamed to have been tricked. He turned around and on his way to his camp laid waste to the areas in the vicinity of the fortress. That night Gazhdaham decided to abandon the castle. But first he dispatched a letter to King Kay Kavous, apprising him of the great threat the young Turanian warrior posed for Iran. He wrote that a prodigious young man who went by the name of Sohrab and who resembled the noble Saum had come forth against the White Fortress. He had easily trounced Hojir in battle and taken him captive. Gazhdaham added that the young Turanian warrior was sure to take the fortress by the next day and that they were preparing to flee under the cover of the night.

The next morning Sohrab took over the deserted castle, set up camp there, and waited for the arrival of the armies of Iran.

The Rage of Kay Kavous

Back at the Iranian court, the king had received the letter dispatched by Gazhdaham. Kay Kavous was beset by anxieties when he considered what could happen if the forces of Turan were led by this formidable new adversary. He called a council of the knights, and they agreed that Rostam should lead the charge against this new menace.

The king dispatched Geav to fetch Rostam. Geav was commanded to be swift in this mission and not to linger in Zabol for more than one night. He carried a letter from the king that began by extolling Rostam for his leadership in the Mazandaran and Hamavaran campaigns. It concluded by stating that the hero's services were again needed to cope with the new threat on the borders of Turan.

Rostam read the letter and put it aside dismissively. Scorning the speculations about the appearance of a new warrior with the qualities of Saum in Turan, he said, "I doubt any Turanian would resemble the noble Saum. I myself have a son with the princess of Samangan. He might resemble Saum one day, but I have recent news from his mother that my son is still a child. He is weaned from milk, but he is still a novice at imbibing wine. At any rate, let us drink to the sounds of pleasant music. In due time we shall go to court to look into this matter."

Rostam and Geav stayed in Zabol, drinking and carousing before returning to court. Four days later, they finally set off. Upon their arrival, they saw that the king was fuming with anger. He had interpreted Rostam's late arrival as a personal affront. Furious, he ordered Geav to take Rostam out to the gallows and hang him for insubordination. The command was so absurd as to be incomprehensible. Geav was stunned and unable to move. Kay Kavous took this as defiance and ordered Tous to hang them both. This command was even more absurd. Now it was Rostam's turn to give full rein to his wrath: "Muzzle your fury, Kavous. You don't deserve to be king. Your deeds are all evil, one worse than the other. You say you want to hang me. Why don't you hang Sohrab if you are so quick to anger?"

Tous rose, not to execute Kavous's command but to lead Rostam out of the court. Rostam sent him flying with one blow of his arm and stomped out. He mounted Rakhsh and said to those who had followed him: "I am the crown giver to this dynasty. Kavous is nothing to me. Why should someone like Tous dare lay hands on me? The earth is my slave; this horse is my throne; the mace is my royal staff and the war helmet is my crown. I light up the dark night with my blade. The sword and the lance are my confederates. I am no one's slave. Let Sohrab come and lay waste to Iran and kill everyone. It will be none of my concern. Contrive a way to save yourselves, for I am taking wing to rise far above this land."

With these words Rostam brought Rakhsh to a gallop and disappeared from view. The noblemen and the knights were dismayed. They sent Gudarz to speak to the king. He reminded Kay Kavous of the services Rostam had rendered. He had twice rescued them all from captivity. Did such a hero deserve to hang in ignominy?

Kavous was contrite. "Words of wisdom issue from old lips. A king must remain impervious to anger. Now you must go to Rostam and speak to him and wash his heart of the poison of my words."

Gudarz immediately went in pursuit of Rostam. Upon reaching the hero, he praised him and said what was common knowledge among the knights: Kavous was reckless and impetuous! He was famously devoid of reason when he was moved to anger. Rostam said that he had had his fill of this foolish king. He had no fear of Kavous. Nor did he need him in any way. Gudarz agreed. "True, but Iranians should not be deprived of your services for the folly of their king. Besides, leaving the battle while Iran is under attack would create the false impression that you are afraid of this new Turanian warrior."

It was this last bit of advice that seemed to finally persuade Rostam to return. When he entered the court, Kay Kavous rose and apologized for his conduct. "You know that I am quick to anger. There is a flaw in my God-given nature. I was so distraught over this new young adversary from Turan that I lost my temper. If you have been offended by my outburst, it is my duty to beg your pardon."

Rostam accepted the apology and pledged his submission to his sovereign. Kay Kavous rejoiced and called for a lavish feast. The next morning he opened the treasure houses and ordered Geav and Tous to ready the army for departure.

Sohrab Confronts the Army of Iran

A hundred thousand Iranian cavalry marched toward the White Fortress to the beat of battle drums fastened to the backs of war elephants. Golden shields and silver lances glittered in a dark cloud of dust that enveloped the immense procession. The news reached the forces of Turan that an army of vast proportions had appeared in the distance. The commanders of Turan ascended to the ramparts of the White Fortress. Sohrab turned to Houman and with the curve of his hand swept the horizon. "Don't fear this multitude, for not one among them can match me on the battlefield. There are many weapons and many hands. But I don't see many heads daring to rise above the crowd. I will vanquish this army in the name of Afrasiab." To show his lack of concern, he called for a chalice of wine to welcome the coming war.

When night fell, Rostam asked Kay Kavous's permission to go on a scouting mission. He wanted to catch a glimpse of the young warrior who had struck such terror in the hearts of the Iranians. The hero wore a disguise and slipped into the occupied fortress with the skill of a lion tracking a dear. There he followed the sounds of a banquet and arrived at a hall where Sohrab was presiding. He was sitting on a throne flanked by Houman and his uncle Zende Razm.

Rostam was amazed by the enormous size and fine proportions of the young hero. Filled with the vigor of youth and endowed with a strong and muscular frame, Sohrab appeared to fill the throne. One hundred warriors and fifty attendants surrounded the champion. As Rostam watched this scene, Zende Razm left Sohrab's side as if he were going on an important errand.

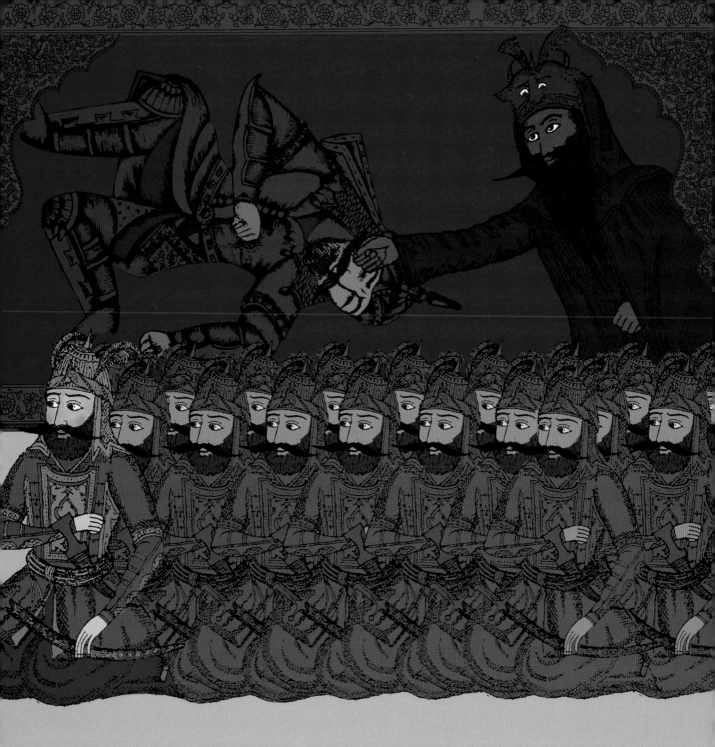

Spotting the large figure of a mysterious stranger lurking in the shadows, he walked behind Rostam and startled him with the command: "Who goes there? Come out into the light and show your face!"

Jolted by this command, Rostam rushed the man and struck him a mortal blow. Zende Razm fell to the ground and died immediately. The hero quickly left the fortress, slinked back to the Iranian side, and went to the king. He told Kay Kavous that Sohrab was superior not only to those around him but also to anyone on the Iranian side.

Back at the White Fortress, the body of Zende Razm had been found. Sohrab was outraged by the sudden and untimely demise of his uncle. He promptly terminated the festivities, appointed sentries to guard all entrances, and swore an oath to avenge the death.

The next day, as the sun fastened its noose on the high wheel of the heavens and began its ascent, Sohrab donned his armor, climbed to the roof of the fortress, and looked out over the massive Persian army that filled the horizon. Without his uncle Zende Razm to point out Rostam, he called for the captive Hojir to join him. Sohrab extolled the virtues of a man who tells the truth and threatened dire consequences for lies. Then he ordered Hojir to identify the Iranian flags and standards. "The mark of an elephant belongs to Tous," Hojir explained. "An embroidered lion on a flag signifies Gudarz. The likeness of a wolf appears on Geav's standard."

Sohrab pointed at the center of the camp and asked, "But who is the mammoth hero at the heart of the army flying a flag with the image of a dragon? Is that Rostam?"

Hojir was surprised at his young captor's accurate guess. But he also feared that Sohrab would challenge Rostam to a duel. If he killed Rostam, and he would, an Iranian defeat would be inevitable. His compatriots would also incur eternal shame, for none among them would be able to avenge Rostam. Life would not be worth living after Iran was defeated and shamed and after his father, Gurdarz, and his entire clan were annihilated. Hojir pondered all this and resolved to deceive Sohrab.

"No, that is not Rostam," Hojir said. "The Champion of the World is in Zabol at this time of the year attending local festivities. The hero you have pointed out must be a Chinese mercenary who has recently joined the ranks of Kay Kavous's knights. I don't know his name."

Sohrab did not believe Hojir; it was unlikely that Rostam would sit out such an important campaign. He tempted Hojir with untold riches if he were to show him the standard of Rostam and threatened to kill him if he insisted on lying. Hojir replied: "If I don't tell you the name of that hero, it is because I don't know it. Besides, why would you want to go against Rostam? Don't you know that only those who have a death wish go against him? Don't you know that he has the strength of a hundred men and that he can slay an elephant just as easily as he kills a man?"

Sohrab was revolted by Hojir's mendacity and cowardice. "What a shame it is for a great knight like Gudarz to have sired an unworthy son like you! You lack might, wisdom, and skill. Nor have you the right to judge strength, as you have not seen a true battlefield. Why do you praise Rostam when you have seen my prowess in battle?"

When Hojir repeated that Sohrab was no match for Rostam, he received a humiliating blow that knocked him off his feet. Sohrab was disappointed that he was not going to encounter his father on this campaign. Now there was little cause to go to war except that he had to avenge Zende Razm's death.

Sohrab Challenges Rostam

Sporting a Chinese helmet, the impetuous Sohrab mounted his steed. With his feet firmly in the stirrups, he held a lance with a tempered tip and galloped through the gates of the fortress toward the Iranian army. Haranguing Kay Kavous, he roared: "What brings you to a battlefield, Kavous? And for what reason have you tagged the royal title of 'Kay' to your name? Last night I swore an oath to avenge Zende Razm by impaling you on my lance or seeing you hanged at the gallows. I shall annihilate the lance holders of Iran, one and all. Who among your men can stop me?"

There was silence in the ranks, as no one had ever seen such a fearsome fighter before. Receiving no answer to his challenge, Sohrab charged the Iranian troops, and as they ran from his assault, he reached the royal camp and cut the ropes of seventy tents. Kay Kavous was shaken. He sent Tous on an urgent mission to call Rostam to the front.

Upon receiving the summons, Rostam complained bitterly. "Other kings would occasionally call on me for feasts and festivities. But Kavous summons me only to suffer the miseries of war."

Rostam issued orders that Rakhsh be prepared. As he watched from his tent he saw that the menial tasks of saddling his horse were not discharged by the stable hands. Rather, it was the high-ranking knights who scurried about, hurrying each other and fussing over the horse. This scene unsettled the hero. He said to himself, "This is the doing of the devil. Why should the fate of Iran revolve around me alone?"

Rostam tightened his belt and galloped to the front lines. He could make out Sohrab's horned helmet in the distance with its plumage fluttering in the wind like a great lion's mane. As he rode closer, Rostam had to admit to himself that the young warrior cut a mighty figure reminiscent of the great Saum.

Rostam approached his opponent. Ignoring all formalities, he immediately proposed that they choose the ground for their combat. Sohrab agreed, then mocked Rostam. He said that the old fighter, impressive as he may have been at one time, no longer seemed to pose a serious challenge. Was he sure he wanted to fight Sohrab alone? Rostam shot back: "The young should be modest in their judgments. The mountains, the seas, and the stars could bear witness to how I have crushed the armies of Turan."

Sohrab replied: "I will ask you a question now. I wish to hear the truth. Are you not Rostam, who is from the seed of the legendary Saum?"

"No. I am not Rostam. Nor am I from the seed of Saum. He is a great knight and I am but a subordinate, without a throne and without a crown."

Sohrab despaired. His bright day turned into a black night: Rostam was not present at this battle. It seemed that his plan to find his father and unite Iran and Turan had come to naught.

The two warriors fought with lances until they broke, with Indian swords until they shattered, and with maces until they tired. The armor was torn from the horses and the parched warriors riding them were soaked in sweat and blood. In utter exhaustion father and son separated to rest and regain their strength.

The world is full of mysteries as it makes and breaks.
Love and wisdom forsook them both, nor did
One of them pause to correct his mistakes.

Fish, onager, and beasts of burden in their mangers
Know their own, but greed so blinded father and son
That they faced each other as strangers.

Tired of the stalemate, Rostam turned from the scene of the duel toward the troops of Turan, causing great disorder in the ranks. Houman, with orders not to move before the end of Sohrab's battle with Rostam, stood his ground.

Sohrab retaliated by tearing into the heart of the Iranian lines wielding his mace. Tous was injured and great knights fled from Sohrab behind a buffer of infantry. Rostam looked back and saw that Sohrab was nearing the standard of Kay Kavous. Fearing for the king's life, he called out to Sohrab, "Why are you fighting the Iranians, you bloodthirsty wolf?"

"But you tore into the ranks of Turan first, attacking those who were not party to our feud!"

Rostam replied: "The sun is setting and it is getting late. You have shown what a young man can do with a blade. This example will live forever. Let us now rest and see what God decrees tomorrow."

The Last Day

With these words they went back to their camps. Rostam went to Kay Kavous with a heavy heart and reported about his difficult battle with Sohrab: "This warrior is formidable. I had never failed to lift an opponent off his horse. But Sohrab was like a mountain of granite in the saddle. We have agreed to wrestle tomorrow, but I am not sure that I will emerge victorious against him."

Fearful for the outcome of the battle, the king prostrated himself to God and asked for divine intervention. Rostam went to his brother, Zavareh, and shared his forebodings with him, adding: "Tomorrow, follow me to the front, carrying my standard. If I am victorious, I will not linger on the battlefield, but if I am defeated, keep your composure. Do not try to avenge me. Go back to Zabol and console my mother. I have killed my share of men, demons, and beasts in battle. Death is our inevitable fate. And unto our father Zaul say that he should continue to obey the royal house of Kay Kavous."

The young Sohrab had a more festive night, as he had dominated the battle against Rostam. But in the morning he shared his misgivings with Houman. "This lion who fights me has all the characteristics of my father, Rostam, as enumerated by my mother. He is as tall and as strong as I am. I am mysteriously drawn to him, and I have a strange feeling that he is none other than Rostam. There are few men like him in this world, after all. If this man is Rostam, I ought not to fight him."

Houman, who had been ordered by Afrasiab to keep Rostam's identity a secret, dismissed his doubts. He agreed that the warrior and his horse were indeed reminiscent of Rostam and Rakhsh, whom he had encountered in previous battles. But he was convinced that the horse was not in fact Rakhsh, as the beast lacked the stamina of the famous steed that Rostam rode to every battle.

Although it had been thrice confirmed that his opponent was not his father, Sohrab was still not persuaded. Grave misgivings had gnawed at him during the night and even in the morning as he put on his armor.

As Sohrab approached Rostam on the battlefield, he once more demanded to learn the true identity of his opponent. "It is my hope that you will die in bed and not by my hands. Let us sit down together this day and drink wine, leaving the fighting to others. My heart longs for your companionship, and I have a sense of shame in fighting you. Maybe you can tell me about your knightly lineage."

Rostam scoffed at the idea, which he considered frivolous. He wanted to get to the business of fighting.

The two warriors dismounted and began hand-to-hand combat. The heroes again found themselves at a lengthy stalemate that lasted for hours. Finally

Sohrab lowered Rostam into the dust like a lion catching its prey. As he sat on his opponent's chest to sever his head, Rostam spoke deceitfully: "But this is not the custom of Iranians. Among us the loser of the first round always gets a respite and a second chance."

Sohrab relented and insouciantly walked away. Confident that he had the upper hand, he went on a leisurely deer hunt in the nearby thicket. Houman, who had been monitoring the wrestling match, was dismayed that Sohrab was so easily deceived and he reprimanded him for being naive. He was sure that Sohrab would not get a second chance at vanquishing his adversary.

Rostam used the respite to rest, wash himself in a nearby stream, and ask God for victory. When he came back for the second round of wrestling, he found Sohrab hunting an onager as if he did not have a care in the world. Sohrab looked up and said, "I see that the one who escaped the talons of the lion has come back for more wounds."

They tethered their horses and started the second round of wrestling. But fortune had deserted Sohrab. It was as if the heavens were holding him back. Shortly he was brought down by Rostam. Knowing well that his opponent would not stay down for long, Rostam acted decisively. He drew his dagger and slashed the side of the young champion.

Sohrab sighed, knowing that he had received a mortal wound. "You are innocent of my blood, for I have been slain by the treachery of my own destiny. My peers are still playing in the sand, and I lie here dying on the battlefield. I will not survive, but nor will you escape the hand of destiny. Soon my father, Rostam, will find you and avenge my death, even if you turn into a fish and hide in the sea; even if you become a star and shine upon the heavens."

Rostam's head swam and the world darkened in front of his eyes. He fainted. After a few moments he regained consciousness and realized the enormity of the disaster that was engulfing him. He asked his victim if he had a sign to prove that he was the son of Rostam. Sohrab said, "So, you are Rostam, aren't you? Why did you hide this from me? Why did your fatherly tenderness desert you when I was pleading to learn your real name? Now, look at this armband that you gave my mother. Little did she know that you would see it after killing me."

Rostam saw the badge. He pulled his hair in anguish, wept, and wallowed in the dirt. Sohrab said that it was too late for sorrows, but he had one last wish. He asked Rostam to prevent the Iranians from attacking the army of Turan. This war was all his doing, and the defeat was only his. Rostam agreed that he had done enough evil for one day. Enough innocent blood had been spilled. He rode back to the Iranian side. His return meant that he had survived the duel, but his bearing was not that of a victor.

Rostam told the knights what had happened and asked them to respect Sohrab's wish. Then he rode back to his dying son.

Three prominent knights, Tous, Gostaham, and Gudarz, followed Rostam. They consoled him and even prevented him from committing suicide in a moment of utter desolation. Rostam knew that Kay Kavous had a magical potion, a panacea that could save the dying Sohrab. He charged Gudarz to plead with the king for the elixir of life that he had in his possession. "Tell the king of the disaster that has befallen me. Tell him that I have mortally injured my son in battle. If I have ever rendered him a service, let him take pity on me now and send along the elixir of life that he holds in his secret vault. My son will get well and serve him, as I have done for all these years."

Gudarz went to the king and pled Rostam's case, but the king had not forgotten the harsh words of Rostam before the conflict when he had accused him of incompetence. What would such an arrogant knight be capable of if he were to join forces with a formidable champion like Sohrab? Who could resist the combined forces of father and son? Kay Kavous thought that this would not bode well for his crown. He refused Gudarz the panacea that could save Sohrab's life. Gudarz rushed back to Rostam with these words: "Kay Kavous's vile nature is a tree hung with bitter fruit. He withholds the magical potion. Rush to him yourself if you want to change his mind."

Rostam prepared a bed for his wounded son, appointed an attendant to care for him, and set off on the road to the king's pavilion. He had not gone far when someone came from behind to give him the news that Sohrab was dead. Rostam sighed and closed his eyes. Then he dismounted and wallowed in the dirt to mourn his son. He wailed: "Who has suffered this misfortune before me? What kind of father kills his own son? How shall I plead my case when Zaul and Rudabeh denounce me? The knights of Iran will curse the progeny of Saum for this monstrous act. Above all, how can I inform the fair Tahmineh that I have killed our innocent son? Who could know that this precocious child would so quickly grow into such a formidable warrior?"

Rostam ordered the body of Sohrab adorned in kingly brocade and placed in a casket. Then he went to his encampment and set fire to it. The luxurious tent and its golden, silk-covered throne burned down. Rostam stood there and decried his fate for its malice. The knights of Iran kept Rostam company. When Kay Kavous came to extend his condolences, Rostam conveyed the wish of Sohrab that there should be no war against the Turanians. The king reluctantly acceded.

Rostam led Sohrab's funeral procession back to Zabol. Unkempt and in torn cloths, he tearfully walked ahead of his son's coffin. A great crowd came forward to mourn Sohrab. Zaul dismounted and said, "No mother will ever give birth to a son like Sohrab."

Rostam came to the palace, opened the casket, and showed his father the face of the grandson he had never met. Everyone came forth and wept loudly, for Sohrab bore an uncanny resemblance to the noble elder of their clan the late Saum. Sohrab was entombed in a magnificent crypt.

Tahmineh heard of the death of her son and died of sadness in less than a year.

The tale of Sohrab brings tears to one's eyes
And a tender heart is enraged at Rostam
Who was most reckless and unwise.

The Martyred Prince:
Siavosh

Sing now learned poet of the eternal law
Of just deserts, weave it into the fabric of verse.
Delight in spreading wisdom and inspiring awe.

The Maiden of the Thicket

At the crowing of the cock one morning, Tous, the son of King Nowzar, led a hunting expedition of the Iranian knights to the plains of Daghuy, near the border of Turan. Using hunting cheetahs and falcons, the group spread out across the lush hunting grounds on their horses. Tous and Geav rode off together into a dense thicket in pursuit of wild boar. Instead of the game they were chasing, they came upon a girl, flawless in beauty and radiant as the full moon, hiding among the bushes.

Tous asked the maiden to explain how she came to be in such a wild place all alone. The maiden said that she was a Turanian princess of the house of Garsivaz, the brother of the Turanian king, Afrasiab. Her father had come home drunk from a feast the previous night and had pulled a dagger on her. She had no choice but to run for her life in the middle of the night. Having lost her horse to exhaustion and her jewels to a band of thieves, she sought refuge in the thicket.

To Geav and Tous, the beautiful maiden was just a slave girl, an object of desire to be possessed. When they could not settle the matter of ownership, they returned to the capital and took up their dispute with their king. Kay Kavous's advice was that the worthy knights would do well to busy themselves with the stories of their hunt and leave the lovely catch of the day in the care of His Majesty. Then the king turned to the girl and asked if she would prefer to serve as his favorite consort rather than as a slave to either of the knights. The matter was settled to the satisfaction of the king.

The next morning the maiden of the thicket was in the king's harem reclining on a sumptuous seat decorated in yellow silk and studded in rubies, lapis lazuli, and turquoise. In due time she grew heavy with child. But sadly she died in labor and did not live to see her radiant son, who was more beautiful than a lavishly adorned idol. The king was saddened by the death of his favorite consort but rejoiced at the sight of his son, whom he called Siavosh, meaning the rider of a black stallion. Royal astrologers cast his horoscope but found little happiness in the stars of the newborn, although the boy was expected to sire a magnificent king. Kay Kavous was disheartened with the prediction but could do little but entrust his son to divine protection.

Rostam had retired to Zabol after enduring the tragedy of the death of his son, Sohrab. A few years passed, and Rostam thought it was time he paid his respects at the royal court. It was during this visit that he first saw the young boy Siavosh.

Upon seeing the marvelous child, Rostam expressed a desire to take him to Zabol and oversee his proper education. The king happily delegated the training of the crown prince to his impeccable knight. In Zabol, Rostam treated his new ward like his own son, protecting him and caring for his every want and desire. The education of the future king started in earnest. Under Rostam's watchful eye, Siavosh soon mastered the arts of riding, combat, and archery, as well as the ways of justice and the finer points of decorum. On completion of his education, the young prince was eager to return to the capital to practice his martial and courtly skills at his father's palace.

Rostam prepared a great celebration, and the city of Zabol was decorated for Siavosh's departure. People lined the streets, and a mixture of gold coins and rare fragrances such as ambergris and musk rained on them from atop the walls and domes of the city. The horses, well groomed and perfumed, marched in the parade to the festive music. Siavosh rode out with Rostam, sad to leave his teacher but also elated at the prospect of being reunited with his father. The Persian court welcomed Siavosh with lavish festivities that lasted a whole week.

For the next seven years the young prince busied himself with refining and perfecting the royal arts that he had learned in Zabol. He tried his best to be a good son and a perfect crown prince.

The Queen's Gambit

Unbeknownst to the young Siavosh, Queen Sudabeh had nursed a secret admiration for the prince as he grew into a handsome, noble young man. Her heart melted like ice by a great fire at his sight, and she felt a sweet melancholy in his presence.

One day Siavosh received a message from the queen indicating that a visit to her private chambers would be welcomed. Siavosh judged this to be an inappropriate invitation from his stepmother and sent word that he was not in the habit of frequenting the women's quarters. Sudabeh tried another approach, telling the king that Siavosh had sisters in the harem who longed to see their gallant brother. The king thought that this was a grand idea and suggested it to his son. Siavosh demurred, contending that visiting the harem would be a waste when his time could be more profitably spent in the company of learned men, great warriors, and adept courtiers. The king praised his son's good judgment but did not relent on his request that he visit the harem. Siavosh gave in despite his misgivings.

On the appointed day, Kay Kavous issued orders for a magnificent welcome for Siavosh at the inner quarters. The doors opened and the young prince was ushered in, walking on a spread of Chinese silk lined with bowls of musk, saffron, and wine. Handfuls of gold coins, agate, and lapis lazuli were thrown at his feet. Sudabeh, fragrant and splendid as a garden of paradise, descended from her bejeweled dais, embraced the prince, and longingly kissed his eyes and his face. Siavosh knew that there was no innocence in her lingering embrace. He cut short his discourse with the queen and walked to where his sisters were sitting. The prince spoke to them for a spell and left the harem.

Siavosh went to the king and pronounced that His Majesty's good fortune had exceeded that of the glorious kings of yore. The king was pleased by these words of praise. Siavosh hoped his visit had satisfied the king and that it would be the end of Sudabeh's invitations.

Later that night, Sudabeh visited with the king in private, extolling the virtues of the crown prince and proposing to arrange his marriage to her own daughter. The king rejoiced, because he recalled that the royal astrologers had prophesied that a magnificent king would be born to Siavosh.

The young prince agreed to wed anyone his father chose but begged to be excused from another visit to the queen's chambers. The king laughed at the awkwardness his son felt around his queen. He insisted that Sudabeh was like a mother to Siavosh and that her advice was crucial in the matter of his wedding. Kay Kavous was confident that he was offering Siavosh sound advice.

False confidence leads a foolish man to slaughter.
He stomps on solid ground but it turns out to be
A layer of straw floating on a puddle of water.

Siavosh had no choice but to smile and bow his head in acquiescence as a great storm raged inside of him. He went back to the queen's quarters, where he was presented with a bevy of nubile virgins, including the queen's own daughter. Although they were shy, none of the girls could take her eyes off the young prince. The girls were dismissed, and Sudabeh turned toward Siavosh and said, "Stop hiding your thoughts. What is your pleasure? Those who see your angelic face can't resist you. Which one of these beautiful girls is worthy of your companionship?"

Siavosh was ill at ease and could not find the words to speak. During this moment of pause, Sudabeh threw off her veil and gushed: "I understand your hesitation. Why would anyone look at the moon when the sun is high in the sky? Why would you choose another when I stand before you in my splendor? Pledge your loyalty to me and I will choose a child bride for you. But I will be the one to love you and serve your desires. And when the king passes from this world you will become my protector. You will love me and spoil me just as he has. Look at me: I am yours, body and soul."

With these shocking words, Sudabeh approached Siavosh, shamelessly held his head, and kissed him with parted lips. Siavosh flushed like a rose. With tears in his eyes, he prayed for strength against temptations of evil. Siavosh would never betray his father. But he also knew that Sudabeh was capable of great mischief. He tried to mollify her. "You are as exquisite as the moon in the sky. You are unmatched in the entire world. Only a king deserves to be your companion. It is honor enough for me to wed your daughter. Ask the king for her hand on my behalf, and I pledge to not divulge what transpired between us today. You are the queen, and I look upon you as my dear mother."

Siavosh left the harem in a hurry, unsettled and in great confusion. Sudabeh continued with her plan and went to the king with the good tidings that the crown prince had chosen her daughter as his future wife. The king opened his treasure house and piled up a heap of precious gifts for the wedding. Sudabeh watched this, but she was absorbed in reveries of terrible vengeance if the young prince continued to reject her. The next day the queen sat upon her throne wearing a precious crown and sent for Siavosh. She said to him: "The king has given you his daughter. Two hundred elephants cannot carry the gifts he has set aside for you. I, too, am giving you my daughter, and I will give you more gifts than the king has. Look at my face in all its beauty, and tell me what possible excuse you could have to turn your back on me. I have pined for you for seven painful years. My sun has been blotted out and my days have been dark for long enough. Come and make me happy; revive me! But let me warn you: if you turn away from me, I will ruin this kingship for you and turn your father against you."

Siavosh replied in great anguish and desperation. "May I never lose my head for a matter of the heart or be so dastardly as to betray my own father. You are the queen, the sun upon the throne. You are above committing a sin like this."

Sudabeh screamed that he did not deserve her trust; that he wanted to betray and defame her. Then she tore her cloths to shreds and scratched her cheeks. The palace reverberated with the sound of her wailing and the king rushed to her chambers to see what had happened. The queen cried and pulled her hair and accused Siavosh of lusting after her. She claimed that his physical assault might have injured her unborn child. Siavosh was stunned. He turned to his father pleading with him not to believe the lies of Sudabeh.

Trial by Fire

To ascertain the truth, the king smelled his wife and found that she was redolent of rosewater, musk, and wine but that there was not a trace of these scents on his son. Siavosh had not touched Sudabeh. She was obviously lying, and the king had no choice but to decide in favor of Siavosh.

Of course, she deserved the edge of the sword for this calumny, but Kay Kavous thought of the dire consequence of executing the daughter of a neighboring king. Besides, how could he kill a woman who had been loyal to him, taken his side and shared his prison cell at her father's castle? What would come of their children after the execution of their mother? Above all, how could he kill a woman he still loved? These thoughts assailed Kay Kavous one after another and prevented him from punishing Sudabeh. Instead he advised Siavosh to keep the matter to himself and forget the terrible event altogether.

But Sudabeh was not content with the quiet resolution of the dispute in favor of Siavosh. She knew a hoary sorceress who was having a difficult pregnancy. To win back the king's sympathy and corroborate her version of the events, the queen convinced the witch to end her pregnancy. Then she placed the sorceress's twin fetuses in a golden basin on display and took to bed feigning a miscarriage.

Suspicious of Sudabeh's claims, Kay Kavous called on astrologers to determine the identity of the stillborn infants. Again, the definitive judgment was against Sudabeh: far from being children of royal parents, the infants were the spawn of the devil. Kay Kavous considered the matter for a week and then broached it with Sudabeh. She refused to admit her guilt and insisted that the astrologers had been suborned by Siavosh. She bitterly wept and said, "There will be no love between us if you take the fate of your perished infants so lightly."

Kay Kavous also wept. Bewildered about who was telling the truth, the king turned to his high priests. They advised that the ultimate test of truthfulness was trial by fire. Either the accuser or the accused had to go through the flames and emerge unscathed to prove his or her claim. Sudabeh refused the trial, contending that the aborted fetuses were her evidence. Siavosh welcomed the occasion to demonstrate his innocence once and for all. The king was reconciled that he would lose either his son or his wife to the fire's judgment.

On the appointed day, a hundred caravans of red-haired camels brought firewood to the palace, and the servants piled the wood into two mountains, separated by a path that could accommodate four horsemen riding shoulder to shoulder. Siavosh appeared on his beloved black stallion Behzad and bowed in front of his father. According to custom, his white shirt was sprinkled with camphor to imply that he was clad in a shroud and was prepared to die. The king was ashamed that Siavosh was facing death over his bad decisions. But the prince comforted him, saying that this was his fate and that he was certain of vindication.

The crowds that had gathered to witness the event hailed the white-clad prince who galloped on a black horse toward the immense, scorching fire. As the mouth of the inferno swallowed the young prince, a hush fell over the multitudes. Sudabeh watched from her balcony full of anxiety and hatred, with a mouthful of curses. She prayed that the prince would never emerge from the mountain of flames. Time seemed to stand still. People shed tears when Siavosh lingered in the flames.

Suddenly Siavosh rode out of the blazing wall of fire unharmed. His face was gloriously flushed, but there was not a speck of ash on his white shirt. A loud cheer went up from the crowd, and the city rejoiced. Sudabeh tore her hair out and clawed her face. The king embraced his son and begged his pardon for doubting his honesty. Lavish festivities commenced, and the courtiers drank with the king and his son for three days.

On the fourth day, the king sat on his royal throne, holding his ox-headed mace and prepared to mete out justice against his devious wife. He summoned Sudabeh and ordered her to put a stop to her lies. The queen confessed that Siavosh had told the truth and that she had earned her just deserts. She only begged the king to forgive her before she was put to death.

Kay Kavous consulted with his advisers. Their unanimous recommendation was announced by the king: Sudabeh was condemned to die. As the henchmen entered to take her away, the king blanched. Realizing that he would be blamed for her execution, Siavosh interceded with his father, asking him to forgive the queen. Kay Kavous immediately granted this wish, as if he had been waiting for an excuse to spare her life. Siavosh kissed the throne and left the court. Sudabeh's attendants ran to salute her for her narrow escape from the gallows.

As time passed, Sudabeh bewitched the king with her love despite her past treachery. Judging from his adoring gaze, Kay Kavous had forgotten the entire affair. And in time, Sudabeh resumed her intrigue against Siavosh.

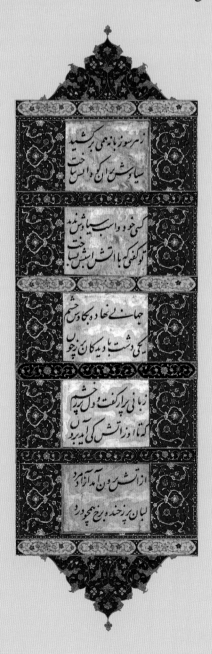

Siavosh Victorious

Kay Kavous was enjoying the seemingly newfound peace in the royal household when Afrasiab, the king of Turan, once again started to stir up trouble by sending a hundred thousand soldiers across the Oxus River, occupying the eastern provinces of Iran. Kay Kavous called the knights to council and announced that he would lead the charge against the enemy. The royal advisers did not endorse this plan. Kay Kavous had twice allowed himself to be taken captive, endangering the safety of the country. The king asked his knights, "Well, then, which brave knight will rise to this worthy challenge?"

When no one spoke up, Siavosh stood and declared that he would expel the Turanian invaders. He was seeking the glories of victory, but he also wished to get away from the royal palace, rife as he found it with Sudabeh's poisonous plots. The king embraced his brave son and praised him. Then he wrote Rostam, appointing him commander of the new campaign. Rostam accepted the charge, as he had nurtured and instructed Siavosh and loved him like a son.

Twelve thousand shield-bearing infantry and as many Baluchi, Parsi, and Gilani cavalry gathered under the command of Siavosh. Five priests carried the standard of Kaveh in front of the army. Kay Kavous traveled one milestone of the journey and embraced Siavosh at the moment of farewell. Father and son cried aloud as if they knew this would be their last embrace. From there the young prince drove his army to the realm of Zabol. He stayed for a month, until the troops of Kabul and India converged with Rostam's army.

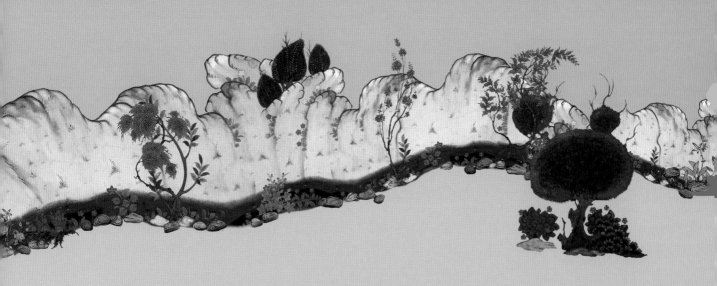

When all was ready, the forces of Iran marched to the city of Balkh, where they faced the army of the Turanian general and Afrasiab's brother, Garsivaz. What followed was a lengthy and intense campaign. Siavosh fought two pitched battles in three days against superior numbers and succeeded to defeat and rout the enemy. Thrilled by his first military success, he wrote to Kay Kavous about his decisive victory and asked for further instructions. The king rejoiced in the triumph of his son but advised caution. Giving chase would risk dissipating the forces of Iran. Siavosh was commanded to sit tight and await another Turanian incursion, whereupon he could wipe them out.

Garsivaz redeployed his forces behind the safety of the Oxus River and rushed to the court of Afrasiab. Wildly exaggerating the numbers of the Iranians, he tried to justify his defeat. Afrasiab shot a murderous look at his mendacious brother and dismissed him with accusations of cowardice and incompetence. Then he called a thousand of his elite warriors to a feast, with the aim of rallying them for an attack. They ate and drank until sleep overcame the king.

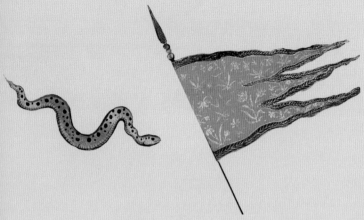

Afrasiab's Nightmare

One watch of the night had elapsed when Afrasiab woke from a nightmare with a deafening scream. The attendants were startled, and Garsivaz rushed to the king's side. Interpreters of visions were called, and Afrasiab related his dream to them: The king found himself in a snake-infested field under a sky swarming with eagles. A wind toppled his standard and the Iranians slaughtered his troops. He was captured and taken to the court of Kay Kavous, where a young prince took a sword and cleaved him in half. It was the pain of this blow that had awakened the king.

The meaning of the dream was not difficult to decipher, but only one among the interpreters dared to speak. First he begged and received leave to address the king without fear of retribution reserved for those who cast bad omens. He said the dream was a warning against war with the Iranians under the command of Siavosh. If the young prince were killed, Turan would be doomed.

Afrasiab was disturbed to hear the news and soon convinced himself of the wisdom of the path of peace. He halted the preparations for war and called a council of knights. In the gathering the king spoke in praise of reconciliation and deplored the depredations, misery, and senseless bloodshed of war. The council enthusiastically endorsed this sentiment and authorized the king to sue for peace.

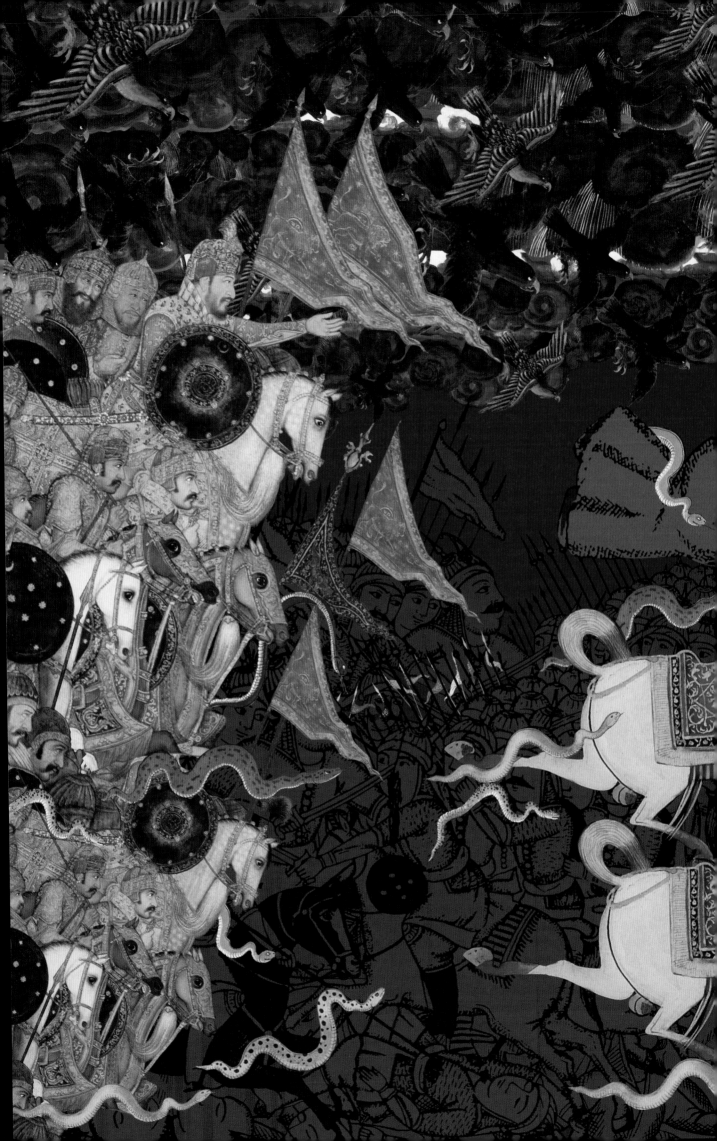

Afrasiab sent a substantial offer of settlement to Siavosh, including rich gifts and a nonaggression pact. Garsivaz acted as the king's emissary and led a caravan of lavish gifts on camelback, accompanied by long trains of Arabian horses and exquisitely attired slaves.

The Iranian prince and his military commander sent word to Garsivaz that they needed time to consider the proposal. The offer of gifts was sufficient, and the pledge to withdraw from the territories west of the Oxus River was acceptable, but Afrasiab could not be trusted given his habit of violating his covenants. To ensure compliance, Rostam drew up the names of one hundred close relatives of Afrasiab. They were to be delivered to Iran as hostages. If the king of Turan were to violate his treaty, the hostages would pay with their lives.

Garsivaz returned to his king and conveyed Siavosh's demand. Afrasiab was hesitant but, knowing he had no option, he complied. Having delivered the hostages, Garsivaz returned to the court and sang the praises of Siavosh, whom he described as a prince unmatched among the highborn. Afrasiab was content that he was close to concluding the peace treaty with Iran.

Flushed with success in the campaign and happy for the extraction of a strong treaty, Siavosh dispatched Rostam with a letter to his father. It explained the new offer of peace backed by the guarantee of prominent hostages to be held in Iran.

When Rostam arrived at the court, Kay Kavous welcomed him and asked for news from the front and the reason for his visit. Rostam delivered the letter to the scribes. As the document was read, Kay Kavous's mood darkened and his face twisted in anger. Outraged at the suggestion to end hostilities with Turan, the king accused Siavosh of naïveté, saying that he had obviously been deceived by Afrasiab's wiles. Surely hostages would be worthless in preventing someone like Afrasiab from carrying out another invasion. The Turanian king would easily forfeit the lives of his lowborn relatives. Kay Kavous commanded that the gifts of Turan be burned on the spot and that the hostages be shackled and sent to the capital for beheading. War had to commence immediately.

Rostam retorted that not blundering into a reckless war was the king's own policy detailed in a previous letter. He added that the king of Turan had sued for peace and that the proposal was sound. Besides, Siavosh would never go back on his word. He would not allow the execution of hostages while Afrasiab maintained his side of the peace treaty.

Kay Kavous unleashed his fury on Rostam and accused him of masterminding the peace proposal for love of comfort and worldly goods. Then the king threatened to relieve Rostam of his command if he refused to carry out the new bellicose policy.

Grievously offended, Rostam resigned his commission and left the court. Kay Kavous appointed Tous in his stead and ordered him to wage war on Afrasiab immediately. He also sent a harsh letter to Siavosh, berating him for his indolence and gullibility. He commanded his son to return to the capital if he failed to burn the gifts, dispatch the hostages, and wage war on Turan.

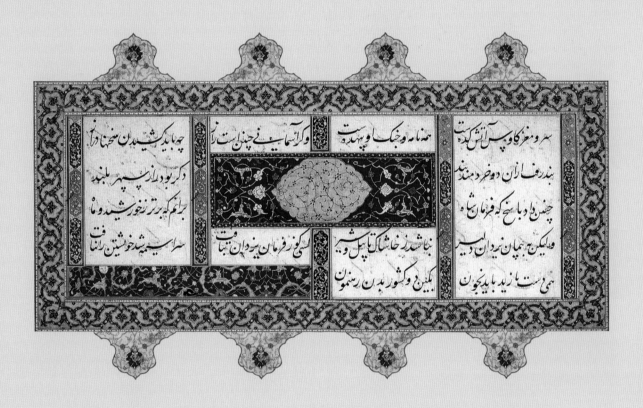

Siavosh in Exile

When Siavosh read his father's letter, he whispered to himself, "Would that my mother had never given birth to me, and, having been born, would that I had died before this day."

To disobey his father's commands would be tantamount to sedition. But obeying his father was inconceivable as well. Allowing the execution of a hundred innocent men was morally repugnant to him. Nor could he bear the thought of abandoning the campaign and returning to the royal palace to face the wrath of the king and the intrigues of the queen.

Torn by this dilemma, Siavosh finally resolved to go forth into exile and spend the rest of his days in obscurity. His trusted friend and lieutenant Bahraum advised against this course. He urged the young prince to remonstrate with the king, ask for the return of Rostam, and, if it all failed, to obey and carry out the king's orders. But Siavosh had made up his mind. He wrote his last letter to Kay Kavous:

I have sought the path of virtue since I came of age. But that woman plotted against me and turned your court into my prison. I had to go through an inferno to prove my innocence, but the torments continued. When I could no longer bear the misery, I went to war, won glory, and brought peace to two nations. But it is all to no avail. You have no love for me. I wish you happiness as I walk into the mouth of the dragon. I do not know what the stars have in store for me.

Siavosh sent a message to Afrasiab asking leave to pass through his realm in search of a refuge. Along with this message, he returned the hostages and the goods offered for peace. The king of Turan was dismayed to learn of the new Iranian position. He was even more shocked by Siavosh's request for safe conduct.

Piran, Afrasiab's cousin and trusted adviser, offered him guidence. He echoed Garsivaz's earlier praise of Siavosh and said that the king would do well to offer the Iranian prince asylum in Turan. Graced with divine sanction and possessed of courage and righteousness, Siavosh deserved to be treated as a royal guest. Kay Kavous was getting old, and his son was sure to return eventually to the throne of Iran. Then the two countries would be united by the friendship that Afrasiab had cultivated at that crucial moment.

Afrasiab listened to Piran and found his words worthy of reflection. But he countered that when all was said and done, one could hardly trust a son of Kay Kavous. Piran disagreed. Siavosh had disobeyed his father on the matter of the hostages at the expense of the throne of Iran. This was proof that he had not inherited the impetuous and unjust temper of Kay Kavous. Afrasiab was persuaded. He wrote back to the young prince, extending a fatherly invitation to come to Turan and remain there as his revered guest.

Siavosh was relieved because he had found a way out of his predicament. But he was also heartbroken that he would spend his life in exile. The young prince delegated the command of the army to Bahraum and ordered him to await the arrival of Tous. With a heavy heart, Siavosh prepared for his journey. He mounted his black stallion Behzad and rode out toward the Oxus River at the head of three hundred of his loyal warriors.

Piran crossed the Oxus River to welcome Siavosh and accompanied him as they rode toward Kang, the capital of Turan. Four white elephants and a thousand attendants were included in the welcoming assembly. Cheering crowds thronged the streets of every town they passed on their way to Kang, plucking on the strings of harps and lutes and singing songs of welcome. All this reminded Siavosh of his joyful return to the capital of Persia upon leaving Rostam and the land of Zabol. Piran noticed the melancholy of the young prince and the sorrow he was trying to hide. In their final rest before arriving at the capital, Piran said, "Among the highborn, you are unrivaled for three reasons. You are from the seed of Kay Qobad. You are utterly truthful. And your face commands love and respect."

Siavosh smiled and said, "Your reputation for loyalty and kindness precedes you, my wise old friend. I know that you will never betray one with whom you have established bonds of friendship. So, allow me to ask you a question. Can I rest assured that I will be safe in this country? For if in your estimation I am not safe, I will travel to another land."

Piran assured Siavosh that he was safe. He said that although Afrasiab had a bad reputation, he was essentially a godly man. As the king's blood relative, his knight, and his adviser, the old warrior claimed to be in a position to judge Afrasiab's character. Besides, Piran reassured Siavosh that his army of one hundred thousand warriors would be on hand should the slightest threat to his safety arise.

Siavosh took comfort in these heartfelt assurances and trusted Piran like a father. When they arrived at the gates of Kang, Afrasiab came out on foot to welcome them. Siavosh quickly dismounted. The king of Turan embraced him and said, "From now on there will be no wars. The ram and the tiger will drink from the same fountainhead. The world has had enough of the discord unleashed by Tur's slaying of his brother Iraj. But in your person, Iran and Turan will finally be reconciled."

Then he took Siavosh by the hand and allowed him to share his throne. The king looked upon the face of the young prince and marveled at the foolishness of old Kay Kavous, who had spurned such a winsome and virtuous son.

Elaborate games were announced in Siavosh's honor, and the entire city came out to see how the Iranian prince fared against the Turanians. The Iranians excelled at polo to the point that Siavosh asked them to go easy on their competitors. At archery none could string the young prince's bow. Even Garsivaz was humiliated as he failed at the task. Afrasiab, who thoroughly enjoyed Siavosh's athletic performance, laughed and said, "Once I had a bow like this. None could string it. But those were the bygone days of my youth."

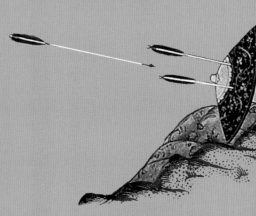

For the next year Afrasiab spent most of his time with Siavosh, to the exclusion of Garsivaz and his advisers, much to their displeasure. Despite this attention, Siavosh could not shake the melancholy of being separated from his homeland. To relieve the young prince's solitude, Piran proposed that his nubile daughter Jarireh serve as a suitable consort. The young prince bit his lip when he cast eyes on the lovely girl. Shortly after this arrangement was made, Piran suggested the daughter of Afrasiab, the stunning Farigis, as Siavosh's wife. Marrying the king's daughter would ensure his success at the court and help him adjust to his new life in Turan. Siavosh demurred at first. Piran insisted that Jarireh would continue to serve him as a loyal consort and that Siavosh deserved to marry the daughter of the king.

Afrasiab had some reservations when Piran broached the subject of the marriage of Siavosh to Farigis. Astrologers had foreseen that the fruit of such a connection would be a king who would destroy the homeland of Turan. Piran, who was in the habit of dismissing such prognostications, convinced Afrasiab to give his consent despite the forewarning of the astrologers. A lavish wedding was arranged, and Siavosh settled into his new life in comfort and good standing. Another year passed, and memories of Kay Kavous and Rostam began to fade.

The king offered his new son-in-law the vast territories that lay between Turan and China. Siavosh left the young Jarireh in her father's care and traveled to his new realm with Farigis. He built the city of Siavoshgerd. The walls were set at three miles in length and width. Its cobbled streets were lined with fields of tulips and hyacinth. At the heart of this new city,

a magnificent palace was built for Farigis. It was topped with several high domes. In his throne room Siavosh commissioned lavish frescoes on opposite walls portraying the knights and heroes of Iran and Turan feasting and fighting. Kay Kavous, Zaul, Rostam, and Geav were portrayed on one wall, and images of Afrasiab, Piran, and Garsivaz graced the opposite wall. At this time a letter arrived from Jarireh. She was proud to have produced a son for Siavosh despite her tender age. The boy was named Forud. Siavosh was very happy when he saw the saffron handprint of the infant at the bottom of the letter.

On a visit to Siavoshgerd, Piran was dazzled by the wealth and luxury of the city. Everything appeared to be going well, but the young prince had an abiding sense that ill fortune was haunting him. He had a strange premonition that his blood would be unjustly spilled on foreign soil. Siavosh shared with Piran the chilling vision of his death and the disaster that would befall Turan after his passing. This prophecy of doom shocked Piran despite his skepticism of visions and fortunetelling. He thought to himself: What have I done? What if he is right? Afrasiab also spoke of this dark future. I am the one who brought him over to this land. I may very well have been the cause of the envisaged disaster.

Upon his return to the capital city of Kang, Piran told Afrasiab of the grandeur of the city of Siavoshgerd. Afrasiab wondered if the young prince had at long last settled in Turan. To be sure of Siavosh's position, he dispatched Garsivaz to the new city with many gifts and asked him to gauge if Siavosh had thoroughly acclimated to his new homeland.

The Wicked Garsivaz

Garsivaz chose a thousand cavalrymen and rode out to Siavoshgerd. He was awestruck by the beauty of the newly constructed city. The more Siavosh showed off his magnificent city, the more envious Garsivaz grew. The excursion ended at the marvelous palace of Farigis, who descended her throne and greeted her uncle, the royal emissary. Garsivaz looked around at the sumptuous palace, begrudging Siavosh the wealth and power he had been granted in Turan. Give it a year or so, he thought, and this man will not regard anyone as his equal.

Garsivaz's resentment was augmented during the welcoming games that were arranged in his honor. First he challenged his host to a contest, but Siavosh refused on the grounds that it would be improper for a young prince to challenge the king's brother. Instead, he called on Garsivaz to designate a substitute. The Turanian knight appreciated the propriety of the young prince and called on his troops for a volunteer. A soldier named Goruy said he would be a proper match for the Iranian prince. Siavosh frowned at the impudence of this suggestion. Garsivaz said that he approved of the match, as Goruy was a worthy warrior. Siavosh disagreed. "Since I won't be engaging the royal opponent, not one but two from among your men must join forces against me."

A second opponent was chosen to assist Goruy, and the two approached Siavosh in an equestrian armed contest. The prince did not lay hands on his arms. He easily clutched Goruy's belt and threw him off his horse into the dust. Then he shamed the second warrior by snatching him off his saddle, carrying him by the neck, and depositing him at the feet of Garsivaz. Siavosh dismounted and climbed the throne with a triumphant laugh.

The royal emissary did not relish the taste of that humiliation and further brooded on the position Siavosh had attained in Turan. Garsivaz thought Afrasiab was wrong to elevate a foreign prince above the men of Turan and blamed him for having allowed an Iranian prince to shame Turanians in their own land.

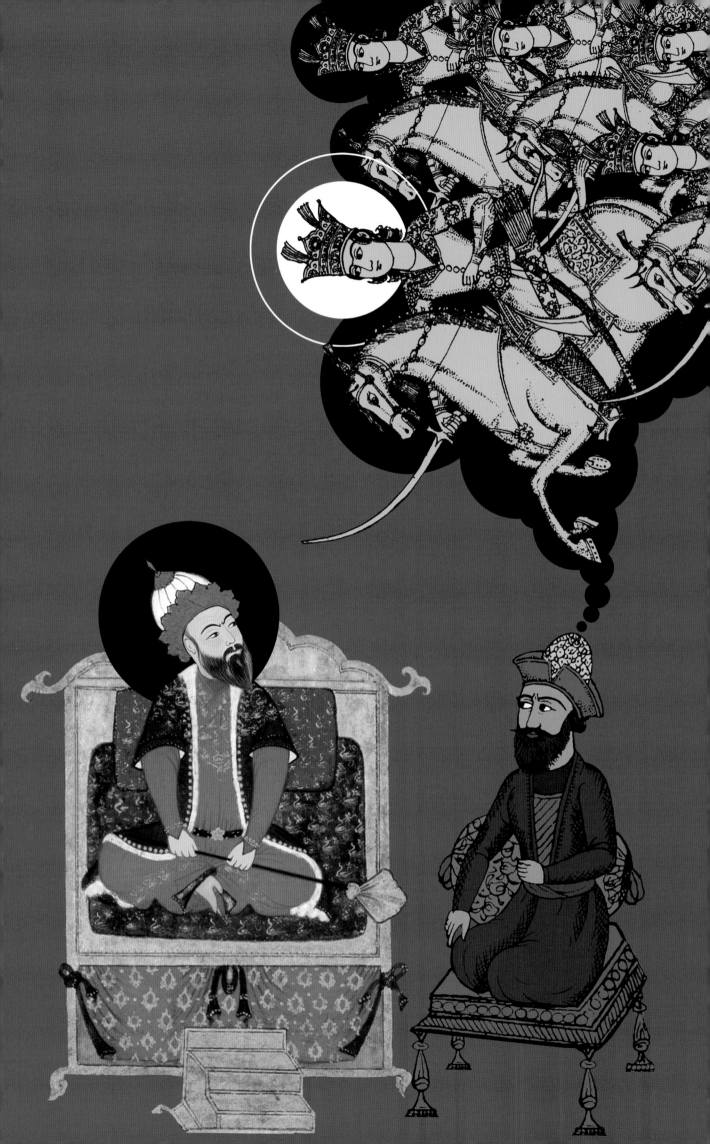

When Garsivaz returned to Kang, he went straight to the court to report to Afrasiab. He spoke of Siavosh as a prince who trafficked with Iran, China, and Rome to foment rebellion. Afrasiab was disturbed by this intelligence and said that he needed three days to think the matter over.

On the fourth day the king called Garsivaz to a private consultation. Despite their misgivings, the fact remained that Afrasiab had admitted Siavosh into his realm and given his daughter to him in marriage. Neither the heavens nor the world would look kindly upon a king who would turn on his son-in-law without cause. Maybe Afrasiab could summon Siavosh to the court and encourage him to return to Iran.

Garsivaz disputed the wisdom of this plan. For one thing, he argued, Siavosh would never accept such an invitation, as he was not the young prince Afrasiab remembered. Nor was Farigis the shy princess of the past. From what he had seen in Siavoshgerd, they now had ambitions of sovereignty. For another, Garsivaz warned, the Iranian prince could not be trusted to go back to Iran, as he knew all the military secrets of Turan. Afrasiab was beginning to regret his kindness to Siavosh, but in the absence of an excuse, he could not act. Garsivaz urged action before the young and popular prince charmed the entire army and reduced the king to a lowly vassal in his own land.

At long last Afrasiab decided to invite Siavosh and Farigis to the capital in order to study the matter. He wrote a mildly worded invitation expressing a desire to see his daughter and to hunt in the company of his son-in-law. Garsivaz was charged to take the royal invitation back to Siavoshgerd.

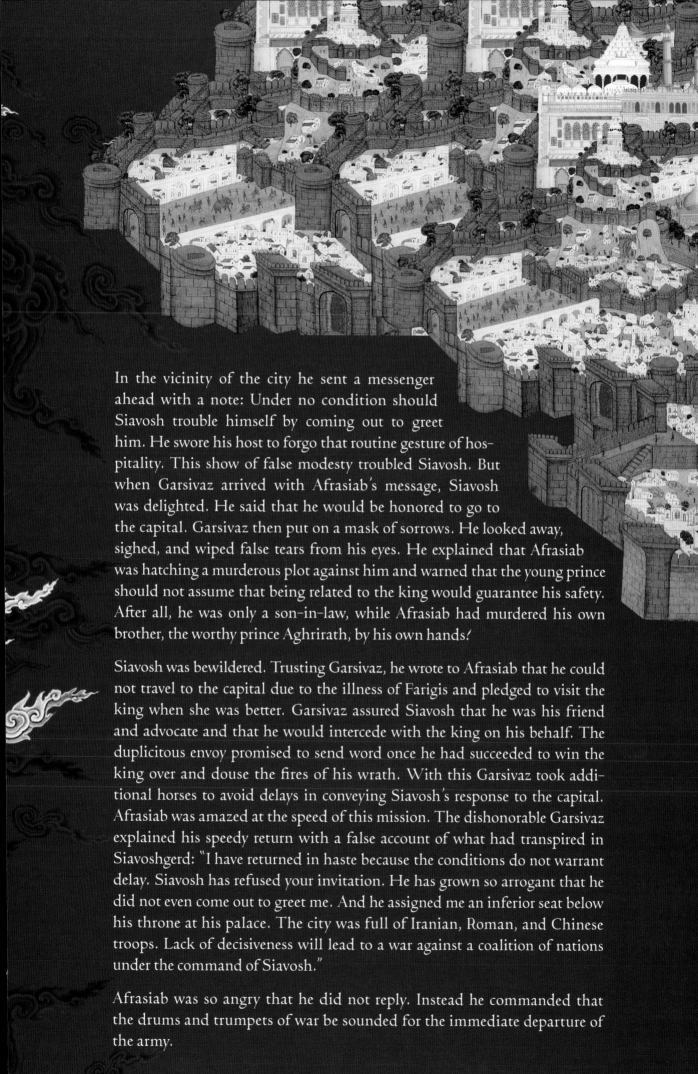

In the vicinity of the city he sent a messenger
ahead with a note: Under no condition should
Siavosh trouble himself by coming out to greet
him. He swore his host to forgo that routine gesture of hos-
pitality. This show of false modesty troubled Siavosh. But
when Garsivaz arrived with Afrasiab's message, Siavosh
was delighted. He said that he would be honored to go to
the capital. Garsivaz then put on a mask of sorrows. He looked away,
sighed, and wiped false tears from his eyes. He explained that Afrasiab
was hatching a murderous plot against him and warned that the young prince
should not assume that being related to the king would guarantee his safety.
After all, he was only a son-in-law, while Afrasiab had murdered his own
brother, the worthy prince Aghrirath, by his own hands!

Siavosh was bewildered. Trusting Garsivaz, he wrote to Afrasiab that he could
not travel to the capital due to the illness of Farigis and pledged to visit the
king when she was better. Garsivaz assured Siavosh that he was his friend
and advocate and that he would intercede with the king on his behalf. The
duplicitous envoy promised to send word once he had succeeded to win the
king over and douse the fires of his wrath. With this Garsivaz took addi-
tional horses to avoid delays in conveying Siavosh's response to the capital.
Afrasiab was amazed at the speed of this mission. The dishonorable Garsivaz
explained his speedy return with a false account of what had transpired in
Siavoshgerd: "I have returned in haste because the conditions do not warrant
delay. Siavosh has refused your invitation. He has grown so arrogant that he
did not even come out to greet me. And he assigned me an inferior seat below
his throne at his palace. The city was full of Iranian, Roman, and Chinese
troops. Lack of decisiveness will lead to a war against a coalition of nations
under the command of Siavosh."

Afrasiab was so angry that he did not reply. Instead he commanded that
the drums and trumpets of war be sounded for the immediate departure of
the army.

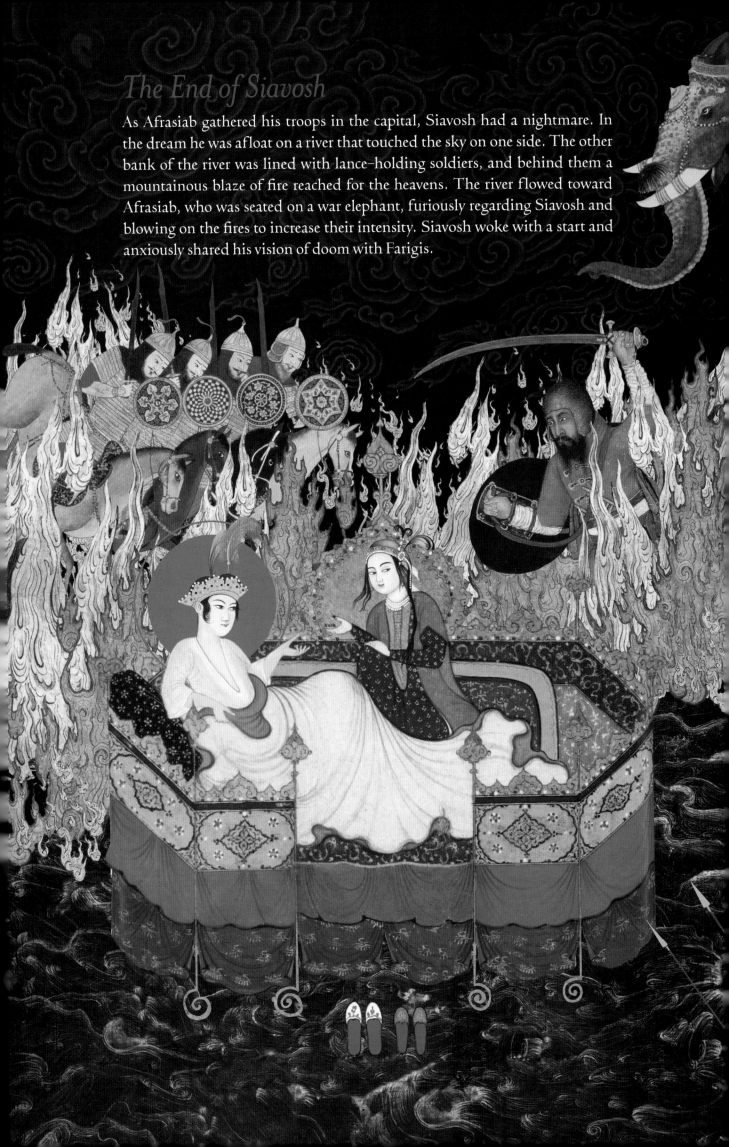

The End of Siavosh

As Afrasiab gathered his troops in the capital, Siavosh had a nightmare. In the dream he was afloat on a river that touched the sky on one side. The other bank of the river was lined with lance-holding soldiers, and behind them a mountainous blaze of fire reached for the heavens. The river flowed toward Afrasiab, who was seated on a war elephant, furiously regarding Siavosh and blowing on the fires to increase their intensity. Siavosh woke with a start and anxiously shared his vision of doom with Farigis.

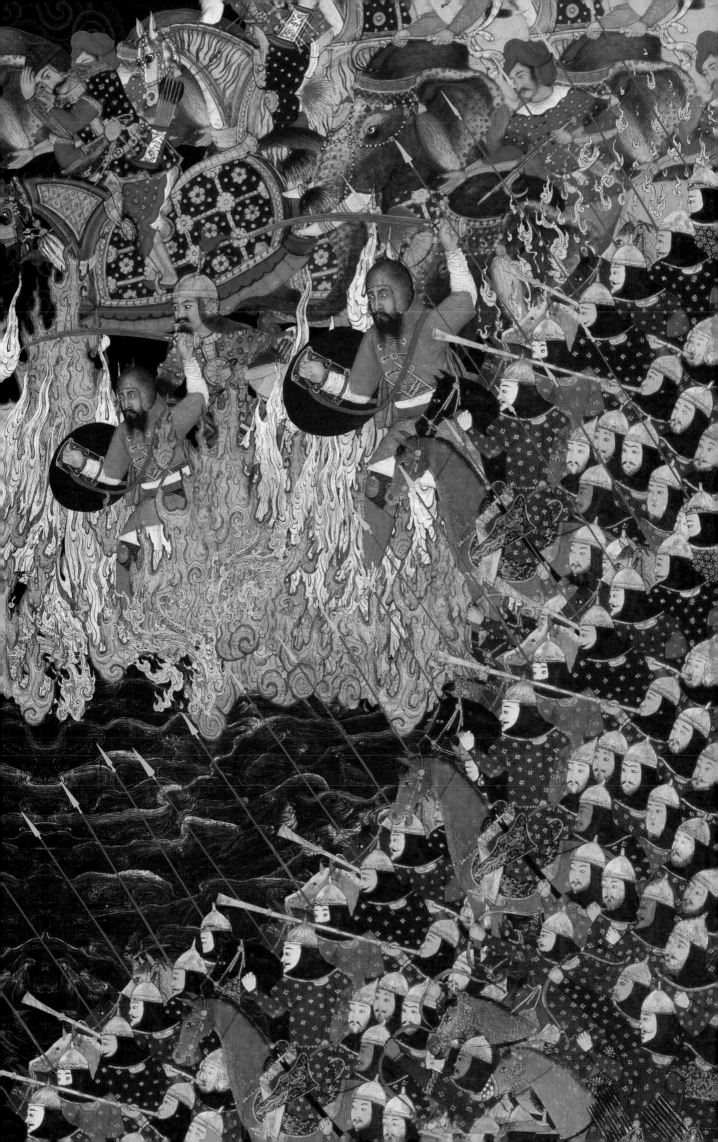

Farigis tried to decipher the dream as an omen against Garsivaz, but Siavosh was not convinced. He put his troops on alert and donned his armor, awaiting word from Garsivaz. As the troops approached the walls of Siavoshgerd, Garsivaz sent this message: "All is lost. My words had no effect on the king. Save yourself if you can."

Still trusting the treacherous Garsivaz, Siavosh gave Farigis the bad news that Afrasiab was nearing with his troops. She cried and clawed at her cheeks. Then she said to him: "Don't think of us at all. Ride your horse and escape with your life. My only wish is that you remain alive."

Siavosh said, "My dreams of doom have come to pass. Men are fated to die, and my time has come. I will be beheaded. My body will not be honored with a burial. No one will weep for me. The king's henchmen will march you off, uncovered and debased. But you shall find succor in Piran's protection. You are five months pregnant, and you will have a son. Call him Kay Khosrow. In time, an Iranian knight named Geav will come and take you and your son beyond the Oxus River. Kay Khosrow shall be king, and he will avenge my death. Now, be strong and prepare yourself for hardship until the appointed day."

Farigis rushed to her husband, held him for the last time, and sobbed.

Siavosh went into the stables, lifted the collar and bridle off his beloved black stallion, hugged his neck, and whispered: "Run away, my dear Behzad. Abandon the comforts of the stable and suffer no one to ride you until Kay Khosrow rises to avenge me. Be his steed as he crushes the cobra's head."

With this he released all the horses and rode out ahead of his trusted warriors toward the borders of Iran, tears streaming down his cheeks. Soon they came against the army of Turan that filled the horizon.

Siavosh addressed the king: "Why have you brought these troops, Afrasiab? Why do you intend to kill an innocent man? You will sow vengeance and animosity among nations."

Garsivaz said, "Silence, you unworthy man! If you are honest, then why have you come to welcome the king in your armor?"

It was at that moment that Siavosh realized that the wicked Garsivaz had deceived him. Afrasiab issued orders to his troops to attack the Iranian warriors. Resigned to die, the Iranians prepared to fight a hard battle. Siavosh said that his time had come and that bloodshed was unnecessary. But it was to no avail. The Turanians massacred the Iranian troops. Siavosh was wounded in the battle. Goruy, who had led the charge, captured Siavosh, tied his hands, and brought him before the king. He put a packsaddle on Siavosh's back to further humiliate him.

Afrasiab condemned Siavosh to death. A brother of Piran's named Pilsam was present at the scene. He tried to prevent the inevitable by urging patience.

He pleaded with the king to wait until Piran arrived. But Garsivaz insisted on his immediate execution on the grounds that it was unwise to delay slaying a wounded snake. He threatened to leave the service of the king if the execution was stayed.

Afrasiab knew that Siavosh's guilt had not been proven. Besides, he had had a dream indicating that killing the prince would spell doom for Turan. But things had gone too far. Releasing Siavosh after all that had happened would also lead to war and disaster.

Farigis, who had heard of the bloody confrontation, arrived on the scene in a dreadful state. She struck her face, pulled her hair, and poured dust on her head. She addressed Afrasiab: "Why do you want to lower me to the dust, Father? Why have you surrendered yourself to lies? Heaven shall not abide killing a young man who abandoned his father and his throne to seek refuge in your protection. Haven't you heard what happens to the unjust? Haven't you heard how Feraydun dealt with Zahhak? Aren't you afraid of what will happen to this land when Rostam and Geav come to avenge their prince?"

With this she looked upon Siavosh's bloody face, clawed her cheeks, and wept aloud. Afrasiab pitied Farigis. He could not bear to see his daughter in such a state, so he had her sent under guard to Kang. Afrasiab could not see a way out of the course the events had taken. He issued the final orders for Siavosh's decapitation and emphasized that he should be executed on barren land where no plants could grow.

Goruy dragged the doomed prince away to the scene of his execution. Siavosh turned to the heavens and prayed that his blood would be avenged. To Pilsam he said farewell and asked that he convey his affections to Piran and to ask him: "Where were your one hundred thousand troops to protect me as the henchmen of Garsivaz dragged me into the dust? I had no one to mourn me as I was unjustly slain."

The shameless Goruy hurled him on the ground. To prevent innocent blood from trickling on the soil and invoking the wrath of the heavens, he placed a golden basin under his victim's head. Garsivaz handed him a dagger and Goruy beheaded Siavosh. A dark wind blew and dust storms covered the sun.

Such is this hoary world and its ways
It takes the breast from the infant's lips
And the innocent traveler it waylays.

We have finished the tale of the fallen prince
And now to the story of a king who rose
To wage wars and seek vengeance.

The steed of the poet's youth is tied to the signpost of fifty-eight.
With thoughts of the end, he trades the reins of the stallion
He rode at youth for a cane and tempers his gait.

His only ambition is that providence give him leave
To finish weaving the epic poem he has started
And allow posterity its ancient legacy to receive.

Return of the King:
Kay Khosrow

Now come back, ye, to the tale that the aged
Farmer told of those who learned of the demise
Of their prince and the wars they waged.

Turan After the Martyrdom of Siavosh

When Farigis heard that Siavosh had been murdered, she clipped her braids, clawed at her face, wailed, and uttered curses against Afrasiab in public. Outraged at this insolence, Afrasiab ordered his henchmen to beat Farigis and show her no mercy. He knew she was with child but he did not care. The king was heard saying: "I want no sapling from that root, not a branch, not a leaf."

Dreading what could befall Farigis at her father's hands, Pilsam rode out to meet Piran, who had heard about Siavosh's troubles and was on his way to Siavoshgerd. When Pilsam delivered the news of the beheading of Siavosh, Piran ripped his clothes and wallowed in the dirt in a gesture of mourning. Pilsam advised that there was no time for lamentations, as Afrasiab was intent on killing Siavosh's pregnant wife as well.

Piran galloped for two days without rest to reach the city of Kang and arrived not a moment too soon. As Afrasiab's minions were beating the defenseless Farigis, Piran intervened and stayed the murderous hands of the henchmen. Then he rode up to the court with Farigis by his side and persuaded Afrasiab that killing his daughter would bring him nothing but infamy in this world and damnation in the hereafter. The king agreed and released his daughter into the custody of Piran on the condition that her baby be brought back to court for the king's final judgment. The wise Piran took the bereaved princess to his palace and entrusted her to the care of his wife, the kind Golshahr.

On a moonless night a few months later, Siavosh appeared in a dream to Piran. He emerged from the sea holding a sword. With his other hand Siavosh held a candle that was lit by the glow of the sun. He turned to Piran with a smile and intoned: "Wake up from this sweet slumber, Piran. Truly this is an auspicious night. A son is born to me. I name him Kay Khosrow!"

Piran stirred to awareness and roused his wife, urging her to attend to Farigis. Lady Golshahr went to Farigis's chambers and found that she had given birth to a beautiful boy. She ran back and said, "Come, my husband, and see the handsome child. He is a veritable king in the cradle."

Piran set his eyes on the radiant infant and bitterly wept for Siavosh. He swore an oath to protect Kay Khosrow from his vengeful grandfather. The next morning he went to the court as he had been instructed and declared: "My glorious king, last night your daughter, Farigis, gave birth to a son. He has your looks. Your divine grace is reflected in his face. He resembles his ancestors Tur and Feraydun. Dispel all evil thoughts from your heart on this auspicious day."

Afrasiab sighed with regret for what he had done to Siavosh. He had not forgotten the prophecy that a king from the lines of Tur and Kay Qobad would spell his doom. But this day the king was in a fatalistic mood. The mortals, he thought, can't undo the decrees of heaven. What is the use of killing an infant?

Afrasiab ruled that the baby must be sent away to the countryside, where he would never learn of his lineage or find out what had happened to his father. Relieved, Piran made arrangements to send the infant to the shepherds once he was weaned.

But growing up in this pastoral environment did not hide the light of Kay Khosrow's royal heritage. At the age of seven, he fashioned a crude bow and arrow and practiced deer hunting. At ten he was hunting wolves and boars, and at twelve he went after lions armed with nothing but a club.

Worried that the lad would be injured in such reckless adventures, the shepherds went to Piran and complained that they were unable to cope with the ambitions of their young ward. Piran smiled, for he had always known that the royal lineage of the son of Siavosh would eventually shine through. He rode out to see the shepherd boy who hunted like a king. Kay Khosrow was summoned, and Piran embraced him for a long time. The bewildered boy found it odd that a knight would deign to treat a peasant with such respect. Piran smiled with affection and revealed to the young boy the truth about his royal lineage. Despite Afrasiab's command, he fitted the boy with a worthy steed and a proper outfit and took him back to live in his palace.

321

A few years passed, and Afrasiab had another disturbing dream that reminded him of the dark prognostications about the son of Siavosh. He ordered Piran to bring Kay Khosrow to court for an audience. Piran feared for his young ward's life. He knew that Afrasiab would not hesitate to kill the son of Siavosh if he sensed the slightest threat.

Before the fateful interview, Piran advised Kay Khosrow to act the part of a dim-witted farmhand. On the appointed day, the young Kay Khosrow went to the court in the company of Piran. The king looked at him with compassion and asked, "How do you care for your flock?"

"There is no game. And I have no bows and arrows to hunt with."

"What is your view of fate, and of what is good and bad in life?"

"If there is a leopard, it is sure to maul people."

"Who are your parents? What do you know of Iran?"

"Even a ferocious lion can't overcome a good dog."

Afrasiab laughed at the apparent idiocy of the simpleton who had been born to Farigis.

Piran's ploy had succeeded, and the king's fears about the future of Kay Khosrow were allayed. He exiled Kay Khosrow and his mother to Siavoshgerd, the city that Siavosh had built many years ago.

In the absence of its founder, the magnificent city of Siavoshgerd had been neglected and was overgrown with thorns. But the people who still revered their martyred benefactor came out to welcome his son. At the place of Siavosh's slaying, where a few drops of his blood had been spilled on the ground, a tall tree had grown. It had a fragrance like musk, and its leaves bore the image of the martyred prince. People routinely gathered in the shade of that holy tree to pray and rest.

Iran After the Martyrdom of Siavosh

When Kay Kavous received the news of the martyrdom of his son, he threw himself on the ground and ripped his royal garments to shreds. Tous, Gudarz, Geav, and the rest of the knights cried for their beloved prince. When Zaul and Rostam heard the news, they too mourned for one week. Rostam swore not to take off his armor, put down his weapons, or even wash until he had avenged Siavosh. Then he traveled to the capital at the head of a great army and went straight to the court of Kay Kavous to harangue him. "The seeds of your wickedness have borne fruit. You have forfeited your royal crown to your recklessness and your infatuation with that woman. Lack of wisdom and excess of power are a deadly combination. You have brought disaster upon our heads. We shall never see a prince like Siavosh again. He was heroic in battlefield and gracious in feasts. I shall go to war with tears in my eyes and avenge my prince."

Kay Kavous was too ashamed to return Rostam's angry gaze. He just sat on his throne and sobbed. Nor did he move when Rostam went to Sudabeh's quarters with a drawn dagger, pulled her out, and slayed her in full view of the court.

When the Iranians concluded their mourning for Siavosh, the raging Rostam led an army to avenge their fallen prince. Tous, Gudarz, and Geav, as well as Rostam's son Faramarz and Kay Kavous's son Fariborz, accompanied the army. Rostam gave Faramarz the command of the forward division, composed of twelve thousand warriors, as they marched toward the Oxus River.

On the borders of Turan, the army of Faramarz came against the troops of a vassal king by the name of Varazan. In a great fury to avenge Siavosh, Faramarz tore into the enemy and killed hundreds of warriors until he came face to face with Varazan. The vassal king asked him to identify himself. Faramarz said that he would not deign to reveal his name to a lowly servant of Afrasiab and felled Varazan with a blow of his javelin. Then he dismounted and beheaded him and set fire to the border territory. Afrasiab was alarmed by the news of this invasion. He responded by sending his favorite son, Sorkheh, with thirty thousand sword-wielding cavalry to stop the forces of Faramarz. The king declared to Sorkheh: "You are my favorite son and the pillar of my kingdom. No one in the army of Iran is your equal in combat. You can lock swords with Faramarz if you wish, but stay away from Rostam."

With his thirty thousand swordsmen, Sorkheh marched forth to stop the Iranian invasion. A furious battle ensued, the two sides clashing to the din of massive drums. Bloody swords glittered within the cloud of dust that arose from the battlefield as steam rises from a cauldron. Spotting Faramarz's standard, Sorkheh left his bow with his son, picked a lance, and went forth to challenge him to a duel. But it didn't take him long to realize the foolishness of that decision. Faramarz struck him with his lance with such force that Sorkheh was knocked out of his saddle. Grabbing onto the neck of

his horse, he tried to escape, but Faramarz caught up to him from behind and lifted him off his horse, bound his hands, and sent him back to the Iranian lines as a captive. Rostam praised his son and curtly ordered Tous to execute the young, handsome prince of Turan. Sorkheh pleaded with Tous. "Why do you want to spill my innocent blood? I was of the same age as Siavosh, and we were friends. I cried day and night for him after that calamity. I cursed his murderers."

Tous took pity on Sorkheh and begged Rostam to spare him. But Rostam's rage knew no bounds. He said that Afrasiab must suffer the loss of his son just as Kay Kavous was suffering. Then he commanded his brother, Zavareh, to carry out the gruesome task.

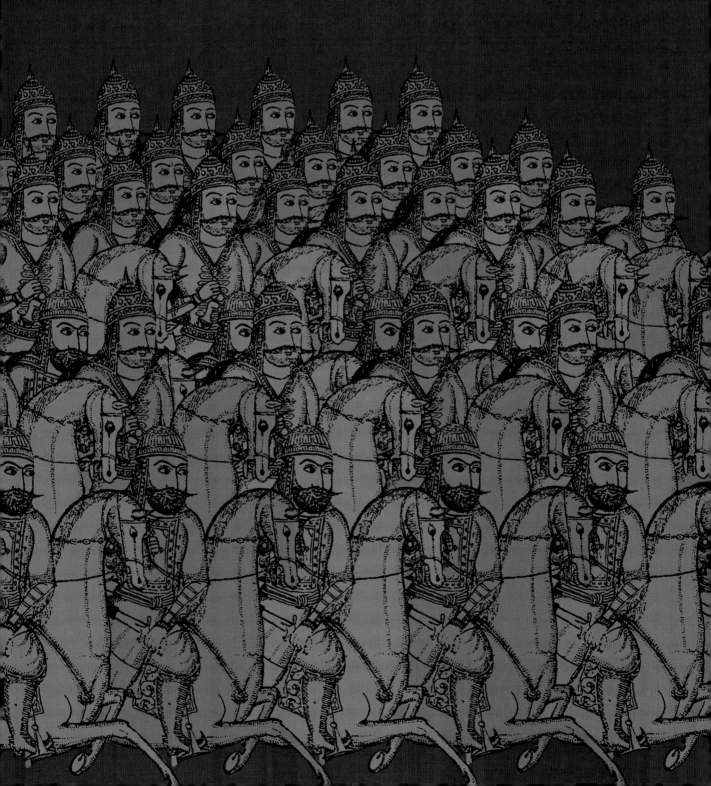

When the news of the demise of Sorkheh reached Afrasiab, the king displayed great sorrow. He called on his troops to avenge the blood of their young prince. Pilsam volunteered to bring down Rostam in a duel if Afrasiab granted him an excellent horse and a set of glittering, well-made weapons from his treasury. Piran objected, pleading with the king to spare his brother from the deadly mission. But Pilsam insisted, and upon receiving his commission, he rode to the Iranian lines and shouted out: "Where is Rostam? Who claims that he is a dragon on the battlefield?"

Geav drew his sword and roared, "The great hero Rostam does not fight anyone who happens to shows up in the arena."

Pilsam threw his lance, causing Geav to lose his hold in his stirrups. Faramarz rode out to help Geav, and for a while Pilsam was warding off two of Iran's greatest knights. Rostam watched the battle from his position and witnessed the power of the Turanian warrior. He knew that the opponent could be

none other than the famed Pilsam. He told the army commanders to hold their ground and galloped to the center of the battlefield, shouting, "Here I am, if you seek me." Then, without delay, he ran Pilsam through with his lance, lifted him off his horse, and dropped him at the front of the Turanian lines. Piran was dismayed at witnessing the quick demise of his mighty brother. He cried bitter tears as the trumpets and the drums of war sounded and the general battle commenced.

In the confrontation that followed, many on both sides were killed. In one of his forays, Afrasiab succeeded in forcing Tous to flee. But Rostam rallied the knights and mounted a counterattack to push back the warriors of Turan. When Rostam spotted the black standard of the king of Turan, he charged and struck him with his lance. Afrasiab was thrown from his horse. His trusted and prominent knight Houman came to his rescue, pounding his mace on

Rostam's shoulder. This blow didn't do any damage. It merely distracted the hero and allowed Afrasiab to escape once again from Rostam's clutches. Soon the army of Turan followed its leader away from the battle. The victory went to Iran.

Rostam in Turan

After Afrasiab fled with the remnants of his army, Turan belonged to Rostam. He reclined on his adversary's throne and delighted in his triumph. He gave away the treasures of Turan to his warriors and divided the kingdom between Tous and Geav. To Fariborz he offered the golden crown of Afrasiab and said, "You are our superior. You are brother to Siavosh. Do not rest until you have avenged his blood." Then he declared amnesty on those who withdrew their loyalty from Afrasiab and submitted to the Iranian conquerors.

For several years, the Iranian knights remained in Turan. They enjoyed the spoils of battle and the comforts of victory. One day, Rostam's brother, Zavareh, was on a hunting expedition and heard his scout say that it was the favorite hunting ground of Siavosh. He collapsed and fell off his horse and released the falcon he was carrying. Having been reminded of the martyrdom of Siavosh, he swore to forsake all the comforts he had been enjoying and to rededicate himself to avenging Siavosh's death. Rostam and the other knights agreed with this sentiment. Forgetting the amnesty they had granted earlier, they waged indiscriminate war, laying waste to the land, pillaging and killing man, woman, and child.

The elders of the land went forth and complained to Rostam. One of the elders said, "We have nothing to do with Afrasiab. Nor do we want to see him even in our dreams. We were not guilty of the innocent blood that he spilled. Nor do we know where he might be hiding, in the clouds or in the mouth of a dragon. Now we humble ourselves at your threshold. Shed not the blood of the innocent in victory. Do not wage war on the heavens."

At this admonishment Rostam ceased causing further bloodshed and called for a war council.

The knights gathered and discussed the troubling rumors that Afrasiab was regrouping to attack Iran. With Rostam and the knights languishing in Turan and the inept Kay Kavous at the helm, Iran was indeed vulnerable. The return was sound strategy, but Rostam was not convinced until a mage came forth with a piece of ancient advice:

Sate your passions and temper your greed
Rein in the demon of excess in this world
And only in the path of justice proceed.

Rostam felt a pang of shame. In short order the knights gathered their booty in horses, slaves, and jewels and went back to Iran.

With the return of the army to Iran, Afrasiab, too, went back to the capital city of Kang and found it a wasteland. Indeed, wherever he turned he found utter devastation, which saddened and enraged him. To avenge the demise of his own land, he broke across the borders and laid waste to the Iranian territory, burning cities and demolishing villages. Iran was also suffering from a seven-year draught. War and natural disasters compounded the misery of the Iranians and reversed the fortunes of the ancient land.

One night, the angel Sorush appeared to Gudarz in a dream riding on a rain cloud. He intoned: "If you want to escape the clutches of misery and the depredations of this foreign invader, seek Kay Khosrow, the son of Siavosh, whose maternal ancestor is Tur. When he sets foot in Iran as king, heaven will fulfill his wishes. He will not rest until he avenges his father. None but your son Geav from among the knights of Iran will be able to find him."

As the sun peered through the raven wings of the night, Gudarz summoned Geav and shared his dream with him. He warned Geav: "Finding Kay Khosrow will be a dangerous and difficult assignment. But what would be greater for a mortal than the everlasting glory of enthroning a righteous king?"

Geav accepted the mission and set off on his lonely quest to the borders of Turan. For seven years, he searched the land and kept his identity a secret by living in obscurity and killing those who might inform on him. He hunted onager for food and wore their skin as his garment. He became a gaunt, wild man. On occasion he came so close to despair that he doubted whether his father's vision about Kay Khosrow was divine or demonic.

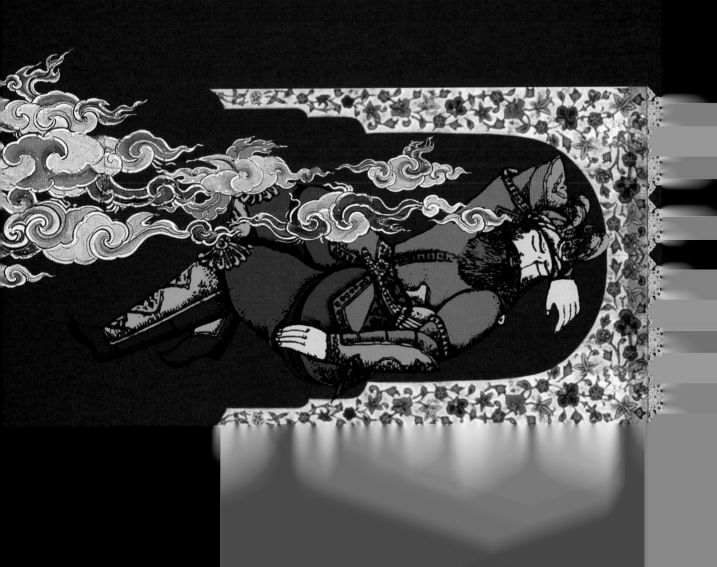

Finally, Geav made his way to Siavoshgerd and wandered into a garden. He was musing on the futility of his mission when he came across a charming lad wearing a garland of flowers and holding a chalice of wine. There was a divine light about the young man, as if he were sitting on a throne wearing the torque and the crown of a king. Geav knew instantly that his quest was at an end and that this young man was none other than his future king. In great excitement, he dismounted and ran to the young man. The man turned and smiled. Geav kissed the ground and said, "My lord and master! We long to utter your name. I am convinced that you are descended from the kings of Kay, and that you are the son of Siavosh."

The young man had surmised the identity of Geav as well. "And I suppose you are Geav, the son of Gudarz."

The knight was astounded. "May you live a long and happy life. Who told you of Geav and Gudarz?"

The young man responded: "My mother has told me the story as she heard it from my father. One day, she promised, Geav would come from Iran to take me back to my father's homeland and make me king."

Geav asked to see the mark of Kay Qobad on the young man's arm and praised God that he had at long last found Kay Khosrow. Then he begged the future king to lead the way back to the house of his mother. Happy to see Geav, Farigis urged great speed and caution. The slightest lapse or delay would alert the enemy and bring Afrasiab and the armies of Turan upon them. As they prepared for their great escape, the banished princess urged her son to ascend to the high meadow beyond the mountains and find Behzad, Siavosh's black stallion.

"My royal son, listen to my instructions. There is a catchment where a herd of wild horses drink. Behzad runs with that herd. When you approach them, hold aloft this saddle and bridle and speak to him softly. No mortal has been able to ride him since the day of your father's demise."

As Kay Khosrow approached the meadow, Siavosh's noble steed neighed but did not move from the spot at the edge of the watering hole. Kay Khosrow enfolded Behzad's neck in his arms, kissed his face, and whispered in his ears the sorrows of his father's last day. Then he saddled and mounted the stallion and returned to Siavoshgerd. Farigis presented Geav with Siavosh's armor as a token of her appreciation, and the three of them left the town swift as the wind.

Escape from Turan

The three fugitives from Siavoshgerd rode hard for many hours, and when they could go no further, they stopped at a small oasis to rest. Geav kept his armor on and his horse ready for battle as he watched over the mother and son he had taken under his protection. In the distance he saw the dust of the approaching warriors of Turan.

Piran had dispatched three hundred cavalry under the command of his brothers Golbad and Nastihan. Fearful that the escape of Kay Khosrow would trigger a new wave of revenge wars, Piran had authorized his brothers to kill Geav and Farigis on sight and bring back Kay Khosrow in chains.

The spirited Geav drew his sword, brought his horse to a full gallop, and fearlessly tore into the enemy lines. The warriors of Turan that surrounded him appeared like a thicket of lances. But Geav turned that thicket into a tavern flowing with Turanian blood. Golbad could not believe his eyes. He consulted with his brother, and they agreed that the only wise course was to withdraw their troops and go back to Piran for reinforcements against the unstoppable knight of Iran. When the two brothers returned, Piran dismissed them as inept and accused them of bringing disgrace to his name.

"How could a single man rout two of my knightly brothers, backed as they were by three hundred soldiers?"

Piran formed his own division of one thousand horsemen and went in pursuit of the fugitives. He forbade rest until the objects of their chase were killed or taken into captivity.

Having repelled the first wave of attacks, Geav was keenly aware of further perils that awaited them. He and his companions rode again for a long time until they crossed a deep but narrow waterway. Exhausted from their long journey, they stopped to rest. This time Farigis kept watch over Geav and her son as they slept. When she spotted a huge army approaching under the banner of Piran, she woke the men with great fear and anxiety in her voice. Geav assured her that he would be equal to the challenge. Kay Khosrow offered to fight along with him, but Geav refused his assistance. "I am a knight, one of seventy-eight sons of Gudarz. There are many knights like me, but there is only one king. If you are killed, my seven-year search will have been for naught. Don't worry. I can handle this army. Just ascend to the top of that mountain and watch over the battlefield."

Geav rode out to the river and challenged the army of Turan to send forth their best warrior. Piran cursed him as an inferior man of low birth who was doomed by his false pride. How did he hope to overcome a thousand soldiers by himself? Geav replied to the boastful fulminations of Piran: "You are a lionhearted commander indeed. It would behoove you to cross this stream and see for yourself how a single horseman of low birth contends with a high-born knight."

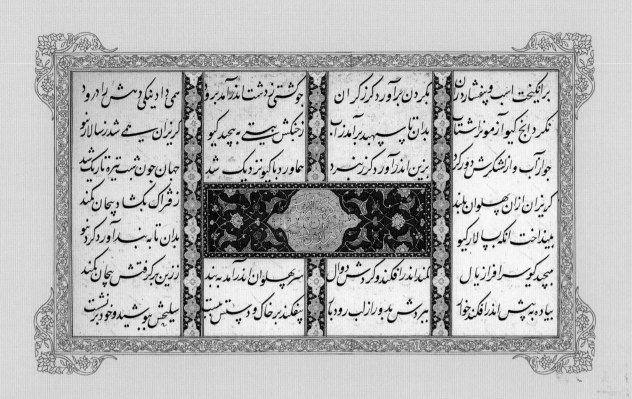

Moved to anger, his opponent crossed the river. Geav did not rush to battle, waiting for Piran to emerge from the water and leave the bank of the river. Then he withdrew to low ground and into a thicket that was well hidden from view. Piran gave chase. Geav holstered his mace and deployed his lariat. Suddenly, Piran found himself ensnared in Geav's noose, as he was caught by the neck and pulled off his horse. Geav quickly dismounted, tied Piran's hands, and relieved him of his clothes and armor. Donning them himself, Geav mounted on his captive's horse, looking, to all the world, like Piran.

The Iranian knight crossed the river in his Turanian disguise to the cheers of Piran's men, who mistook him for their leader coming back in triumph. They realized their mistake only when Geav tore into their ranks, wielding his mace and killing anyone who was not quick enough to escape.

When the forces of Turan were thoroughly routed, Geav crossed the river back again and dragged the helpless Piran to his future king. He called Piran a faithless wretch who had richly earned his impending demise for deceiving Siavosh. Piran kissed the ground when he saw Kay Khosrow and begged him to spare his life. But it was Farigis who interceded with Geav: "You have seen many hardships and traversed long distances for us. But know that this old man is righteous and wise. After God, he is the only one who stood between us and certain death."

Geav replied: "But, my lady, I have sworn an oath to the moon to paint the earth crimson with his blood."

Kay Khosrow said, "Keep your oath, then. Pierce his ear and let his blood run."

Geav obeyed. Piran begged for his horse, for otherwise he had no hope of catching up with his men. Geav agreed but bound his captive's hands to the saddle. To ensure that he would no longer hound them, Geav made Piran swear that none but his wife, the kind Golshahr, would untie his hands. With this he sent Piran across the river to follow the tracks of his retreating soldiers.

When Afrasiab heard of the flight of Kay Khosrow and the ensuing disastrous skirmishes, he gathered an army to pursue the fugitive prince himself. First he came to the battlefield where Golbad and Nastihan had been defeated. Disheartened, he demanded to know how a knight and his entire army had been allowed to cross into Turan without notice.

One of his commanders answered that this was not the work of an army under the command of a knight. One single knight, the gallant Geav, had fought that battle against the forces of Golbad and Nastihan. Afrasiab said, "May no one ever rely on the advice of Piran. I would not see this day if I had killed and buried that lad. And who, I wonder, brought the intelligence about the existence of Kay Khosrow to this son of a demon Geav?"

Moving forward, Afrasiab came to the second battlefield and saw Piran leading his army back. First Afrasiab rejoiced, as he thought they were returning in triumph. But as they came closer, he saw Piran's bound hands and blood-spattered face. Piran explained what had happened. Afrasiab dismissed him with a disdainful bark.

Then the king of Turan gave full rein to his rage and swore an oath to bring down the fugitives even if they ascended to the clouds. He pledged to mince their flesh and feed them to the fish of the sea.

Afrasiab appointed Houman commander of the pursuit and reminded him one last time of the urgency of the chase and the prophecy that when a mixed-blood king from the seeds of Kay Qobad and Tur rose, Turan would turn into a field of thorns.

Crossing the Oxus

Geav, Farigis, and Kay Khosrow reached the Oxus River ahead of the armies chasing them. Geav asked the boatman for a ship with new sails fit to carry a king across the river. The boatman replied that the river did not know king from servant. Geav said that he would pay the price, whatever it might be. Sensing their desperation, the boatman demanded a heavy ransom for rides across the river, swollen as it was by the angry torrents of spring. He wanted to keep either the prince or his mother, and, failing that, he demanded the black stallion that Kay Khosrow was riding or the armor of Siavosh's that Geav was wearing. Geav said, "You are a thief and a brigand, even if you don't carry weapons. You ask a heavy ransom for your meager services. Keep your boats, for we are taking on the river ourselves."

Turning to the prince, Geav charged: "If you are truly Kay Khosrow, you shall gain from challenging the

346

waves as a testament to your divine sanction. King Feraydun ascended his throne only after he had humbled the mighty waves of the Arvand River. We shall follow in your wake, but you must not care if we survive the crossing. We have been put on this earth to bring about the day of your ascending the throne as king. But follow you we shall, for remaining on this side would mean certain death."

Kay Khosrow said a prayer and rode his black stallion into the angry waves of the river. Geav and Farigis followed him as the incredulous boatman watched. When the three safely emerged on the Iranian bank of the river, the troops of Turan appeared on the horizon. Afrasiab was harsh with the boatman for his assistance to the fugitives. The boatman defended himself, saying: "I had nothing to do with it. They defied the river on their own. No one has ever seen horsemen in full armor crossing the river in the height of the spring."

Afrasiab ordered the boatman to prepare his ships. He wanted to chase the fugitives into Iran, but the prudent Houman dissuaded him. Going into Iran would count as an invasion, and they were not prepared for that.

Once on Iranian soil, Geav escorted Kay Khosrow and Farigis to Isfahan, the realm given to his clan. He sent letters ahead to his father, Gudarz, and King Kay Kavous with the good tidings of their safe arrival. Gudarz rode eighty miles to welcome the new prince, saying: "May your father rest in peace. As God is my witness, I would not be so happy if I saw him alive."

In Isfahan they celebrated for seven days, and on the eighth they set off to the winter palace of Pars. The city was decorated in honor of Kay Khosrow's arrival. King Kay Kavous cried tears of joy as he descended his throne to place kisses on his gallant grandson's eyes and face. Then he asked about his exile in Turan and the adventures of his rescue.

Kay Khosrow told his stories and denounced his maternal grandfather, Afrasiab, for killing his father. Then he related Geav's heroic labors in rescuing them from the land of Turan.

All the knights, with the exception of Tous, pledged their allegiance. Tous favored Fariborz as the crown prince and the next king of Iran, for he was the son of Kay Kavous from an Iranian mother and hence of pure blood. Conversely, Kay Khosrow was considered impure, for his mother and grandmother were Turanian princesses.

Geav, however, firmly stood by Kay Khosrow. This confrontation brought Iran to the brink of a civil war, as the two knights contended for their favorite successors and gathered armies in preparation for war. To resolve the stalemate, Kay Kavous arranged a contest to conquer the enchanted castle in Ardebil. Fariborz failed in the effort, and Kay Khosrow took the castle with the help of his loyal friend Geav. As the matter of succession was resolved, Tous and Fariborz submitted to Kay Khosrow and pledged their allegiance to him. Kay Khosrow reciprocated the gestures of Tous and his uncle Fariborz and graciously honored and maintained them as the commanders of his armies.

Kay Kavous recognized his glorious grandson as king
Sat him on his throne and endowed him with his crown
And the royal torque and the sovereign's ring.

Rostam came from the land of Zabol to pay his respects. The young king was thrilled to meet Siavosh's mentor and sent forth Geav, Gudarz, and Tous, wearing their ceremonial golden boots of knighthood, to welcome Rostam.

Trumpets blared and drums beat as the hero was ushered in. Rostam kissed the ground and wept because Kay Khosrow bore a great resemblance to his father, the noble Siavosh. The new king descended the throne with tears in his eyes and embraced the great hero. They stayed up, drank wine, and told stories both bitter and sweet of times past.

Kay Khosrow established the mountaintop fire temple of Azar Goshasp and prayed there in seclusion for a year. Then he came back to the winter palace of Pars to reside there, naming his mother, Farigis, the Queen of the World.

The fickle world, capriciously grants
Favors and ever inflicts unjust pain.
Fortunate is the one who supplants

Worries for serenity of the heart, calms
His covetous nature and shares his wealth
Without fears and petty qualms.

351

The Wrong Path:
Forud

Four things are required for excellence in rule
Noble birth, talent, skills, and practical reason.
The prince who is highborn and talented must school

Himself in royal skills and train hard
To master the arts required of a king but above
All he must discipline his mind and reason to guard

Against unwise choices and only at this stage
Can he be an impeccable king like Kay Khosrow
Who was noble, gifted, skillful, and sage.

The Second Invasion of Turan

Before placing the golden crown on the head of his grandson, Kay Kavous extracted an oath from him to pursue and punish his father's murderers. The young king made a solemn promise to avenge his father and immediately opened the treasure houses to prepare for war. He gave generously to those knights who vowed to bring down the house of Afrasiab. Geav, Gudarz, and Bizhan got the lion's share of the gifts.

Kay Khosrow sat in state and watched his knights march past the throne in a display of might. Fariborz, the son of Kay Kavous, led the procession at the head of one hundred and ten knights from the Kay royal house. Zarasp, the son of Tous, led eighty knights of the house of the late king Nowzar. Then Geav and his seventy-eight brothers marched behind the standard of their father, Gudarz. One prong under Faramarz, the son of Rostam, was sent to

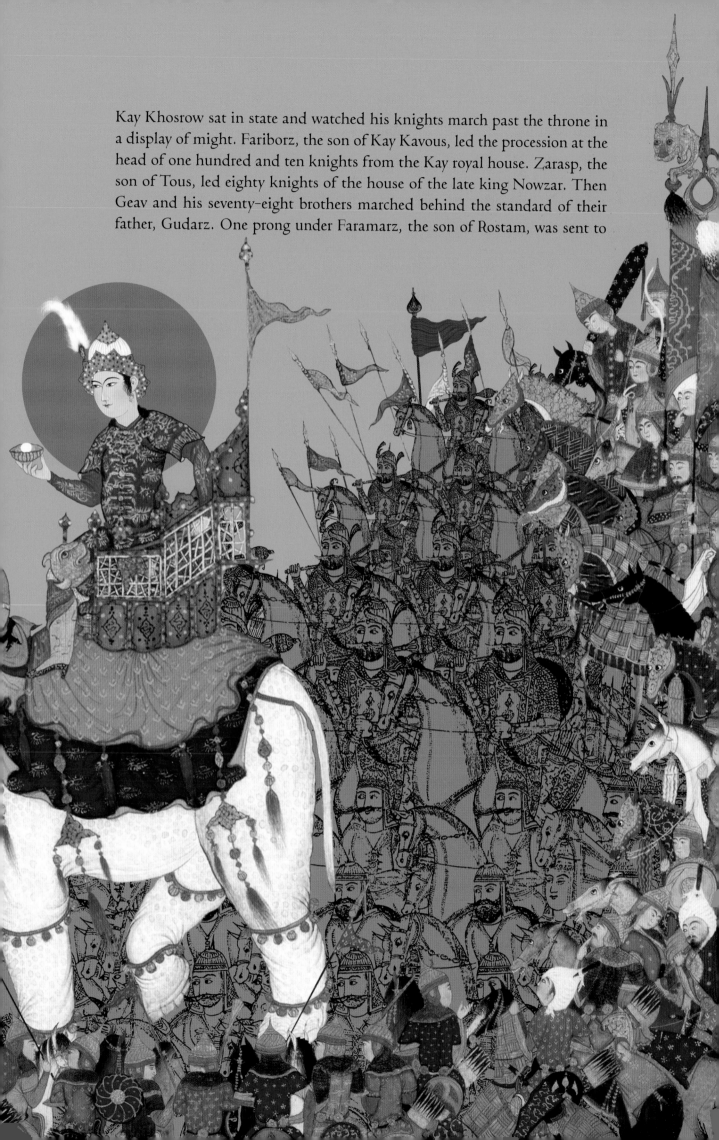

the southeast to recapture a province in the vicinity of the land of Zabol. On the day of the departure of his forces Kay Khosrow sat on a war elephant and viewed the departing legions. He advised Faramarz against waging war on those who wished to stay in peace. He enjoined him to protect the poor and the weak: "Be generous and resist the temptations of wealth. Remember that a good name is our only lasting legacy in this world."

The Northern Prong

After the departure of the first army, Kay Khosrow summoned his field marshal Tous, who had earlier opposed his kingship, to head up the second prong toward the north, where Afrasiab was laying waste to the Iranian land. Before dispatching the expedition, the king issued strict instructions against harming noncombatants. Peaceful peasants and artisans were not to be abused or harassed. "Such is the way of ruling as a just king: ordinary people must be protected from harm as an army marches to war."

The king also warned Tous to avoid the mountain path toward the enemy lines. That path would take the army to the impregnable castle of Kalat where the formidable Forud resided. There was no reason to confront the mighty Forud for he was the king's half brother born to Siavosh's consort Jarireh. He bore no animosity for Iran and was indeed disposed to help Kay Khosrow avenge their father. Tous pledged to obediently follow these instructions and set off for battle.

A few days into their journey, the army reached a fork in the road. On one side lay an expanse of difficult and parched terrain. On the other stood the lush mountains of Kalat. Tous was tempted to take the easier route. Against the advice of Gudarz and in clear violation of his promises to the king, he led the army through the mountain path, which would bring him to the gates of Forud's castle.

As the Iranian legions climbed the mountains approaching Forud's castle, scouts brought news of an advancing army. The young lord of the castle pulled back his flocks of sheep, camels, and horses and locked the gates of the fortress. Then he sought the counsel of his mother, who had long mourned Siavosh and resented Afrasiab for causing the demise of her beloved husband.

Jarireh advised her son to join forces with the army of his brother, Kay Khosrow, and help avenge their father's death.

"Your brother, Kay Khosrow, is the new king of Iran. He knows you well, for you are from the seed of the same father. Siavosh asked Piran for my hand and took me as his first Turanian bride. You are noble on both sides, and if Kay Khosrow seeks vengeance for his father's death, you too must be bold and lead his armies. As the elder brother it falls upon you to avenge your father's death. Put on your armor and pick up your weapon. Be a new avenger at the service of a new king."

She further counseled her son to seek out Bahraum, who was the loyal and trusted lieutenant of Siavosh. As Forud did not know the Iranian knights, Jarireh appointed a guide named Tokhar to accompany him on the scouting expedition to assess the approaching army. Forud and Tokhar rode up to the peak of a crag to inspect the forces of Iran. The valley of Kalat was filled with thirty thousand warriors whose golden helmets, maces, shields, and belts shone in the sun as they marched to the sound of heavy drums. From this position Tokhar identified the standards of all the knights leading the legions of Iran. The standard of the elephant belonged to Tous, and that of a shining sun signified Fariborz. Geav's flag bore the likeness of a black wolf, and Bizhan flew a flag with the image of a horned moon.

Down in the valley, the commander of the Iranian army, Tous, espied the two equestrians on the lookout point and roared with rage. "Go and see who they are. Who dares spy on my army? If they are our own men, let them be punished with two hundred lashes. If they are the enemy, they must be killed or brought to us in chains."

Bahraum rode out to discharge Tous's command.

Forud asked Tokhar about the identity of the knight who was boldly approaching them. Tokhar wasn't sure, but judging from the appearance of his helmet and armor, he appeared to be a knight from the clan of Gudarz.

Bahraum shouted: "Who goes there on that peak? Do you not see that an army is approaching and hear the sound of drums and horns? Are you not afraid of the field marshal who commands that army?"

Forud retorted: "Speak softly, for we have not offended you. Do not carry on as a lion pouncing on an onager! You are in no way superior to me. Let us speak as equals. What is this army, and who is its commander?"

Bahraum replied: "This is the army of Iran, led by Tous. The formidable knights Gudarz, Geav, Bizhan, and Gostaham ride under his command."

Forud asked: "Why have you not mentioned Bahraum, who is also of the house of Gudarz? He alone would delight us if fortune allowed us to meet."

"How do you know Bahraum?"

"It was my mother, Jarireh, who told me of Bahraum. She advised me to seek him out for he was like a brother to my father, Siavosh."

"Then you must be Forud, the exalted son of Siavosh," Bahraum said.

"I am indeed Forud, and I am a branch that grew from that mighty trunk before it was felled."

"And I am Bahraum. May you live forever, and may your spirit remain radiant. But to prove your claim, show me the birthmark that distinguished the line of your father."

Forud bared his arm to display his birthmark. The two warriors dismounted, embraced, and rejoiced to see one another. Forud said that the reason he had come forth was that he wished to speak to the commander of the army of Iran and invite him and his troops to a banquet at his castle.

Bahraum said he would convey this message to Tous. Then he reluctantly added, "Tous is not a man of reason. Proud of his wealth, skills, and nobility, he is disdainful of the directives of his king. Not long ago he scorned Kay Khosrow, preferring instead to enthrone Fariborz because he was of pure Iranian blood. The clan of Gudarz stood against him and won the day. But Tous is still resentful. He commanded me to come to this peak and speak to you only in the language of the mace and the dagger. Now, I shall return to him with your message, but beware that he is likely to turn his back on you.

"If I manage to persuade him, I shall return to you with the good news. But if he sends another man, know that he means you harm. Go back to your fortress and close the gates."

As a parting gift, Forud presented the noble Bahraum with a mace covered in gold and studded in turquoise and bid him farewell.

Bahraum went back and reported that the man on the mountain was none but the king's brother and the lord of Kalat castle, accompanied by a lieutenant.

"Know that it is Forud, the son of our martyred prince Siavosh. I have seen his resemblance to his father and his birthmark."

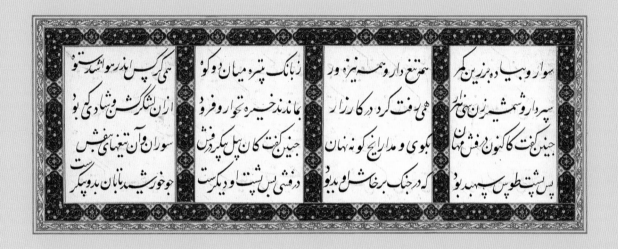

Forud Fights Five Knights

Tous was livid. He had no interest in the identity of the men who had insulted him by daring to scout his army from their high position on the mountain. Furious that Bahraum had neither fought nor brought the men down for questioning, Tous reprimanded him for insubordination and heaped scorn on the house of Gudarz for what he considered to be Bahraum's cowardice. In his rage, Tous called for brave warriors to go up to the look-out point and behead the men who had dared to spy on the armies of Iran. Tous's son-in-law Rivniz was the first to volunteer for the mission. Bahraum warned the volunteers that they would be fighting Forud, a mission that was at once dangerous and dishonorable. "If you ever wished to see Siavosh, you must look upon the face of his son Forud, who stands on that mountain. He is brother to our king. One hair on his head is worth a hundred knights."

Forud knew that Tous had rejected his overture when he saw that the man coming at him was not Bahraum. He pulled an arrow from his quiver and asked Tokhar to identify the man. Tokhar said that he was named Rivniz and that he was a servile man, the only brother to forty sisters. Forud was not moved to compassion. "I will not take pity on this warrior of Tous. I shall send him to lie with his sisters."

Tokhar agreed that Rivniz didn't deserve to be spared. Tous had to be taught a lesson for his disrespect. As for Rivniz, he had forfeited his life by accepting the mission. Forud pulled at the string of his bow and loosed an arrow that went through Rivniz's head, piercing his Roman helmet on both sides. He collapsed from the saddle in full view of Tous.

Astounded, Tous ordered his son Zarasp to avenge his fallen brother-in-law. But he, too, was quickly dispatched when Forud's formidable arrow split his armor below the waist. As Zarasp fell, a collective cry went up from the Iranian troops. Consumed with rage, Tous donned his armor and rode out to face Forud with tears in his eyes and hatred in his heart.

When Tous approached, Tokhar identified him as the field marshal himself. Maybe it was best to go back to the castle, he warned Forud. But Forud would have none of it: "I don't care if it is a host of wild elephants, tigers, and whales. When the battle is raging, one must feed the fire of the warrior's courage, not smother it in mud!"

Tokhar advised that killing Tous would mean challenging the entire army of Iran. "Thirty thousand men would descend on your fortress and raze it to the ground. Besides, this would divert them from their main mission, which is avenging the death of your father, Siavosh."

This good advice should have been offered before.
An inept counselor led Forud to risk his life
In vain and lose everything in a futile war.

Withdrawing at that point was not an easy decision. Forud could not turn back and run in full view of the entire army of Iran, not to mention his eighty attendants and consorts, who were cheering for him from the ramparts of his castle. Tokhar's next piece of advice was that his lord shoot Tous's horse—a knight would not fight without his steed. Forud agreed, notched another arrow in his bow, and proceeded to unhorse the commander. A cheer went up from the ramparts of the castle as the proud commander was sent staggering back to his troops on foot.

The Iranians were happy that Tous had not lost his life, but Geav was outraged. The loss of Rivniz and Zarasp and the disgrace of Tous proved too much to take even from a son of Siavosh. As the formidable Geav rode out, Forud sighed in despair and said, "It appears that this pugnacious lot is bereft of common sense. I am afraid they will not succeed in their mission to avenge my father unless Kay Khosrow comes to Turan himself. Then the two of us will join forces to defeat our enemy. Now tell me, who is this horseman whose fate must be mourned?"

Tokhar said, "He is the man who brought your brother, Kay Khosrow, out of the land of Turan, singlehandedly fighting entire armies that gave chase. He is the one who tied the hands of your grandfather Piran and crossed the Oxus River on horseback. He wears Siavosh's armor, which deflects shooting arrows and slashing blades. None dares confront him. Target his horse."

Forud pulled an excellent arrow from his quiver and shot Geav's horse through the heart. Another roar of laughter and derisive calls from the battlements followed as Geav made his way slowly down the slopes on foot. Bizhan reproached his father for turning back. Geav said that he had no choice but to retreat—that it was not fitting for a knight to fight without his steed. Bizhan was furious. He said that he would have to see to the affair of punishing Forud himself. Then he insolently turned around to walk away. Suddenly he felt the sting of his father's horsewhip on his head.

Geav said, "Have you not heard that discretion is the better part of valor, you insolent boy?"

Bizhan was too angry to heed the pain of the horsewhip or his father's reprimand. He swore an oath not to take the saddle off his horse until Zarasp's death had been avenged. Acquiring a worthy and well-armored horse from one of the commanders, Bizhan prepared for battle. Geav, who realized that Bizhan was determined to confront Forud, was constrained to send forth his famous armor to protect his son against Forud's deadly arrows.

As the fifth Iranian warrior made his way up the mountain, Tokhar informed his master that the new challenger was none other than the peerless Bizhan, the audacious son of Geav, who was liable to pursue combat even without his horse. And indeed, the young warrior continued his climb wielding a glittering sword even after Forud had felled his horse. Forud loosed a second arrow that pierced Bizhan's shield but did not go through his armor. As Bizhan rushed forward on foot, the young lord of Kalat turned his horse around to gallop toward the castle. A desperate cry went up from the ramparts. Bizhan gave chase and slashed at Forud's horse near the gates of the castle. The horse fell, but Forud managed to slip inside. The sentinels quickly shut the gates and rained rocks down on the bellicose Iranian knight.

Now it was Bizhan's turn to taunt: "So, where is your courage now? Mounted on a horse, you ran away from a man on foot. You should be ashamed."

Bizhan returned to the Iranian camp in triumph. Tous swore an oath to raze the castle and soak the rocks of the mountain with Forud's blood.

Forud's Last Stand

That night Forud's mother had a dream in which a fire devoured their fortress. Troubled at the meaning of her vision, she ascended to the ramparts and found the surrounding mountains crowded with enemy soldiers. Then she went down and told Forud that their fate was sealed.

Forud said, "We cannot fight fate. My time has come. My father died unjustly at the hands of Goruy. Bizhan will be the name of my killer. But I shall not beg for mercy. I will die free."

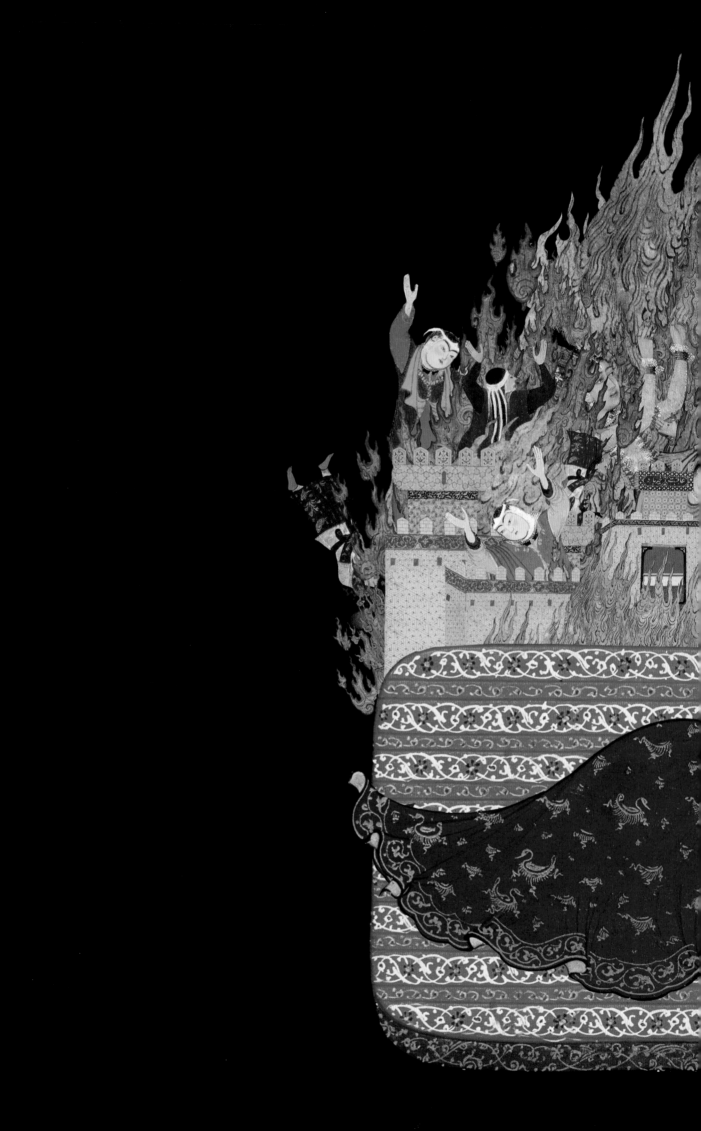

With this he armed his men and suited up for war. As the sun rose on the dome of heavens and the trumpets of war blared, Forud led his men out the gates of the castle. They fought a heroic battle until the sun reached its zenith. When all of his men had fallen, Forud turned around and galloped to the gates of the castle to escape the tightening circle of the enemy. But he rode into an ambush Bizhan had set for him. As they engaged in combat, a companion of Bizhan's by the name of Roham came up from behind and slashed at Forud, severing his arm. In great shock and severely wounded, Forud escaped the ambush, galloped to the gates of the castle, and barely managed to slip in. Then he dismounted and collapsed on the ground, in a pool of blood that gushed from his wound.

Jarireh came to the side of her dying son. As he took his last breaths, she silently lamented that her son was dying without having reached the age at which he could inherit the crown. Forud looked up at his mother and whispered his last request: "Nothing should go to the enemy as the spoils of their victory. Bizhan should not gloat over our treasures and women after he takes the castle."

Jarireh promised to fulfill her dying son's last request. Following their master's wish, Forud's loyal consorts and attendants committed suicide by flinging themselves from the ramparts of the castle. Jarireh burned all the treasures in a great fire and killed or hamstrung all of the horses in the stable. Having denied the enemy the spoils of that unjust war, she stumbled back to the side of Forud, spattered as she was with the blood of the horses that she had killed. Jarireh lay down, put her face on her son's cold cheek, and split her side with a dagger.

When the Iranians entered the castle they found the dead bodies of mother and son. There was no one to enslave and nothing to plunder. Bahraum wept at the scene of Forud's death and rebuked his companions Tous, Gudarz, and Geav. "Forud died more tragically than his father. Siavosh did not share his deathbed with his mother. Nor were his companions and belongings destroyed. Are you not afraid of the curse of the heavens? Are you not ashamed of disobeying your king's strict orders? How are you going to face him now that you have murdered his brother?"

Gudarz, Geav, and even Tous were moved by the scene of the death of mother and son. Tous was remorseful, although he tried to justify the misadventure as a punishment for Forud's slaying of Zarasp and Rivniz. Bahraum retorted that they were the victims of Tous's own impetuosity and insubordination to the king's direct orders. Tous fell silent and later ordered a royal burial for Forud. After three days of rest, the army of Iran moved forward to discharge its mission of confronting Afrasiab.

Defeat and the Retreat

Once Tous's army left Kalat, a weeklong blizzard impeded their advance. Then Tous locked horns with a Turanian general named Tazhav, who was married to Afrasiab's daughter Espanouy. After a brief skirmish Tazhav escaped, carrying his wife on the back of his horse. Bizhan gave chase, but Tazhav evaded capture because he left his wife behind to be taken by Bizhan. Espanouy was known for her beauty and had been considered one of the most valuable prizes of the campaign even before it started.

Tazhav returned to the Turanian capital and reported the invasion to his king. Afrasiab appointed Piran to lead a counterattack. With thirty thousand battle-hardened warriors, Piran moved rapidly but silently toward the Iranian lines, with the aim of waylaying the invaders. His spies came back with news that the Iranians were drunk and asleep as he closed in on their camp. Tous's army had spent the night drinking and merrymaking, celebrating their easily won victory against Tazhav. In their hubris and self-confidence they had not posted sentries to protect them from a raid.

Thus the entire army was caught naked, inebriated, and unprepared for the deadly Turanian raiders, who struck in the middle of the night. Only Geav and Gudarz were sober, and they valiantly fought back. In the morning the scale of the massacre was evident. The plain was covered with the dead bodies of Iranian soldiers. Tous was driven to the brink of madness by the enormity of the disaster. Gudarz lost many of his sons to the slaughter.

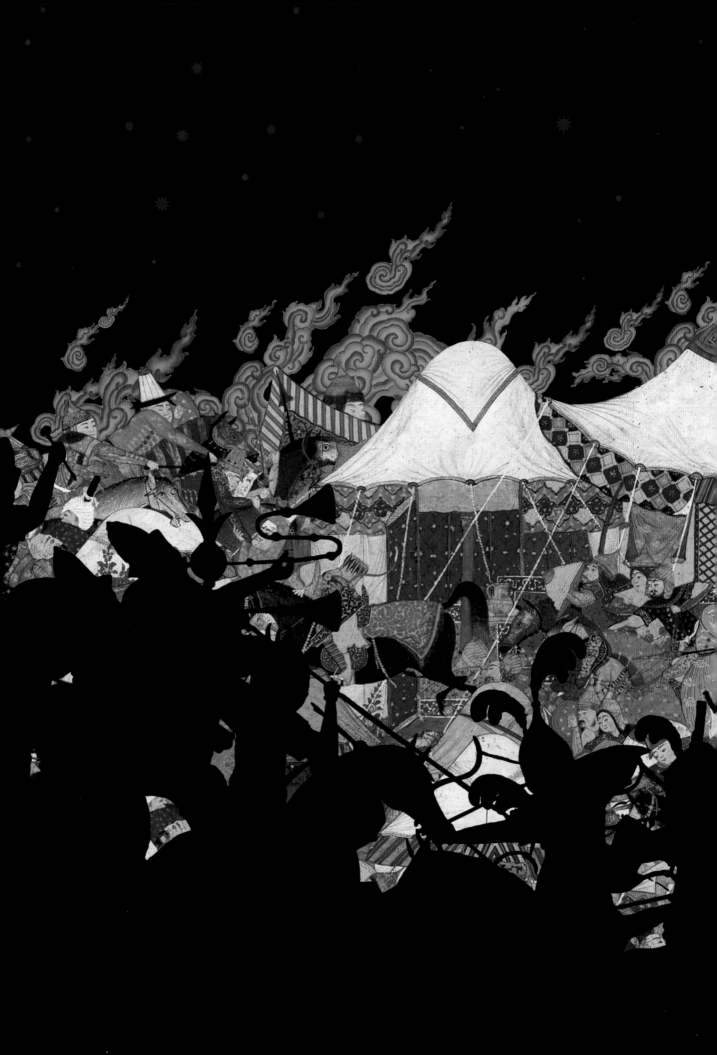

When Kay Khosrow heard of the catastrophe, he relieved Tous of his command and ordered him back to court. Fariborz, the son of Kay Kavous, was dispatched as the new commander of the army, and he was cautioned to remain sober and avoid unnecessary confrontations. Fariborz proposed a one-month truce to the Turanian commander. Piran agreed and after the month had elapsed, the two sides met at the battlefield of Pashan.

In the bloody and heavy battle that ensued, the Iranians were defeated again. Fariborz withdrew to higher ground, and a rout was avoided only because of the heroic determination of the knights of the clan of Gudarz. Geav and Bizhan kept the line and saved the army from a disgraceful collapse, but the casualties were heavy and the battle was lost. Only eight out of the scores of knights and warriors of the clan of Gudarz survived the battle. The worthy Bahraum was among the casualties, as was Fariborz's eldest son. The house of Kay lost eighty of its knights and warriors in the battle of Pashan as well. The victors also suffered enormous losses. Piran lost nine hundred of his children, grandchildren, and kinsmen. Afrasiab lost three hundred.

The Iranian expedition that had started with the misadventure of Kalat and the killing of Forud had foundered. After the disaster at Pashan, the Iranian army lost its spirit and retreated. Piran received a hero's welcome at the Turanian court. Afrasiab celebrated the triumph for two weeks, and lavish festivities were arranged in honor of his victorious general Piran.

Back at the Iranian court, the knights stood with arms folded. They hung their heads in shame. The army had returned in utter defeat. More importantly, they had disobeyed the king in taking the Kalat route to Turan and unjustly killed his brother. Kay Khosrow was despondent. He cried tears of sorrow and fury, reprimanded his defeated generals, and said that a thousand of them richly deserved public execution for their insubordination and incompetence. This was a fitting punishment indeed, but he would not mete it out, if only out of pity for them and for the sake of his piety.

Kay Khosrow averred that none among the knights deserved beheading more than the villainous Tous, who had brutally and recklessly slain Forud and brought heaven's curse on the entire expedition. The king excoriated Tous in public. "Have you no shame before God and the assembly of knights? Did I not warn you against taking the mountain path? After your senseless murder of Forud, you continued your march of folly and allowed yourself to be waylaid. Why would you treat the battlefield like a banquet, drinking to excess and leaving yourself vulnerable? Your evil deeds have brought immense loss to the clan of Gudarz. You are a fool. You belong in a madhouse. You are lower than a dog in my sight. Only your white beard and royal lineage save you from beheading. Now be gone from my sight and let your house be your prison."

Then the king exclaimed: "I can't tell friend from foe anymore. I was mourning my father. Now I have to mourn my brother. How dare you disobey me? I dispatch a great army headed by forty knights in their golden boots, and I reap nothing but disaster."

With this the great king dismissed the assembly of knights and barred them from his audience. He forbade himself a life of leisure and happiness as well.

Such is the nature of war
One finds a narrow grave and another
Glory and riches galore.

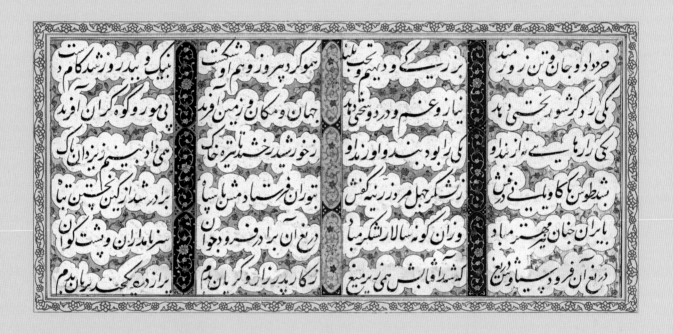

The Great War of Nations:
Iran Besieged

Before the story of the battle against Kamus, let us say grace
To the creator and then laud the magnificent warrior
Rostam, whose heroic deeds we can't properly praise.

The Third Invasion

When Rostam heard about the failed invasion of Turan and King Kay Khosrow's dismissal of the assembly of the knights, he traveled from his native Zabol to the capital and requested an audience with the king. He spoke on behalf of his fellow knights. "I beg the king who has honored the throne, the crown, and the royal ring to forgive the lapses of Tous. The confrontation with Forud was an unfortunate blunder. Tous is reckless by nature. Witnessing the demise of his son and son-in-law by the hand of Forud drove him to madness. Such was the decree of fate."

Then Tous came forward in abject humility to offer his apologies: "I am ashamed, in the sight of the king, as the most guilty among the knights. Forud, Rivniz, Zarasp, and Bahraum were slain for my mistakes. But if it pleases the king, I shall redeem myself by avenging Siavosh's death. I wager my life on it."

Kay Khosrow declared that the second Turanian campaign that ended with the battle of Pashan was a stain on the reputation of Iran and sought to set the matter right and take revenge for the fallen. The knights pledged their commitment to the new campaign. Tous was once more appointed to lead the invasion—on the condition that he consult Geav in all his decisions.

Drums rolled, and the army moved behind the standard of Kaveh toward the borders of Turan. Piran was distraught when he heard that a new invasion had been launched, as he knew the Turanian armies were not prepared for war. In desperation, he sent a message to Tous: "After all my care and mourning for Siavosh, and after the services I rendered to Farigis and Kay Khosrow, is this the bitter harvest I deserve to reap?"

Tous took pity on Piran and sent word that, should he leave with his troops and come to the Iranian side, he would be forgiven and rewarded with knighthood and a crown of honor.

Piran responded with a deceitful reply stating that he needed time to persuade his clan of the wisdom of defecting to the other side. At the same time he dispatched a swift messenger to his king asking for reinforcements.

Afrasiab sent an army so enormous as to blot the earth and blind the sun. The Iranians were outnumbered two hundred to one. With the arrival of fresh troops, Piran put aside all pretense of peace and moved on in full force. Tous and the Iranian knights realized that they had been deceived.

As the two sides faced off, Houman rode up and challenged the Iranian army. Tous went up to answer the challenge. Houman expressed his surprise that a commander would come in person to fight. Tous answered: "I am both commander and warrior. You and your brother Piran should come over to our side. The king has advised me against harming the clan of Piran, the son of Viseh."

Houman responded: "Piran's hands are tied. He does not fight this battle of his own accord. He is loyal to his king just as you are to yours."

While they were engaged in this discourse, Bizhan rode out and harangued Tous for fraternizing with the enemy rather than speaking in the language of the sword. Houman addressed Bizhan: "It is true that your clan of Gudarz was nearly wiped out in the battle of Pashan. You have every right to be angry with us over the death of your brother Bahraum as well. But you have no right to tell Tous what to do. If you are so eager to fight, let us draw our swords. Death is our ineluctable fate, and it is best to die on the battlefield."

Bizhan accepted the challenge and the two fought with spears, swords, and bows and arrows. They were equally matched, and neither emerged as victor. Both warriors went back to their own sides, and the general battle commenced in full force. As valiantly as the Iranians fought, they could not prevail, and the number of casualties swelled. Gudarz lamented his fate as he continued to lose close relatives and members of his clan. Tous was heard saying: "Would that my royal father, Nowzar, had not planted my seed, so I would not witness so many friends and kin lying lifeless on the battlefield."

The battle was going badly, and Tous had no choice but to withdraw under the cover of night to the Hamauvan Mountain and to send word to his king for reinforcements and, above all, for the assistance of Rostam.

When Piran heard of the Iranian withdrawal, he knew that they must be crushed before Rostam's arrival. Piran, too, sent for reinforcements.

Houman rode out to the retreating army and scolded Tous and Geav. "You came from Iran with war elephants and a great army to avenge Siavosh's death. Are you not ashamed to run to the mountains like wild game?"

Piran knew that if he could surround the Hamauvan Mountain, he would be able to starve the Iranians into surrender. With this intention he asked Afrasiab for massive reinforcements. The auxiliary forces came in the form of a great coalition of ten nations. Kings from India and China and champions from the lands of Koushan, Sind, and Rome joined the armies of Turan. Soon a sea of warriors with the flags of many nations filled the horizon around the mountain where the army of Iran had taken refuge.

Tous was close to despair. The situation looked grim, and he was unsure if reinforcements would reach him in time. Provisions were in short supply and morale was low. All attempts to break the siege had failed.

At the nadir of this hopeless situation Tous had a dream of Siavosh, whose face was luminous. He reclined on an ivory throne enveloped in the glow of a candle that emereged from watery depths. Siavosh addressed Tous: "Keep the Iranians in this place, for victory is yours and do not mourn for the fate of those lost to the clan of Gudarz. We are drinking wine in a bower of flowers and we shall drink forever."

Tous interpreted the dream to mean that Rostam was on his way to rescue them. He shared this vision with Gudarz, and the two knights took heart and believed that their troubles would soon be over. But the next day, the enemy had multiplied and closed in on them. Gudarz climbed to a high peak and saw the enormity of the coalition that had assembled against them. He wailed: "Bitter misfortune is my lot. My chalice is filled with poison. I had an army of sons and grandsons. They have all been killed to avenge Siavosh's death. I have lost hope, and my day has turned to night. Would that I had never been born."

Rostam at Hamauvan Mountain

Gudarz ordered his horse to be saddled and his grave to be dug. He prepared to wade into enemy lines in a morbid search for heroic death. It was at that moment that a lookout shouted that an army was approaching from the Iranian side, flying a standard that bore the image of a dragon.

The troops on the horizon were indeed the forces of Iran. Having heard of the siege at Hamauvan Mountain, Kay Khosrow had dispatched Rostam and Fariborz. Fariborz came first, with a message from Rostam that they should refrain from desperate attempts to break the siege until his arrival.

The Iranians were relieved. Tous and Gudarz rejoiced. With Rostam on their side, the tide would certainly change against the Turanians.

Piran was discouraged when he heard of the approaching Iranian forces. He said to his knights: "I am filled with despair. I truly hope that it is not Rostam who has come to the aid of the Iranians."

When Rostam arrived on the scene he was disheartened to hear that one of the heroes of the Turanian alliance, Kamus of Kushan, had unhorsed and humiliated two of the greatest Iranian knights, Tous and Geav. As Rostam arrived on the front lines of Hamauvan, another Kushanian champion, Ashkabous, was holding forth and taunting the Iranians. Scandalized by the failure of his fellow knights, Rostam picked up his bow and a quiver of arrows and walked out into the arena on foot. He could not go to battle in full gear, because Rakhsh was tired from the long journey. The overweening Ashkabous sneered: "Speak your name and tell me, who shall cry over your headless body?"

"You will not last long enough to benefit from knowing my name. But if you must know, my mother named me 'Your Death.'"

"So where is your horse? What manner of knight comes to war on foot?"

"Tous sent me here on foot to take Ashkabous off his horse. Surely someone of your stature will fight much better on the ground."

"So where are your arms? You speak in jest and make a mockery of battle."

"This bow is all I need. Allow me to show you its use."

With this Rostam loosed an arrow that struck Ashkabous's horse and brought him to the ground. Rostam laughed: "You were so proud of your horse. Now why don't you mourn your companion somewhere away from the battlefield?"

Badly shaken, Ashkabous sent a barrage of ineffective arrows at his opponent. Rostam kneaded the string of his bow with relish and advised him not to fatigue himself in a useless exercise. Then he took a long shaft from his quiver. No sooner had the arrow kissed Rostam's fingertips than it went through Ashkabous's backbone, killing him on the spot.

The king of the Chinese, one of the allies of Afrasiab in the great coalition of nations, looked upon this scene with amazement and sent someone to retrieve the unknown Iranian warrior's arrow. Upon examining the missile, he turned to Piran: "You belittled these people, calling them a ragtag army of worthless warriors. Who would use arrows longer than a lance?"

Piran's heart sank when he saw the arrow, as he knew that it could only belong to Rostam. But Kamus of Kushan had not lost his confidence. He swore an oath that he would vanquish the owner of the long arrow that had killed his compatriot Ashkabous.

At the dawn of the next day Rostam donned his tiger skin over two coats of chain mail, wore his helmet, and rode up to the front of the Iranian army. He advised the troops to forget their ties to this world and seek glory on the battlefield. Kamus came forth and in the first battle of the day slew one of Rostam's chosen lance holders. Rostam unfurled his lariat and roared with fury. He approached Kamus and challenged him to a duel. The champion of Kushan replied: "Why are you haranguing us? Lower your pitch and pray tell what you are intending to do with that string you have wrapped around your arm."

Rostam said, "How can a lion not roar when he sees a herd of onager? As of this string, you are about to see its use." Kamus rushed Rostam and slashed at him with his sword. The blade landed on Rakhsh's neck but did not go through his armor. Rostam quickly ensnared Kamus in his lariat that was fastened to Rakhsh's saddle. In one magnificent movement Kamus was unhorsed and captured. Unable to fulfill the promise he had made to the Chinese king, he lost the gamble on which he had wagered his honor and his life.

The king of the Chinese called for a champion to avenge Kamus. A man named Changash rose to the occasion. He donned his armor and rode to the Iranian side with much bravado, shooting arrows and calling for the undefeatable warrior to show his face. Rostam came forth and presented himself. The fearsome visage of the hero struck such fear into the heart of Changash that he fled the scene. Rostam gave chase and cut the distance with his fleeing opponent until he was able to grab the tail of his horse. The Turanian army watched in amazement as Changash threw himself on the ground and begged for mercy. Rostam dismounted and beheaded him, disregarding his pitiful pleas.

It was obvious that the tide of the battle was turning in favor of Iran. The Chinese king told Piran that it was time they spoke to the mysterious warrior to see whether he could be appeased in any way. Houman was charged with gathering the intelligence about the identity and intentions of the man.

Embassies of Houman and Piran to Rostam

Houman rode out to Rostam incognito, gave him a false name, and professed to be on the verge of defecting to the Iranian side. Then he asked the mighty Iranian warrior his name and intentions. Rostam replied: "You don't need to know my name. But be advised that I am here to wreak havoc on those who spilled the innocent blood of Siavosh and annihilated the progeny of Gudarz. To end this war, you must surrender the wicked Garsivaz, who plotted against Siavosh, and the shameless Goruy, who beheaded the noble prince. Then you must surrender the children of Viseh: Houman, Lahak, Farshidvard, Golbad, and Nastihan—all except the noble Piran, whom I love and pity. He alone is moderate among the race of Turanians. He was the only one to mourn Siavosh. Now send me Piran, for I wish to speak to him immediately."

Houman trembled with fear and swiftly went to Piran and said, "Our days are numbered, as this hero is without a doubt Rostam. He knows us all by name and demands our surrender. My name is at the top of his list. You are the only one for whom he has respect. He wants to have a word with you."

Piran went to the Chinese king and reported that the man who had killed Kamus was indeed the great hero Rostam. Then he rode out to the Iranian side and addressed Rostam: "Exalted commander! I have heard that you asked for me. Here I am."

Rostam said, "State your name and business."

"I am Piran. I have been told that you wish to see me. Would you kindly state your name?"

"I am Rostam of Zabol."

At hearing this, Piran dismounted, kissed the ground, and asked about the health of Rostam's close family members Zaul, Zavareh, and Faramarz. He also inquired about Farigis and Kay Khosrow. Then he said, "If you will indulge

me, I wish in all humility to share my troubles with you. I planted a tree, but its leaves have turned into poison, and its fruit is blood. Siavosh loved me like a father, and I was his shield against all evil in the world. It is true that I failed him. But it was I who saved his wife, Farigis, and held her in my own house. And I protected their son, Kay Khosrow. Hardships aplenty have been visited upon me since that day. I am crying tears of blood. For all my labors I am now caught between two kings. I have already lost my dear brother Pilsam and many of my kin to these wars of revenge. The soldiers who are standing here have nothing to do with the death of Siavosh, and yet their lives have been forfeited. What is the point of living if I cannot prevent this bloodbath?"

Rostam replied: "I have seen nothing but honesty from you. I offer you two solutions. Either you can send me those who are responsible for the blood of Siavosh, or you can come to our side, where the king will compensate you tenfold for all that you will lose in defecting."

Piran despaired. He knew that he could not deliver Afrasiab's close relatives to expiate the blood of Siavosh. Nor could he hand over his own five brothers as ransom for the brothers Gudarz lost in the previous battles. So he asked for a reprieve to convey the offer of surrender of the guilty ones to Afrasiab.

Piran shared all this with his clan. He then met with the commanders of the coalition of Turan and confirmed that the mysterious hero who had appeared on the other side was none other than Rostam. Neither the Chinese king nor the commander of the Indian contingent, King Shangol, seemed to take the matter as seriously as Piran did. Indeed, Shangol displayed some bravado, saying that he would slay Rostam in the next day's battle. Piran was not heartened by his empty boasts.

He said to himself: I could see this day when I advised Afrasiab against alienating Siavosh, an unrivaled prince brought up by Rostam. But he listened to the worthless Garsivaz instead of me. Now Rostam has come to avenge his beloved prince's death, and none can resist him. I pity my brothers who will be killed in this conflict and my homeland, which will be devastated.

On the Iranian side Rostam had similar presentiments about the demise of the clan of Piran. He said to Gudarz: "The warrior who is favored by fortune must avoid acts of injustice and take the path of righteousness in life. Piran protected Farigis and Kay Khosrow. My heart goes out to him, but I am afraid he and his brothers will be slain before this affair is over. I am loath to stain my hands in the blood of this old and righteous man."

Gudarz reminded Rostam of Piran's earlier treachery, when he had asked for time to surrender while dispatching messengers to Afrasiab for reinforcements. Rostam agreed that Piran was a cunning warrior but said that nonetheless he would not wage war on the old knight unless he rejected his terms.

The next day's battles confirmed Piran's suspicions. The Indian king, Shangol, came to the arena riding his well-adorned war elephant, which was decked out with a colorful parasol. A massive army followed him in well-ordered flanks. Rostam mounted an immediate frontal attack at Shangol's elephant. The king panicked and turned back, causing his men to flee in a disgraceful rout. Rostam's next target was the Chinese king, who was not able to escape. He was taken captive by Rostam after a brief but decisive encounter. With these reversals, the coalition of Turan started to unravel. Piran and his brothers were reduced to flight. The remainder of the armies of Turan milled about like a shepherdless flock and then surrendered. Rostam declared victory on the fortieth day of his arrival at Hamauvan Mountain and claimed the enormous booty left behind by the Turanian alliance for his king. He allowed the enemy soldiers to disarm and leave in peace.

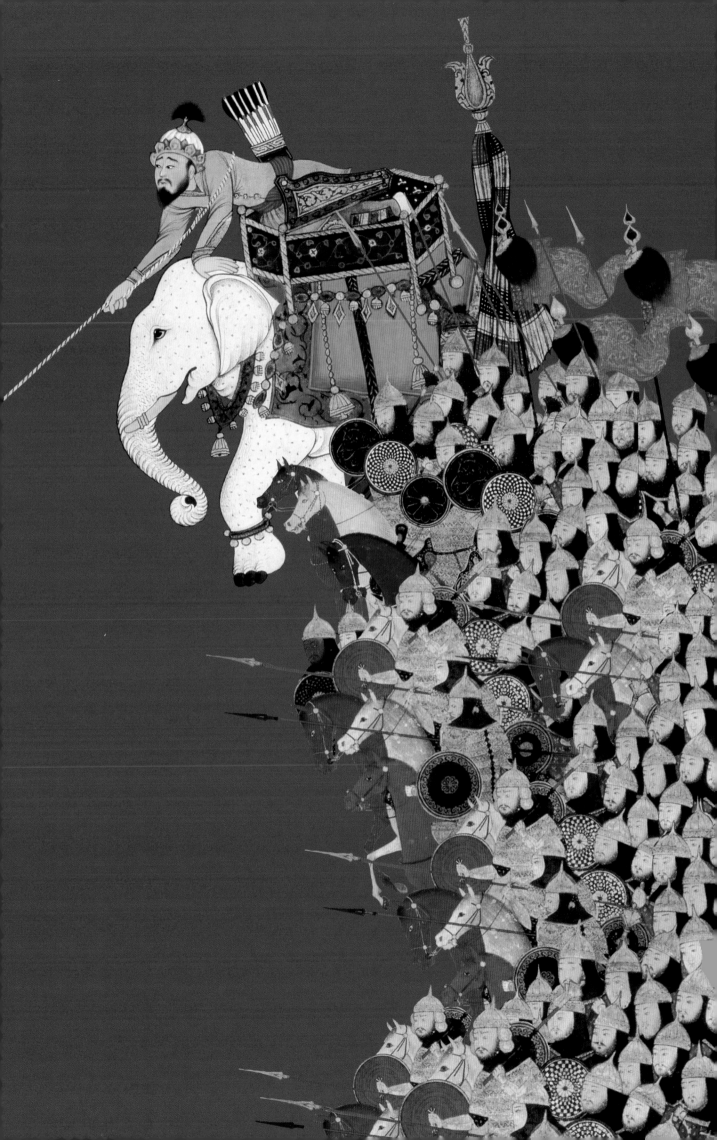

The Challenge of Puladvand

Afrasiab, who was disheartened by the news of the Iranian victory over his enormous coalition, mounted a desparate counterattack under the flag of a local king by the name of Puladvand, who was famous for his heroic frame and his prodigious talents in the use of the lariat and the mace.

Puladvand led a huge mass of warriors to where the Iranian army was camped and challenged them to a fresh battle. In response, Rostam ferociously tore into Puladvand's troops, killing many on the right flank.

Puladvand rode up to the front and unfurled his lariat. Tous responded to the challenge but was captured in the enemy's noose. Geav, Roham, and Bizhan went forth to rescue their fellow knight, but they too were ensnared by the Turanian challenger. To add insult to injury, Puladvand breached the Iranian lines where the sacred flag of Kaveh was raised and managed to tear it in half.

A wave of panic shook the Iranians, and all eyes turned to Rostam for help. Gudarz personally went to Rostam, crying that he was about to lose two more of his sons and his grandson. Rostam beheld the enormous size of Puladvand and knew why he struck such fear into the hearts of the Iranians. He also knew that with four of the top champions of Iran in bondage, a loss to Puladvand would doom the cause of Iran. Rostam stepped up to challenge the mighty Puladvand.

After exchanging taunts, the two champions pounded each other with their heavy maces until it was clear that they were in a stalemate. They agreed to settle the contest by wrestling, on the condition that both the Iranian and Turanian sides would refrain from interfering in the contest.

Afrasiab was worried for Puladvand and made plans to breach the compact of honor by sending a few warriors to assist Puladvand. His son Shideh advised against such a dishonorable act. But before Afrasiab's plan could be implemented, Rostam lifted his opponent high upon his neck and pounded him on the ground with such force that he was left there for dead.

The sound of drums and trumpets rose up from the Iranian side for the victory of their champion. Rostam, who thought he had killed his opponent, rode his steed back to the Iranian side but Puladvand, who had regained consciousness, quickly jumped to his feet and ran away. Afrasiab, too, dropped his standard and escaped.

The troops of Turan tried their best to escape, but the Iranian army gave chase. Finally Rostam declared: "Let them go and stop the killing. It is time for peace." And thus ended the third cycle of Iran's wars of vengeance.

> The tortuous tale of Kamus comes to an end at last
> I have succeeded in recording every detail
> In this opulent edifice of prose I've cast.

A Curious Foe:
Akvaun the Demon

Life is full of mysteries to ponder
None can unravel this riddle
Of existence, so don't squander

Your labors on the surface of the stories.
Look instead at the truths behind the signs
Where faith and reason are at peace.

Wrestling with Akvaun the Demon

During a reprieve from the wars with Turan, Kay Khosrow sat in a pleasure garden drinking wine in the company of his knights. Suddenly a shepherd happened upon the gathering in utter bewilderment with this report: "A strange creature has appeared in the herd. It resembles an onager, but it is the bright golden color of the sun and has the mane of a lion. It is taller than a horse, and a black line runs from its head to its tail. The creature runs amok like a demon on a rampage."

Kay Khosrow knew that the beast was demonic. Surely no onager could surpass a horse in size. The king charged Rostam with investigating the matter and removing the threat. Rostam accepted the mission and went to the place the creature had been sighted. After three days he finally spotted the strange-looking beast. Rostam brought Rakhsh to a gallop and attempted to capture it with his lariat, but the thing vanished into thin air.

It was apparent that the beast could not be anything but the famed demon Akvaun. Rostam chased the creature with the golden mane for three days and three nights until he came to a fountain. Hungry, thirsty, and in need of sleep, the hero dismounted, relieved his horse of its bridle and saddle, and lay down to rest.

As Rostam slept, Akvaun crept up and lifted him high above his head. The demon now appeared in his true form as a fearsome giant. He was so tall that his head scraped the heavenly spheres. Rostam awoke to discover that he had been captured and was being held aloft. He was filled with regret for the lapse that had brought him into such peril. Akvaun asked: "Now I grant the great knight one wish. Which way shall I throw you? I could hurl you far away into the sea or high upon the rocks."

It was obvious that Rostam would not survive if he were thrown on the land from that height. But there was a chance of survival if he were to be thrown into the sea. Knowing the demon's contrarian nature, the hero replied: "It is said that the one who is drowned at sea will never attain salvation. So, now that you are granting this wish, throw me to the land so I can show the leopards and the lions how courageous men fight."

To spite Rostam, the demon turned toward the sea, roared, and flung him to the farthest blue horizon. Upon splashing into the water, Rostam unsheathed his sword to defend himself from the predators of the depths, all the while swimming toward land. When he reached the shore, he swiftly dried his clothes and went in search of his steed.

With his master gone, Rakhsh was taken in by Afrasiab's stable hands. Rostam stole close to the herd and spotted his trusted stallion cavorting with Afrasiab's mares. Quickly he roped his horse in, saddled it, and galloped away. A great number of shepherds gave chase, but Rostam turned around with his blade in his hand and attacked the posse, killing two-thirds of them. The rest turned back and went to Arfasiab to report the theft of the horse from the royal herds.

"This is humiliating, Your Majesty. Have we been so degraded in the world that a single man dares to raid our horses and ride away with his choice of the herd?"

Afrasiab gathered an army along with four white elephants and gave chase. When Rostam realized that he was being followed, he confronted the soldiers with a torrent of arrows, forcing them to retreat. He took Afrasiab's prize war elephants and returned to the fountainhead where he had first encountered the demon Akvaun.

When Akvaun saw Rostam approaching, he taunted him. "I see that you escaped the perils of the sea to come here for more punishment."

This time Rostam was ready. He swiftly caught the demon in his lariat and pounded his head with a heavy mace. Then he cut off its head, took the booty he had won from the Turanians, and returned to the pavilion of his king.

Kay Khosrow was elated to see Rostam return in triumph and gave thanks for having such a competent knight. They feasted for two days. Then Rostam asked leave to visit his father, Zaul, promising to return, as the task of avenging Siavosh's death was incomplete. Kay Khosrow endowed Rostam with many gifts and went along with him for two milestones before bidding him farewell.

Demons of stories stand for evil people given to vanity
And those who deny God's blessings and spurn
The common decency of our humanity.

A Perilous Adventure:
Bizhan and Manizheh

It was a pitch-black night that swallowed the stars
The moon was anemic, and occluded
Were the planets Mercury, Saturn, and Mars.

Not even the sound of a bird or beast broke
The dense silence, and my desolation was
Complete under the night's raven cloak.

I rose with a start and asked my beloved for a light
She brought me a candle and food aplenty
To heal my despair and allay my fright.

With a tray of quinces, pomegranates, and wine, to my delight
She amused me with the tale of a Turanian princess,
Manizheh, who fell for Bizhan the gallant Iranian knight

On the condition that once she was through
I would render the tale in Persian verse.
This was a fair trade and a pact I agreed to.

The Armenian Boar Hunt

With the conquest of Turan, Kay Khosrow celebrated his victories in the company of his knights. In the midst of the revelries, the court chancellor announced the arrival of a group of petitioners from Armenia who lived close to the border of Turan. The envoys kissed the ground and complained of an infestation of wild boars that had ruined their crops and decimated their herds. Unable to cope with the savage beasts, they came to seek the assistance of their king. Kay Khosrow took pity on the petitioners and challenged his brave company of knights. "Who from among you volunteers to rid my subjects of the wild boars that plague them?"

To induce volunteers to step forth, the king ordered a spread to be set down filled with precious jewels. Ten horses with golden bridles were also added to the prize for the champion who would exterminate the boars of Armenia. Only Bizhan stepped forward to claim the treasure trove and volunteer for the dangerous mission, much to the chagrin of his father, Geav, who said,

"Why would you set foot on a path that is unfamiliar to you? Stay your hand and do not be reckless."

Bizhan reminded his father of his past heroic deeds and said, "I may be young in years. But I am a seasoned warrior. I shall exterminate these beasts. Am I not Bizhan, the son of Geav, the destroyer of armies?"

Kay Khosrow entrusted the mission to Bizhan and said, "The king who has a knight like you will never fear an enemy."

The king sent along another knight who was familiar with the Armenian plain as a guide. His name was Gorgin. Bizhan embarked on this mission with a light heart, taking falcons to hunt partridge and pheasant and cheetahs to catch mountain sheep and onager. In this manner the two knights jauntily rode out to the Armenian border. As they approached the thicket of boars, they found it heaving with the sound of the unseen beasts.

421

Bizhan suggested that his companion collaborate in the hunt by accompanying him into the thicket or else stand outside with his mace and dispatch the boars that would try to escape.

"This was not our agreement," Gorgin said. "You are the one who took the kingly gifts to exterminate the boar that infest this thicket. This is not my business."

Offended by this remark, Bizhan tore into the thicket alone, holding a single dagger. A large swine attacked him, tearing his armor with its tusk. Bizhan stabbed it and cut off its head. Then he set to work killing the entire sounder until he had made a hill of the tusks of the slaughtered boar.

Bizhan returned to his camp and showed off the boar tusks that he had taken from the slain animals. Seething with jealousy, guilt, and remorse, Gorgin asked what he intended to do with the tusks. Bizhan said that he would take them to the king as a victor's trophy.

Gorgin pretended that he was happy for Bizhan, but his heart was dark with evil thoughts. He knew that if Bizhan returned in triumph, everyone would learn of his refusal to assist in the labor of the boar hunt. This would diminish him as much as it would raise Bizhan in the eyes of the king and the knights. For this reason Gorgin plotted to ensnare Bizhan in an ignoble affair that would surely tarnish his success.

Bizhan at the Festival of Turan

Gorgin told Bizhan that he had been to the area before and knew of a fabulous Turanian festival that would convene every year in a gorgeous meadow not far from where they were. Afrasiab's daughter the beautiful Manizheh would come to preside over the festivities in the company of a hundred of her pretty attendants. Surely capturing a few beauties for the king's harem would make for a better trophy than just a heap of swine tusks. Bizhan was seduced by the descriptions of the event and agreed to make the one-day journey to the lush plain where the festivities were held.

The two rode out toward the appointed place, one moved by the dreams of youth and the other nursing dark treason in his heart. Upon arriving on the scene, they busied themselves with hunting for two days until the colorful tents of the revelers were erected in the distance. Bizhan said that he wished to go for a closer look. He donned his favorite golden crown, which was decorated with a lammergeier feather, and rode his black stallion to the vicinity of the sumptuous pavilion of the Turanian princess. Under a cypress tree he dismounted to rest.

Manizheh looked out from her pavilion and saw the handsome knight. She was smitten with Bizhan and made no efforts to hide her feelings. To her lady-in-waiting she said, "Go forth this instant to this young man and find out who he might be. It is my guess that he is either the prince Siavosh incarnate or some angel in human form. Find out why he has come this way, and invite him to honor us with his presence at the festival."

Manizheh's lady-in-waiting took the princess's message to Bizhan. She duly asked: "Who are you, Siavosh incarnate or an angel? What business brings you here? Pray tell, on whose authority are you so recklessly breaking the hearts of the onlookers at this festival? Won't you come and join our revelry? I have never seen a winsome prince such as yourself as long as I have been coming to this festival."

Bizhan replied to Manizheh's handmaiden: "My fair lady, I am neither Siavosh incarnate nor an angel. My name is Bizhan. I am the son of Geav and a knight of Iran. I came here to rid the locals of the plague of wild boars, and I have succeeded in that labor. I have heaps of boar tusks to prove it. The reason I came further was to catch a glimpse of the beauteous daughter of Afrasiab. I will offer you a crown, a belt, and earrings of gold if you lead me to her."

The emissary took this message back to Manizheh and sang the praises of Bizhan. Manizheh immediately sent her back with this message: "Rejoice, for you have found what you came here to seek. Come to me this instant and fill my dark life with the light of your presence."

The lady-in-waiting led the young knight to the pavilion of the princess of Turan. As he entered her chambers, Manizheh embraced him and took his belt in a gesture of hospitality. "Why are you marring your handsome visage by formal outfits?" she asked. "And why are you carrying a mace? You have no enemies here. Eat and drink and be merry as our honored guest."

As Bizhan partook of the old wine that was served in crystal chalices, he was overcome by the joy of being in the company of the seductive Manizheh. For

three days and nights they ate and drank to the sound of beautiful musicians until sleep and inebriation took their toll on the young lovers. They sat there with a sense of melancholy, as they both knew the time of departure was nigh. The lovers had to go back to their respective homes soon.

Despite the mandate of inevitable departure, the princess of Turan found herself unable to let Bizhan go. Secretly Manizheh had her attendants lace the young knight's drink with a soporific drug. When the potion took effect, she ordered them to wrap the sleeping Bizhan in soft sheets and place him in her sumptuous litter, which was carried atop an elephant. She hid him under a blanket, and arranged the trip so they would enter the capital of Turan at night. In this manner the bold princess spirited her beloved into her quarters in the heart of Afrasiab's palace.

Bizhan woke from his slumber to find himself still in the embrace of the lovely Manizheh. Frightened to be without a weapon in enemy territory, Bizhan cursed Gorgin for ensnaring him in such a trap. Manizheh put his mind at ease, saying: "Don't worry, my love, over what has not happened yet. Be merry, for the future is no more real than the wind. There is a time for pleasure and a time for war."

Bizhan surrendered to Manizheh's temptations. At her command, beautiful girls skilled in playing musical instruments from every corner of the earth entertained the couple for the remainder of the day and many more days.

427

Bizhan Bound

The gatekeeper at Manizheh's palace heard the rumors that a stranger was being hosted in the princess's inner quarters. He probed the matter and learned the identity of the secret guest. Afraid for his own life, he went to the king and said, "Your Majesty's daughter has taken a companion from Iran."

Afrasiab was outraged. He would have acted precipitously had it not been for the advice of a wise counselor who enjoined him to investigate the matter first. After all, relying on rumors had served the king badly in the affair of Siavosh. Afrasiab turned to his brother Garsivaz with these words: "Fate keeps tormenting me with disobedient children and the Iranian enemy. Go to the palace of Manizheh and look into this sordid business. If you find an intruder, bind and bring him to my presence immediately."

Garsivaz surrounded the palace of Manizheh with three hundred soldiers. The music of the harp and lute and the sounds of merrymaking filled the air. When they tried to enter, they found that all the doors were locked. In a great rage, Garsivaz tore the palace door off its hinges and burst in to find three hundred servant girls with musical instruments and chalices of wine surrounding Bizhan and Manizheh.

When Bizhan saw the intruders, he jumped to his feet in great anguish. He thought: "How can I defend myself without my horse and weapons? Now only God can help me."

He pulled out a dagger that he always carried in his boot and addressed Garsivaz and his men: "I am Bizhan, the son of Geav. None will lay hands on me unless his body has tired of the company of his head. Nor will anyone see my back in flight. You know the reputation of my warrior clan, Garsivaz, and you have heard of my heroic deeds. Many of your men will die by my dagger. And yet this could be avoided if you promise to spare my life and advocate for me in front of the king."

Garsivaz knew that Bizhan meant what he said and agreed to the conditions. He disarmed and brought the Iranian intruder to the presence of Afrasiab.

Bizhan addressed Afrasiab: "Greetings to the great king. If you ask me why I am here, I will say that I did not come here of my own accord. Nor is anyone to be blamed for my presence in your palace. I came here from Iran on a boar hunt. I lost a falcon and followed it to your borders. Then I fell asleep under

a cypress tree. A genie spread its wings over me and spirited me away. We passed over many caravans until we came to a group of Turanian riders who were escorting an elephant on which a litter had been fixed. A beautiful lady was asleep in the litter. The genie mentioned the names of the minions of the devil and dropped me in the litter. Then he recited an incantation over the lady to keep her from waking. That is how I entered your palace. I have not offended you. Neither had Manizheh anything to do with my presence here. This is all the doing of that accursed genie."

Afrasiab replied: "Your bad luck has finally caught up with you. You came here with a blade and a lariat to seek battle and make a name for yourself as a man. Now you tremble before me like a woman. Look at you, standing there with shackled hands, trying to save yourself with ridiculous tall tales."

Bizhan said, "Now listen to a sober assessment, great king. The boars and the lions fight with their tusks and claws. The warriors, too, need their swords and maces to fight. I am disarmed and my hands are tied. If the king wishes to know my mettle, then let him provide me with a horse and a mace. I shall take on a thousand of your men, and if I suffer one of them to live, don't call me a man."

Afrasiab turned to Garsivaz in disbelief. "Now this devil of a man thinks that I am obliged to provide him with the means of glorious contest, so he can kill more Turanians. He supposes he hasn't done enough evil already. What else can we expect from the Iranians? Take him out and hang him from the gallows. Let this be a lesson to those who covet what is ours."

431

As they dragged Bizhan out to the gallows, he cried out: "I don't complain of my fate if indeed an early death is written for me. I am afraid of what the knights of Iran will say when they hear that I was hanged with a body unscathed by wounds of battle. I dread the shame I will bring to my forefathers."

But Bizhan's luck had not run out. As they dug the holes to erect the gallows, the wise Piran arrived on the scene and asked the reason for such activities. Garsivaz said that the man intended for execution was Bizhan and that he had violated the borders of Turan as well as the sanctity of the royal palace. Piran took pity on the young knight and asked him for his side of the story. Bizhan told him everything, including the part about the disloyalty of Gorgin. Piran stayed the hand of the executioner and went up to the king to plead for Bizhan.

In the palace, Piran was received according to protocol. Afrasiab smiled and commanded the old knight to state his pleasure and pledged to grant his wish. Piran said, "All I have is due to your generosity, great king. I am here not to ask favors for myself but to advise you on a matter of importance. I warned you in the past over the affair of Siavosh. I said that killing the son of Kay Kavous would spell disaster for us, and it did. You have seen what they have done to the land of Turan to avenge Siavosh's death, have you not? The unsheathed sword of Rostam is still dripping with blood over that feud. No one knows the power of Geav and Gudarz on the battlefield better than Your Majesty. Shedding the blood of their young scion would bring a fresh disaster on our heads. It is not wise to create new causes for animosity with Iran."

This enflamed Afrasiab's anger. "But you have no idea how Bizhan has shamed me in my own land," the king said. "He has dishonored my daughter and I am a laughingstock among nations. If I let him live, wagging tongues would never stop and my honor would never be restored."

Piran recognized the king's quandary but still advised prudence. "Put heavy chains on Bizhan and suffer him to serve as an example to others. This imprisonment will be a living death for him. Lock him up and let his name be wiped from the records."

Afrasiab accepted this advice. He charged Garsivaz with fixing chains on the young knight and lowering him into a deep well, where the rays of the sun and the moon never reached. He said, "Cover the mouth of the well with a huge boulder that the demon Akvaun hurled from the bottom of the ocean onto the land. Then go with your men and plunder the palace of Manizheh.

"Convey the following rebuke to that insolent girl: 'You have ruined my good name. You do not merit the golden wreath of a princess. Go and attend your lover as a devoted servant at the edge of that well. Let him delight in your presence from the depth of his confinement. Be content, for if you look deep inside the darkness of the well, you can behold the man you once placed on a golden dais.'"

Garsivaz did all this. Then he brought the pitiful princess, who had only rags for clothes, to the desert of Khotan, where Bizhan had been imprisoned, and said, "Settle in this desert in eternal servitude to your lover."

By dusk the tearful Manizheh had found Bizhan's well. She lay beside the opening, pushed her arms through the crack between the boulder and the edge of the well, and wept for the fate of her beloved until the sun rose on the horizon. Then she wandered around the nearby villages and begged for scraps of bread. At night she came back and pushed the meager morsels through the opening of the well and wept for their wretchedness. This was how Manizheh spent her days and nights from that day forward.

Gorgin's Return to Court

Back at the camp, Gorgin was desperate. Bizhan had not returned, and he was beginning to feel the pangs of guilt for his disloyalty. He went to the site of the festival and found only Bizhan's unkempt black horse. Gorgin lingered there for a few days unsure of what to do. Full of regret, he finally went back to Iran.

When Geav learned that Gorgin was returning alone, he rushed out to demand an explanation. Gorgin dismounted at the site of the prominent knight and humbled himself, saying: "I am so ashamed that an exalted knight like you has come out to welcome me. I am even more ashamed that I have returned without your son. But do not worry. He is alive and I will provide you with a full account of his disappearance."

Geav was distraught when he saw that his son's horse had come back without his master. He dismounted, ripped his knightly garments, and wallowed in the dirt, saying: "God, please take me to the abode of the blessed souls if I am to endure life after my son." Then he demanded Gorgin's report: "Tell me where you lost track of my son. Did he leave you? Did you see what manner of evil overcame him? Where did you find Bizhan's distressed horse?"

Gorgin replied: "Open your ears wide and listen to my full account. When we got to Armenia, we found a deforested land that had become a breeding ground for wild boars. We went to work clutching our lances and drove them all from their lairs. They attacked us in droves, but we overcame the innumerable beasts and heaped up a hill of their tusks as the trophy of our triumph.

"Then we happily set off on our trek back to Iran, hunting as we went along. Suddenly an onager appeared whose chestnut hide resembled that of Gudarz's horse. Its head, ears, and tail were reminiscent of Bizhan's black steed. The creature had the muscular legs of the fabulous Simorgh, the neck of a lion, and hooves of bright steel. It was swifter than the wind. One would think it was descended from Rostam's famous steed, Rakhsh.

"Bizhan caught the head of the powerful creature in his noose, but it pulled at the rope and the two of them disappeared in a cloud of dust. I tracked them for a long time but could only find Bizhan's horse. It is my guess that the onager must have been a demon."

The account sounded hollow. Gorgin's eyes were shifty. He was pale, and he stammered through his account. Geav was so sure that the entire account was a fabrication that he contemplated killing Gorgin on the spot in revenge for whatever he had done to Bizhan. Geav roared: "Enough of these lies. You have stolen the sun and the moon from my sky. How can you sleep with the weight of all this treachery? I will search the world for my son. But I will be sure to report your misdeeds to the king and claim the right of a father to avenge his son on the man who has caused his demise."

Geav went to the king and related the transparent lies of Gorgin and demanded justice. The king comforted Geav with these words: "Stop your worries and rejoice in a prophecy I heard from a learned man. There will come a day when I will fully avenge my father in the land of Turan. The name of Bizhan is among the list of my companions on that day."

Geav was distraught. He retired, worried and troubled for his son.

When Gorgin entered the royal court he found it empty. The knights had all gone to comfort Geav. Gorgin sheepishly approached the throne carrying the boar tusks and stood before the king. Kay Khosrow asked him about the adventure and the story behind Bizhan's disappearance. Gorgin lost his composure in the presence of the king and confabulated, producing an

even more incoherent and contradictory account than he had given to Geav. The king flew into a rage at the mendacity and impudence of Gorgin and dismissed him from his presence with these words: "Have you not heard the old wisdom that even a lion shall not escape harm if he should nurse ill will for the clan of Gudarz? I would have you beheaded for this treachery were it not for fear of my salvation and good name."

Kay Khosrow ordered blacksmiths to fashion chains of iron for Gorgin and had him locked away in a dungeon. He told Geav: "Wait until Nowruz, the arrival of the vernal equinox. When the flowers bloom and the green blanket of vegetation is unfurled, I shall stand before God and ask for his sanction to use my enchanted grail. I shall then reveal to you the whereabouts of Bizhan."

Geav thanked the king and left the court with renewed hope.

When Nowruz arrived, the king called Geav to his presence. Arrayed in his ceremonial garb and cap, he sat on the throne, praised God, and denounced evil. Then he picked up the royal grail, which was filled with wine, and peered inside. The images of the seven realms of the world and the twelve constellations were etched inside the chalice. The signs of the sun and the planets Saturn, Mars, Venus, and Mercury were also engraved around the bowl. The mark of the moon appeared beneath them. The king looked into the grail and found Bizhan languishing in a dark jail somewhere near Bactria. He gravely smiled and addressed Geav. "Let your heart be glad, for Bizhan lives. He is in a dark prison cared for by a princess who weeps for his plight. Your son has grown thin as the switch of a willow tree. He has despaired of the help that might come from friend and kin. Bizhan prays that death delivers him from his torments. It seems that his rescue is a task for Rostam alone.

"Rise now and go to the land of Zabol. Do not breathe a word of this to anyone."

The king called a scribe and dictated a letter, addressing Rostam as the victor of Mazandaran and the seeker of vengeance for the blood of the innocent Siavosh. He asked him to rise to the occasion one more time and help a friend in his hour of darkness. Rostam promptly obliged this request.

Geav returned to the capital to bring the good tidings that Rostam had agreed to champion the cause of Bizhan. The king sent his prominent knights Gudarz and Tous some distance outside the capital city to welcome the hero. At court, Rostam greeted the king and prayed that the angels would shower their blessings on him. He stated that he was born to serve a king like Kay Khosrow and that he considered it an honor to be of assistance to the clan of Gudarz. All were merry and drank to the glory of the blooming flowers of the spring.

Gorgin, who was languishing in prison, also heard of the arrival of Rostam. He sent word to the hero, complaining of his fate and expressing regret for betraying Bizhan. "I will go into the flames to restore my name. If you solicit the king on my behalf, I will go with you to fight for you and grovel at the feet of Bizhan to beg his pardon."

Rostam felt pity for the wretched prisoner. He sent word to Gorgin that the monstrosity of his deeds was evident to all but that he nevertheless would plead for him at court. He added: "You had best pray that we find Bizhan alive. If we don't, Geav is sure to seek the right of revenge for your betrayal of his son."

Rostam waited for two days without mentioning Gorgin's case to the king. On the third day he asked for a special audience and broached the subject. Kay Khosrow scowled. "You are making matters difficult for me. I have sworn an oath on my crown and throne to mete out nothing but harsh punishment to that malevolent man. Ask me anything else and it shall be granted. But not this."

Rostam insisted and then asked that the king forgive Gorgin as a special favor to him. At long last Kay Khosrow, who did not want to turn down such a direct request from his most prominent knight, relented and issued orders for the release of Gorgin.

Rostam to the Rescue

Kay Khosrow proclaimed that he would spare no expense in providing Rostam with the military means necessary for the emancipation of Bizhan. Rostam preferred a covert mission to direct confrontation; he felt that Afrasiab would be prone to fly into a rage at the suggestion of an invasion and kill his captive. The king opened his treasures to Rostam. The hero chose a huge quantity of precious stones to be carried by one hundred red-haired camels. The plan was that a few knights would penetrate the Turanian borders in the guise of merchants. Then they would search for Bizhan and rescue him. A contingent of one thousand soldiers was chosen, and seven knights, including Gorgin, volunteered for the rescue mission. Rostam stopped the army at the border and ordered them to wait and stay on alert. He and his knights wore the disguise of merchants and crossed the Turanian border near Bactria.

The sound of the bells of the long train of camels filled the desert air. The caravan stopped at the city of Khotan where Piran had a palace. Rostam took a goblet of precious gems and two well-caparisoned purebred Arabian horses and went to greet him. Luckily for Rostam, Piran did not recognize him in disguise and addressed him as a merchant: "Who are you? Identify yourself."

"I am a seller of merchandise as well as a buyer of goods. I am carrying a load of gems and hoped that I could garner your protection, as this would be an excellent place to set up my business for a while."

With these words, Rostam presented the prominent knight with his generous gifts. Piran was pleased and offered his protection and his son's house to the merchant. Rostam said that he preferred living close to his merchandise and chose a spacious house with plenty of room for displaying his wares. He settled in and started his activities. Soon a great number of people were attracted to the new merchant from Iran, turning the corridors of the showhouse into a veritable bazaar.

Manizheh, too, heard of the Iranian caravan and came searching for news. The tearful princess, still clad in rags, entered Rostam's chambers and pleaded with him. "You have ventured far from your home and I pray that you win the fruits of your labors. May your fortunes increase and may you return in success to the beautiful land that is Iran. Tell me the news of the king and his knights. Do they not seek their beloved Bizhan? Does the clan of Gudarz not miss their young scion, who has been lost to the land of Turan? His hands and feet are bruised by the heavy chains that he wears. I do not cry for my own poor soul. All my tears are reserved for the fate of Bizhan."

Rostam did not trust the young woman who spoke to him so boldly of Bizhan. He yelled: "Stop your rambling and be gone, for I know no king and have never heard of the clan of Gurdarz."

Manizheh sobbed: "It is not becoming of a man like you to be so callous. If you don't wish to speak to me, at least don't throw me out. Is it the custom of Iranians to abuse the unfortunate?"

Rostam regretted his severe tone and said, "I was harsh because you interrupted my business. I am afraid I was too preoccupied with my trade. To answer your question more properly, I don't live in the city where Kay Khosrow resides. Nor have I gone to the realm of the clan of Gudarz. I simply don't know them."

Rostam ordered his cook to set a delectable spread in front of the distraught woman. Then he asked about her story and the reason for her interest in the king and knights of Iran. Manizheh said, "Now you are interested in my story? I had nursed the hope of being treated with kindness by this Iranian caravan. But you spurned me. I had traversed such a distance from the well of my miseries to seek refuge in your protection. But you yelled at me as if I were a warrior on the battlefield.

"I am Princess Manizheh, the daughter of Afrasiab, if you must know. The sun had never seen me unveiled. Now, I am naked and exposed to the world. I am reduced by harsh fate to beg door-to-door for a crust of bread smeared with whey. But my pain is nothing next to that of my beloved Bizhan, who languishes at the bottom of a well. He is bound in heavy chains, unable to tell day from night.

"My request is that upon your return, you convey the fate of Bizhan to the clan of Gudarz. Try to find Geav or Rostam soon and tell them to do something if they want to see Bizhan alive."

Rostam shed tears for the fate of the princess and advised her to seek intercession from her father's friends. He added that he would have helped her immediately if he did not fear the wrath of Afrasiab.

Rostam ordered the attendants to wrap a roasted chicken in bread for Bizhan, slipping his signet into the package. Manizheh ran back with the delectable morsel that she had procured for her beloved. Bizhan was surprised by the rich

offering and asked his beloved where she had gotten it. As she was telling him about the Iranian caravan, a wave of happiness washed over Bizhan because he had found Rostam's signet ring. Manizheh was alarmed when she heard Bizhan's exclamations of delight from the depths of the well and feared for his sanity.

"How can you be so happy in your dark misery?" Bizhan said that he would tell her the secret of his happiness but that she had to swear an oath to keep the secret. Manizheh was offended. "There is no end to my wretchedness. I have abandoned my father and my fortunes for Bizhan. I have offered him my body and my reputation, but he still does not trust me to keep a secret."

Bizhan regretted what he had said. "I should have known that you would keep this important matter hidden. I am in need of your guidance, for suffering has diminished my wisdom. The truth is that the merchant has come here for the sole purpose of rescuing me. God has taken pity on my plight, and it seems that the day of my liberation is nigh. Now, go to the man whose cook gave you this food and ask him this question: 'Are you the master of Rakhsh?'"

Manizheh ran faster than the wind to the merchant and conveyed her lover's question. Rostam knew that Bizhan had entrusted the girl with his secret and said, "Yes, my fair lady. Tell Bizhan that the master of Rakhsh has come from Zabol to Turan only for him. And tell him that we have longed for him and suffered in his absence. Soon he shall see how I will fling that boulder that blocks his well to the cluster of the Seven Sisters in the sky."

Rostam instructed Manizheh: "Go and collect firewood by day. When night comes, light a big fire at the well. And be discreet until then."

Manizheh flew on the wings of air back to the well and told Bizhan that the merchant was the one he had suspected. She also told him about her instructions to light a fire by which the men from Iran could find their location.

Bizhan said, "Carry out your instructions. By the glow of that fire we shall escape our perpetual darkness. And know, my lovely girl, that I shall reward your loyalty. When we go back to the land of my ancestors I shall serve you as a slave."

Manizheh set to work gathering firewood. She climbed the trees like a bird and scurried about in search of kindling as her eye monitored the sinking of the sun on the western horizon. At dusk she breathlessly awaited the coming of the darkness, when she would set fire to the mountain of firewood she had gathered. Finally, when night fell Manizheh stoked the fire that illuminated the desert like a sun. Soon she heard the sound of the approaching hooves of Rakhsh.

Free at Last

Rostam rode out into the desert with the seven knights guided by Manizheh's fire. At the well, the knights were charged with removing the great boulder that blocked it. They applied themselves to the task but were unable to budge the stone from its ptosition.

Rostam dismounted and hitched up the edges of his coat of mail under his belt and lifted the boulder over his head and threw it away. The impact of the boulder shook the ground. Then he shouted into the well: "Your portion of the world was a goblet of clear wine, my dear Bizhan. Why did you take a chalice of poison from the hand of fate?"

Bizhan responded from the unseen depths of the well: "When I heard your voice, the poison of fate turned into clear wine in my veins. With chains of iron below and a mountain of stone above, I had given up the desire to live."

Rostam replied: "God has taken pity on you. You are restored to the world. But I have a request before rescuing you. Forgive Gorgin for my sake and forget his treachery."

This was a hard request. Bizhan replied: "But you have no idea what has transpired between us. You don't know what he has done to me. I can't give up on seeking revenge."

Rostam said, "In that case I am going to ride Rakhsh and leave you in this hole."

Bizhan roared back: "It seems that friends, kin, and the knights have abandoned me. I have suffered much, but I hereby forgive him and cleanse my heart of hatred."

At this Rostam lowered his lariat and pulled Bizhan out of the well. His body was naked and smeared with blood. His unkempt hair was overgrown and his nails had turned into claws. Bizhan still had chains on his hands and feet. Rostam tore the chains off his body and led Bizhan and Manizheh back to his headquarters. The young couple entrusted the hero with their tale of woe as they traversed the distance to safety. When they reached their destination, Rostam had Bizhan bathed, cleaned, and clad in a fitting garment. Gorgin came forth and groveled before his former companion and asked to be pardoned for his act of betrayal. Bizhan granted this wish.

The Last Raid

Rostam announced that it was time to return to Iran. Camels were loaded with what they had brought, and one of the knights took the leadership of the returning caravan. Rostam advised Bizhan and Manizheh to go with the caravan back to Iran, as he and the rest of the knights had unfinished business in Turan. "We shall not sleep tonight until we make a laughingstock of Afrasiab before his nation," Rostam proclaimed. Bizhan dispatched Manizheh but refused to go, for he was the main cause of the raid.

Bizhan and the rest of the knights rode to the palace of Afrasiab and forced their way in. Rostam harangued the king of Turan. "This is the voice of Rostam, the son of Zaul, advising you to rise and lead your men against those who have entered your palace. For many nights you slept on your royal bed as Bizhan languished in a well. Now I have broken him out of your prison."

Bizhan joined in. "Do you remember," he asked, "how you preened yourself on the throne as I stood in front of you with shackled hands? Now I am free to roam your land, and none dares confront me."

Afrasiab attempted to rally his men to drive away the marauders who had impudently penetrated the inner sanctuary of his palace, but they were all killed in the attempt. Afrasiab was reduced to escaping his quarters, leaving behind many of his concubines. Later, these beautiful women were seen walking out of the palace holding hands with the Iranian knights. The war party made haste to escape the land of the enemy with its spoils, as Afrasiab was sure to gather an army and give chase. The Iranian knights galloped west and made it across the border, joining their own troops that had stood on the ready. As they turned around, a cloud of dust rose on the eastern horizon, indicating the approach of a huge army.

The great general Piran led the Turanian army of Afrasiab that was approaching. Rostam was not concerned by the prospect of being outnumbered. He stood in front of the army and addressed the king of Turan. "For how long do you intend to hide behind huge armies? Time and again you have learned the painful lesson that numbers do not make a victory. A lion never fears if the entire horizon is filled by flocks of onager."

The armies stood against each other. Piran and his brother Houman were at the left and right flanks, and Garsivaz and Shideh, the son of Afrasiab, stood at the heart of the army of Turan. Rostam and Bizhan were at the heart of their army. The battle began and the Iranians emerged victorious. Afrasiab fled the scene and Rostam chased him for two miles before returning to the site of the Turanian defeat and distributing the war booty.

The Return in Triumph

When the king heard of the success of Rostam's expedition rescuing Bizhan and defeating a Turanian counterattack, he prostrated himself before God in a gesture of thanksgiving. Geav and Gudarz welcomed the hero with a huge army, which marched to the sound of trumpets and drums. Colorful standards were carried behind the two prominent knights of the house of Gudarz. Upon reaching the returning army, they dismounted and addressed Rostam. "You have rendered a great service to our family. From now on consider this clan your servants."

The king, too, delighted in meeting the triumphant Rostam. The hero ceremonially took Bizhan by the hand and delivered him to the king. Then he presented the captives, who numbered one thousand. Kay Khosrow said, "Your father, Zaul, and the people of your town, Zabol, must be proud of you. But they can't possibly be as proud as I am of having such a worthy knight. Geav, too, must be thankful for being reunited with his son, thanks to your heroic deeds. Surely the Creator chose Rostam as an instrument of Bizhan's deliverance."

Geav agreed and praised both his king and his friend and fellow knight Rostam. Kay Khosrow called for a banquet, and the company spent a delightful night in merrymaking. The next day, when Rostam came to ask permission to leave, the king presented him with lavish gifts, including ten lovely consorts and ten slave girls to attend them. All wore golden belts and coronets. Kay Khosrow also endowed rich offerings to Bizhan. These were meant as a gift to Manizheh in appreciation of her loyalty. He added: "Be kind to her and do not break her heart. Fate lifts one to the turning heavens and lowers another to the depths of a lonely well. Do not chase worldly goods and wealth. It is much better that a man avoid harming others as he lives on this earth."

Thus the tale of Bizhan and Manizheh comes to an end
Time to speak of Gudarz's last campaign in Turan, which
Decimated his clan and put an end to Piran's legend.

The Fall of a King:
Afrasiab

A man who desires a good life must feed
And sustain his family and have enough to be
Generous toward his friends in need.

Beyond this he must abhor
Worldly possessions and dreams of power
That rot the tree of his life to its core.

The Battle of the Eleven Champions

Afrasiab set in motion the fourth cycle of wars of revenge when he brought an army of three hundred thousand warriors to the Oxus River. When the news reached Kay Khosrow, he sent Tous to stand against Afrasiab. Then he sent three armies into the eastern borders of Turan and entrusted the central force of one hundred and ten thousand soldiers to Gudarz in order to resume the battle with Piran. The king advised his general to be merciful with noncombatants and moderate in his decisions.

When Gudarz arrived at the Zibad River, he sent his son Geav with a harsh message for Piran. "It is our aim to avoid bloodshed. Cleanse your heart of the love of Afrasiab. Bring to us the murderers of our martyred prince in chains, submit your horses and weapons and treasures of gold, and send forth your sons as hostages. Comply with these demands before it is too late."

Piran received Geav and the message just as thirty thousand sword-wielding troops reached his camp, with a charge from Afrasiab that the goal of the current war was to wipe out the forces of Iran once and for all. Piran felt assured of his position. He sent Geav back with a terse response that he was not in a position to deliver the culprits in the death of Siavosh. Nor would he surrender his close relatives or belongings. Expecting this answer, Gudarz deployed his army in a favorable position between the two valleys of Gonabad Mountain, intending to draw out a frontal attack by the forces of Piran.

Piran arranged his forces on the flat plain. Although he had more troops than the Iranians, he was reluctant to initiate hostilities, given the enemy's superior position. He wanted to fight on open ground that would allow him to encircle the smaller forces of Iran. The two seasoned commanders bided their time and kept their armies in check for a week as each waited for the other side to make the first move.

The spirited Bizhan tried to dissuade Gudarz from maintaining his defensive posture on high ground, but to no avail. On the Turanian side, the warriors were pressuring Piran to initiate the war as well. Finally Houman broke rank. Disobeying the strict instructions of his commander and elder sibling Piran, he rode out to taunt the knights of Iran. They refused to fight on the grounds that they could not disobey their commander. Houman flew into a rage and turned to Gudarz. "Is this what you promised your king? You came in the name of avenging Siavosh. So why are you cowering here like a ram hiding from a lion? What is your excuse for not fighting me?"

Gudarz flatly refused the challenge. His plan was to avoid wasting time on individual contests and draw out the Turanians into general war, which would allow him to exploit his superior position on higher ground. Holding the greater goal in mind, he coldly refused Houman's challenge and told him to go back to the Turanian side, claim victory, and collect his prizes. But refusing a direct challenge was more than some Iranian knights could take. They asked permission to fight Houman, but Gudarz did not allow them to go forth and stand against the boastful enemy. Furious that the Iranians would not answer his challenge, Houman shot four Iranian sentries blocking his way to a nearby plateau. Upon reaching the high ground, he swung his lance around his head and declared himself the uncontested champion of the two armies. The Turanians rejoiced as the sweat of shame appeared on Gudarz's forehead.

Bizhan heard of what was happening on the front lines and complained to his father, Geav, that Gudarz had become senile. How could he allow such effrontery? Geav told him to be calm and respect his grandfather. But Bizhan ignored him, rode out to the front, and addressed Gudarz. "I have heard a strange story. I have heard that my commander has allowed a common Turanian to ride up and down these lanes, shaming our heroes and haranguing our commander. I hereby ask your permission to teach Houman some manners. Have you forgotten my prowess as I went against Forud and again in the battle of Pashan? If you don't permit me to fight today, I shall protest this to my king."

Gudarz relented and gave Bizhan leave to engage Houman. Geav, too, was forced to drop his opposition and approve his son's duel with the man who had taken the lives of scores of his brothers. He called for Siavosh's famous armor. Bizhan donned it and galloped through the ranks toward Houman's position. He caught up to the Turanian knight as he was descending the high point whence he had boasted victory. Houman saw Bizhan and laughed aloud. "Has your body tired of the company of your head? I will send your corpse back to Geav and let him mourn you as he mourned his other brothers. I will snuff your life as a hawk snatches a pheasant off the branches of a cypress and picks it apart into a bloody mess of feathers. Alas, it is too late tonight. Come back tomorrow and we will resume what you have started."

Bizhan replied: "Follow the devil back to your men. When tomorrow comes, say farewell to your king and kinsmen, for they will never see you again."

The next day, Bizhan and Houman sought flat land near the Turanian lines. The battle ensued and the two warriors fought for a full day with lances, javelins, maces, and swords. Finally, tired of fighting, they took a break and then settled on wrestling. Houman was stronger, but in misfortune virtue becomes vice. As Houman lurched forward, Bizhan pushed him on the right side of the neck while pulling his left leg. Houman stumbled and collapsed like a heavy camel. Bizhan swiftly drew his dagger and beheaded his opponent. He could not believe that he had overcome the formidable champion who had killed so many of his uncles. He then tied the severed head to his saddle string and went galloping back to the Iranian lines as the sun sank under the western horizon. Geav, who had worried about his son, rejoiced. The Iranians celebrated the demise of one of their most challenging opponents.

Piran tore his garments and bitterly mourned the death of his brother. To exact revenge, he sent his other brother Nastihan on a night raid against the Iranian camp. Anticipating this attack, Bizhan set an ambush and waylaid the raiders. They were slain to the last man. Piran was inconsolable. In a short time he had lost two brothers who were also his top commanders. In desperation he sent his son Ruein to Gudarz with a letter:

If it was vengeance you were seeking, well, you have taken your revenge on my dear brothers, whose headless bodies you have left on the battlefield. Why should so many lives be lost to avenge the death of one man? Is it not time to end the bloodshed? If it is territory you seek, I will give you all you want, from Kashmir to Kandahar. Don't suppose that I write this letter out of weakness, for I am superior to you in manhood and riches. But as our hair turns gray, it behooves us to avoid senseless carnage.

If your bloodlust is insatiable, let us limit the war to a contest of champions. We shall designate ten mighty warriors from each side and suffer them to fight in close combat unto death. You and I shall meet as the eleventh pair. We shall stand and fight to the bitter end. Let the side that wins these contests claim victory. But we must pledge that the conqueror should let the troops of the conquered return in peace.

Gudarz received Ruein with respect and affection, but his answer to Piran's overture amounted to a harsh rebuke. The lands Piran had promised, Gudarz wrote, were already conquered by the three other prongs of the Iranian army, and the terms Piran offered fell far short of the goal of the campaign that was bringing the murderers of Siavosh to justice. Further, Gudarz wrote: "Your words are a mirage of falsehoods. Your side started the hostilities with the murder of Iraj and the execution of Nowzar. Siavosh walked into the Turanian trap because he listened to your lies. You speak of correct behavior in old age. My only regret in the hereafter would be to have left the deaths of Siavosh and my sons unavenged."

Piran sent a letter to Afrasiab describing the dire conditions at the front. He also begged forgiveness, for it was his compassion for Farigis and Kay Khosrow that had precipitated the resumption of the wars of revenge. Afrasiab was gracious in absolving Piran of guilt. He chose instead to blame fate for what had happened. Regarding Piran's worries, Afrasiab advised him to take heart. Iran, he averred, would be conquered, and that would put an end to the interminable wars. Piran conveyed the king's message to the troops to restore their confidence, but he had a feeling of impending disaster. In utter desperation, he turned to God in prayer:

"How strange is the fate you decree for us! Who would have thought that Kay Khosrow would become such a powerful king? Why should there be such a bloody vendetta between grandfather and grandson? Armies face each other because kings want to settle scores. Grant that I die in my armor rather than live to see the day Afrasiab has been slain. It is better to perish than to see my homeland lost and the ways of my forefathers abandoned."

Gudarz, who had initially rejected the idea of ten champions dueling in lieu of war, finally decided that it was a good way to proceed. First he sent a missive to Kay Khosrow, apprising him of his recent victories. Then he picked the ten warriors who would go against their Turanian challengers.

The battle of the ten champions ended with total victory for the Iranians. Among the victors were Bizhan, who killed Ruein, the son of Piran, and Fariborz, who killed Golbad, Piran's brother. Roham, Hojir, and Gorgin also vanquished their Turanian foes. The only survivor on the Turanian side was Goruy, Siavosh's executioner. Geav, who had gone against Goruy, spared his life as death on the battlefield was too good for such a low man.

Finally it was time for Gudarz and Piran to face off. Piran looked at the field, which was dyed with the blood of the best of the Turanian warriors. The end was nigh and there was no hope. But he had to be impeccable in discharging his duty as a soldier.

The last battle started with a shooting contest. Gudarz loosed a deadly arrow that pierced the armor of Piran's horse, giving his opponent no chance of disentangling himself from his mount. The horse collapsed and rolled over Piran, breaking his arm. Injured and without a horse, Piran fled from his mounted rival, knowing that he would not live to see the end of the day. Gudarz wept to see the play of fate that had humiliated the exalted commander of Turan.

"Famed warrior and pillar of Turan's strength! Your might, manliness, arms, riches, and wisdom have deserted you. Where is your army? Why isn't someone coming to your aid? Don't you see that the time for battle is over? Why don't you beg for mercy, so I can spare your life and take you to my king?"

Piran staggered among the rocks, hiding behind his shield. He replied: "May that day never come that I beg for my life. Death is our destiny, and there is no shame in dying with honor."

With these words he flung a dagger that sliced Gudarz's arm. A rivulet of blood issued from the wound. Moved to anger, Gudarz threw a javelin that penetrated Piran's armor, went through his liver, and impaled him. Coughing blood, Piran fell with a sky-splitting roar. He shook as he lay on the rocks until death made him still. Gudarz addressed Piran's corpse: "You were the best of the knights of Turan, a courageous lion. But this world has seen many like you, and it will not be faithful to the likes of us."

Gudarz dismounted and dyed his face in Piran's blood in a gesture of revenge for the death of Siavosh and his own sons. But, vengeful as he was, he could not bring himself to sever Piran's head. Instead he planted the fallen hero's standard by his body, placed his head in the shadow it cast on the ground, and rode back to the Iranian lines. Gudarz issued orders that the body of Piran be brought back with due honors and be prepared for interment.

The lookouts on Mount Gonabad brought the good tidings that the royal standard of Kay Khosrow had appeared on the horizon. The king arrived at the scene and viewed Piran's corpse. He reminded the company of the good deeds of the fallen Turanian commander. "This is not the fate I wished for this kindly man. He mourned for my father with all his heart, took me under his wing in my youth, and gave me refuge. We tried to win him to our side, but he was loyal to his king. Fate brought him low as he went against Gudarz and lost everything." Kay Khosrow decreed that a royal crypt be built for Piran. His body was covered in tar mixed with rosewater, musk, and camphor. Clad in Roman silk, he was entombed with his belt and helmet.

On the king's orders, Goruy was executed for his wretched crimes. The Turanian army that had lost their leaders to the battle of eleven champions came to ask for quarter. King Kay Khosrow graciously forgave them and allowed them to return home. The two remaining brothers of Piran, Lahak and Farshidvard, however, refused to surrender.

Gostaham Pursues Lahak and Farshidvard

The Iranian scouts on Mount Gonabad detected a small contingent of the Turanian army leaving the scene of the battle under the leadership of Lahak and Farshidvard. Gudarz was troubled by this intelligence. If they were allowed to escape, they could raise an army to avenge the death of Piran.

Gudarz immediately called on the Iranian knights to pursue the fugitives. But they were mostly tired or wounded. Only Gostaham rose to offer his services: "You appointed the other knights to fight splendid duels against their Turanian challengers. They all won fame. I alone was left behind to protect the camp. Let this be my chance to seek glory."

Gudarz assented with a smile and Gostaham quickly went in pursuit of the runaway knights. Horrified to hear of Gostaham's lonely quest to subdue two of the most formidable warriors of Turan, Bizhan raised his voice in protest against the recklessness of the appointment. Gudarz countered that Gostaham was the only choice for the mission and that he was equal to the challenge of the fugitive knights. Bizhan disagreed with this underestimation of the prowess of Lahak and Farshidvard. He pleaded to be allowed to join Gostaham on his daring assignment. Gudarz said, "There is no need to endanger your life and cause fresh worries for your father, Geav."

Bizhan retorted: "Do you not remember how Gostaham and I fought together in the battlefields of Pashan? Our fates have been joined together since those days. I don't wish to live one day if Gostaham dies."

Gudarz was once again constrained to give his blessings to one of Bizhan's daring ventures. Bizhan wasted no time in going to the aid of his friend. Riding out all day and for part of the night, he finally came upon a thicket where he could hear the weak moans of an injured man.

Gostaham was lying supine by a fountain, having fallen off his horse and lost a great deal of blood. He weakly greeted Bizhan and said that he had succeeded in his mission. He had killed Farshidvard with a single arrow but received grievous wounds in the fight against Lahak. He said with a sigh: "I know that I am mortally wounded. But take me back to the camp so I can look upon the face of my king before I pass from this world. And bring along the heads of the men I slayed as trophies of my campaign." Bizhan ripped his garments to shreds to make tourniquets for his friend's wounds. Then he found Gostaham's horse, which had wandered away.

In his search for the bodies of the fallen Turanian knights, Bizhan captured an enemy soldier and dragooned him to help keep Gostaham on his horse during their journey back to the Iranian camp. Upon their arrival, King Kay Khosrow came to see the wounded knight and offered him a magical healing potion that he had inherited from the kings of yore. He prayed for Gostaham, laid healing hands on his wounds, and appointed skilled physicians to care for him. Within two weeks the brave knight had completely healed. The speedy recovery of Gostaham was a cause of great amazement. The king called the two valiant knights to his audience, praised God for the recovery of Gostaham, and rejoiced at their gallantry, loyalty, and deep friendship.

The Final Battles

When Afrasiab heard about the defeat of Turan and the slaying of Piran and his illustrious brothers, he flew into a rage. In short order he regrouped and crossed the Oxus River with the intention of avenging Piran's death. His brother Garsivaz and his sons Jahan and Shideh led the charge. Kay Khosrow, too, gathered a formidable coalition and rose to the challenge, outnumbering the Turanian troops. Intimidated by the Iranian forces and apprehensive about the coming confrontation, Afrasiab desperately called on his fortune-tellers to foretell the end of the war. He remembered the dreams he'd had many years before that Turan would fall to Kay Khosrow.

His son Shideh objected. "You are an exalted king. A mountain of steel turns into a sea of water when your name is uttered. You treated Siavosh like your son but rightly turned on him as he became treasonous and nursed ambitions of grandeur. You reared his unworthy son instead of consigning him to the grave. Now he has fled Turan like a bird of prey. Forgetting the kindness of Piran, he has slain our exalted knight and brought an army against us. Iranians are not worthy of your concern. Why should you call on fortune-tellers rather than your warriors in this matter? Our troops are arrayed on the left and the right flanks. I ask leave to slaughter the enemy to the last soul. It is my hope to be able to confront Kay Khosrow. I shall vanquish this upstart king and drag his body and good name in the mud."

Afrasiab advised his son to be calm and not to underestimate the power of the enemy. Besides, he added, if Kay Khosrow wanted to fight a duel, he would pick his equal, a king, as his opponent. Shideh said, "You have five sons. God and the army would not approve that you fight while we live."

Afrasiab relented and endorsed Shideh's proposal, sending him to the Iranian side to challenge Kay Khosrow to a duel. When the news arrived that a man by the name of Shideh was challenging the king to a duel, Kay Khosrow wept. He said to the knights who were in his presence: "I know Shideh. He is my maternal uncle, a splendid warrior and my equal in battle. Proposing a duel in lieu of war means only one thing: Afrasiab regrets crossing the Oxus River."

The leaders of the army believed that the duel posed a great danger to the Iranians. Losing a king would throw the Iranian side into disarray and end the Kay dynasty. The assembly was silent for a while. Then Kay Khosrow announced that his mind was made up. He said that he would accept the challenge and sent word to Shideh to prepare to lose his life in the upcoming battle.

When the appointed time came, Kay Khosrow and Shideh chose a corner away from the armies to avoid interference by others. They fought on horseback until Shideh realized that he was no match for Kay Khosrow and proposed that he and his opponent wrestle. Although normally a king would never fight on foot, Kay Khosrow accepted the challenge. Shortly after the hand-to-hand contest commenced, the king took Shideh off the ground and smashed him on the rocks, shattering his backbone. Then he drew his sword and killed him. Kay Khosrow issued orders for the proper interment of Shideh: "This man was my uncle, brash and reckless as he was. Honor him in death all the same, and bury him in a fitting crypt with all the proper ceremony due royalty."

In the next day's general battle the Iranians routed their enemies and pursued them as they withdrew. After a few more skirmishes, the Turanian king realized the futility of fighting against the superior forces of Iran and sent his son Jahan with a proposal of peace. Flattering Kay Khosrow as the king of the world and reminding him of their filial bond, Afrasiab pleaded that he had been led astray by the devil in the affair of Siavosh, and he proposed to remove himself from office and go into solitary exile if the Iranians withdrew.

Kay Khosrow's response was acerbic. "Don't ply me with lies, for I am only a son seeking to avenge his father's death. Regarding your filial rights, remember that you had my mother beaten to induce a miscarriage. Had it not been for the wise Piran, you would have killed both of us. Later you intended to behead me if you found me worthy of challenging you in the future. And remember how you murdered your own brother Aghrirath, and the king of Iran, Nowzar, as well as my father, Siavosh. Your excuses that a devil misled you are not new. The serpent king Zahhak and the haughty King Jamshid also made this plea to justify their evil acts. The righteous man never strays from the straight path. Stop your flattery and deceptions and prepare for war."

When the battle commenced, Kay Khosrow overpowered the enemy with little effort. Afrasiab's brother Garsivaz, who had conspired against Siavosh, was captured alive, as was his son Jahan.

Kay Khosrow took over the palace of Afrasiab, but he refused to enslave his female relatives, disregarding the custom. Wagging tongues accused the king of favoring his maternal grandfather in spite of his obligations to avenge his father. The magnanimous king explained his act of mercy to the womenfolk of the house of Afrasiab by declaring: "We ought not do unto others what we are unwilling to bear. My mother suffered such indignities. I shall not visit those on the womenfolk of my enemy. And to my soldiers I say: 'Do not kill the innocent; keep your hands from defenseless women and the property of your enemy. This is how you turn an enemy into a friend.' "

Afrasiab's next desperate move was to send a message challenging Kay Khosrow to a duel. The Persian king accepted the challenge. "If it is a battle he seeks, let him have it. When king can fight king, why should we fill the battleground with soldiers?"

A messenger returned to Afrasiab with Kay Khosrow's response, but he did not pursue the matter as he had decided to try his luck at another ambush. Kay Khosrow, who had foreseen this move, ordered the Iranians to douse their fires and lie in wait. Thus the army that had come to waylay the Iranians was itself ambushed and routed. This was Afrasiab's final stand. After this defeat he fled to the farthest reaches of Turan, abandoning his army, his family, and the crown of Turan. He sought refuge in a lonely cave close to the Sea of Chichast.

The End of Afrasiab

One night the divine angel Sorush visited a hermit named Houm and told him where Afrasiab was hiding. The monk sent word of his dream to the Persian court and then traveled to this far-flung refuge in pursuit of the deposed king of Turan. When he arrived at the cave, the hermit could hear Afrasiab lamenting the loss of his kingdom. Houm rushed in and captured the fugitive king. He tied his captive's hand and led him out. Afrasiab started to complain of the tightness of his binding and Houm took pity on him and loosened the rope. Afrasiab used this opportunity to slip from the grasp of the monk, jump into the waters of the Chichast, and escape.

The hermit was standing by the sea, looking for signs of his captive, when the exalted knights of Iran Gudarz and Geav arrived. Houm explained that he had caught Afrasiab but had lost him due to his trickery. Houm conspired with Geav and Gudarz to release Garsivaz from captivity in order to lure Afrasiab out of hiding.

Garsivaz was brought to the shore and released as Houm and the knights hid from view. The prisoner was in agony and cried aloud from the wounds he had suffered while in captivity. Afrasiab, who could not bear to see his brother in pain, emerged from the water and addressed him. "I have taken refuge at this wilderness to avoid witnessing scenes like this. How dare your captors inflict such pain on you, a prince who is descended from Feraydun? I have come out because I don't care about my own life anymore when I see you in such pain."

Garsivaz, too, was moved to tears when he saw that his brother was reduced to such ignominy. "My royal brother and king of the world! What happened to all your power and glory? Your fortunes are reversed and you have traded your throne room for a watery hiding place."

As the brothers were engaged in this discourse, Houm came out of his hiding place, threw his lariat, and caught them both. Then he bound his captives, submitted them to the Iranian knights, and went back to his own hermitage.

Kay Khosrow arrived shortly after the capture of Afrasiab. When the hapless king of Turan saw Kay Khosrow, he cried: "I have seen this day in my dreams. Now tell me, you vindictive man, why would you kill your own grandfather?"

Kay Khosrow replied: "Where do I start? With the blood of your own brother Aghrirath that you spilled in vain or your regicide of King Nowzar? Or maybe we must speak of my father, Siavosh, whom you beheaded like a lamb?"

Afrasiab said, "My king, the past is behind us. Suffer me to see my daughter Farigis one last time."

Kay Khosrow replied: "I was in my mother's womb when you killed her husband. Now the day of revenge is at hand, for God has decreed that evil deeds should be repaid in kind."

With this he beheaded Afrasiab. Garsivaz watched his brother's white beard turn crimson with his blood and knew that his time had finally come as well. He too was slain by the executioner's sword.

The king of Iran and his knights returned to the royal court victorious. The death of Siavosh had been avenged, with Afrasiab paying the ultimate price for his horrific deeds. Kay Khosrow gave the throne of Turan to Jahan, Afrasiab's remaining son, and advised him to respect the boundaries set by Feraydun between Iran and Turan. The king withdrew to the fire temple of Azar Goshasp and gave a fortune in alms, for God had granted his ultimate desire. It was at this time that Kay Kavous passed from the world, thankful to have lived long enough to see Siavosh avenged.

Kay Kavous was solemnly consigned to his crypt.
Death does not exempt king or prophet, nor does it
Spare the sage most learned, the soldier well equipped.

The Dynastic Shift

The reign of King Kay Khosrow was short, for at the age of sixty he grew anxious about his fate. He was descended from Kay Kavous on one side and Afrasiab on the other. These were impetuous men, given to passions, greed, and injustice. How could he be immune from their errors? Even such mighty kings as Zahhak, Tur, Salm, Jamshid, and Nowzar had succumbed to evil temptations and lost their divine sanction. Their names were blackened by their deeds. Kay Khosrow feared that he, too, might lose his way and lean toward iniquity.

With these thoughts Kay Khosrow spent a week in solitude and prayer. Then he emerged, called on his knights to pray for divine guidance, and went back to his private chambers for another five weeks. He prayed to pass from this world while his spirit was untarnished. The knights were troubled and worried. The king had grown pale, and his straight back had curved like an old man. They consulted fortune-tellers and sent for Zaul and Rostam to come to the capital without delay. Upon arrival, Zaul opined that the king had probably grown weary of his office and that good advice and companionship would help him recover from his malaise.

In his seclusion Kay Khosrow continued his fervent prayers to God, asking Him: "What good is this kingship to me if I lose your favor?"

He fell asleep and had a vision of Sorush, the divine messenger. The angel intoned: "You shall find all that you seek and a place by the supreme God if you leave this world. Don't linger in this darkness. Give away all that you have and appoint a successor, for your day of departure is at hand."

Kay Khosrow woke to find himself soaked in perspiration and tears. Swept up by a torrent of joy, the king prostrated himself before God. He knew that he had to make haste in order to receive all that he was promised. Thus he wore a new garment, avoiding the crown and torque of his office, and sat on the ivory throne. The king admitted the noble knights in their golden boots and gave them the startling news of his imminent abdication.

The knights were dismayed. Rostam beseeched the king to reconsider but Kay Khosrow was steadfast. "You are the first among the knights and the Champion of the World. The kings of this land have been in your debt since the days of Kay Qobad. For five weeks have I been praying to God to forgive my sins and take me from this world lest I turn to injustice. At dawn the divine messenger Sorush came to me with the good tidings that my soul's dark night has ended. Time has come for me to abdicate the throne and unburden myself of the yoke of this life."

Zaul turned to the knights and said, "This is not right. Reason has deserted this man. I never heard this sort of talk. Now I shall speak the truth to him even at the expense of my life."

The knights agreed to support Zaul, and he rose in protest: "Now hear the bitter truth from an old man, and don't quarrel with what is right. You were born in the land of Turan, to a daughter of Afrasiab, a man who trafficked with demons in his dreams. Your paternal grandfather was the malignant Kay Kavous, who schemed to trespass the gates of the heavens. I admonished him then as I tell you the truth now. Kay Kavous did not listen to me or repent his sins until he crashed from the skies. In your battle against Turan you were reckless as you went against Shideh. You did not care that Iran would lose the battle if you were killed. God saved you and us from certain ruin in that battle. Now you bring this fresh disaster upon us. You stray from the path of God and endanger your divine sanction. If you persist in this conduct, people will abandon you. Your office will be lost and your name shall be blackened. Listen to me and come back to the path of God. Use your good sense and make reason your guide."

Kay Khosrow was silent for a spell. Then he spoke. "It would displease God if I spoke to you with the harsh tone that you have taken against me. Besides, I don't wish to offend Rostam by insulting you. I will speak gently lest I break your heart. It behooves you to speak with caution and be mindful of your station. I swear that I have not strayed from the path of God or inclined to the ways of the devil. You disparaged my Turanian lineage. I am the son of Siavosh, the progeny of the kings of Kay. I am also from the seed of Afrasiab, who is the son of Pashang and a descendant of Feraydun. His fear killed the appetite of Iranian knights, and his terror caused them to dread bathing in the waters of the Oxus River. Regarding the heavenly adventure of Kay Kavous, know that kings are not faulted for their will to conquer the unknown realms. I avenged my father and slew the evildoers of the world. And if I went against Shideh, it was because I did not find a knight who would rise to confront him. That was a battle I won with the aid of my divine sanction.

"I have meditated for five weeks and importuned God to rid me of this world of misery. I have had my fill of this office and wish to unburden myself of these worldly concerns. You have suggested that the devil has misled me. I know not where and when you shall be repaid for this sinful slander."

Zaul was shamed by the magnanimity of the king. He rose in the assembly of the knights and said, "You are pure and wise, my righteous king. Forgive me, for I was the one who was misled. If I have been unjust, it is because I love my king and can't bear the thought of being separated from him."

Kay Khosrow took Zaul by the hand, sat him on the throne, and accepted his apology. Then he ordered the knights to take the royal standard of Kaveh and set up a pavilion outside the capital. In the midst of colorful tents and banners, the king came out and gave away his worldly possessions. His gardens went to Gudarz, his garments to Rostam, his weapons to Geav, and

his armor to Fariborz. He confirmed the stewardship of the lands of Zabol to the house of Zaul, and those of Isfahan and Khorasan, respectively, to the houses of Gudarz and Tous.

Then Kay Khosrow called for a knight by the name of Lohrasp to come forward and accept the crown as the next king. The company was surprised by this choice. Zaul objected to conferring the kingship on the obscure Lohrasp. "He came with nothing but a horse, and you endowed him with troops and the standard and belt of leadership. I see in him neither talent nor lineage. Who has known a king like this?"

The assembly of knights tended to agree with this estimation. They protested that they would not recognize the new king. Kay Khosrow countered the charges and vouched for Lohrasp as a man of reason, nobility, and lineage, intimating that he was descended from King Hushang. Zaul relented, and the assembly of knights ratified the dynastic shift from the Kays to the house of Lohrasp.

After a week Kay Khosrow started his journey up the slopes of the mountain that had been signified by Sorush, the divine messenger. One hundred thousand Iranians accompanied their king to the highlands, which were covered in snow. The king advised his knights to return as he started his lonely ascent.

Gudarz, Zaul, and Rostam returned. But Fariborz, Tous, Gostaham, Geav, and Bizhan followed Kay Khosrow up the windswept inclines until they reached a fountainhead. The king bathed in the waters of the spring and advised his five companions that he would go into occultation the following day and that they must go back, as a snowstorm was approaching.

The next morning Kay Khosrow had disappeared. Astounded at this, the knights searched for their king but could not find the slightest trace of him. They spent the next day there, reminiscing about times past and extolling the virtues of Kay Khosrow. In thus lingering, they disregarded the king's warning about the snowstorm. Soon the flurries started in earnest. As the five knights of Iran commenced their descent, they were caught up in a blizzard. Drifting snows covered them one by one. Each tried to dig his way out, creating a deep well in the snow. But finally they all succumbed to the snowstorm and died.

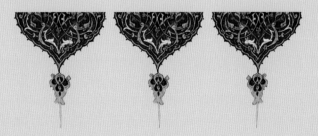

There is no parity between joy and grief in this den of strife
One thing remains after we're gone: a good name,
And that's the lesson of Kay Khosrow's life.

Gudarz mourned his loss sprinkling ash
On his head for his clan was decimated
In the wars waged to avenge Siavosh.

The Thirst for the Crown:
Esfandiar

Kay Khosrow's tale is done and that of Lohrasp has not yet begun
Now we shall set the opulent throne of the man who followed
Feraydun in becoming king on the festival of Mehregan.

Lohrasp and Goshtasp

With the installation of the new dynasty, King Lohrasp ascended the throne on the holiday of Mehregan. He remained loyal to the saintly Kay Khosrow and followed his instructions and his example. His reign over Iran was long, and it would have been uneventful had it not been for his son Goshtasp's greed for power and his impatience to succeed his father on the throne. Twice he suggested that his father give up the crown and publicly call him king. When Lohrasp denied him this brazen request, Goshtasp abandoned the court and took refuge in India. After some years he went to Rome and married the daughter of the Caesar. With his raised status Goshtasp threatened his father that he would invade and take the crown by force. Tired of his son's niggling harassment, Lohrasp finally abdicated. He retired to the city of Balkh to pursue a life of solitude and prayer. At long last Goshtasp was able to quench his thirst for power and assume the Iranian crown. He entered the capital with his Roman queen, Katayun, and their sons, Esfandiar and Farshidvard, at his side.

At this time a prophet by the name of Zarathustra had come to prominence, calling people to the worship of the one God. King Goshtasp eagerly converted to the new Zoroastrian faith and made it the official religion of his realm. Goshtasp's son Esfandiar was a great proponent of the new prophet as well and he blessed the young prince with a protective talisman that shielded him from harm.

At the time of King Goshtasp, all the neighboring kingdoms were pacified. But Turan had prospered under a new king by the name of Arjasp. Indeed, it had grown so powerful as to levy a tax on Iran. Zarathustra advised Goshtasp against accepting the dominance of the pagan king of Turan. This led to another confrontation between the two countries that had lived in peace since the death of Afrasiab.

The Battle of Arjasp and Goshtasp

The Turanians sent a huge army against Iran. The war went badly for the Iranian side, and King Goshtasp lost many of his sons and his brother Zarir to the battle. In his desperation Goshtasp asked for the assistance of his son the brave Esfandiar, who was renowned for his righteousness, invincibility, and extraordinary strength. In exchange he promised his ambitious son the crown. Elated by the prospect of becoming king, Esfandiar eagerly routed the Turanian troops and forced King Arjasp to withdraw.

Esfandiar returned to court expecting to receive the crown, but instead Goshtasp sent him on a new mission to propagate the Zoroastrian religion. He accomplished this commission as well, but the king was still disinclined to surrender his office. The royal court was alive with the tension between father and son over Goshtasp's unfulfilled promises.

In an attempt to divert himself from the affairs of the court and to forget his troubles, Esfandiar went on a hunting expedition with his sons. They were at the hunting grounds when the king's trusted adviser and astrologer Jamasp came with an urgent letter calling the crown prince to return to court.

Esfandiar confided in his sons that the king's heart was set against him; that he would be walking into a den of intrigues by going to court. "But why?" asked his son Bahman. "What have you done to deserve the king's enmity?"

Esfandiar replied: "I have only served him, cleansing the world of enemies and propagating our religion of the righteous path. But he has been led astray by some devil. He wants to destroy me."

Jamasp confirmed Esfandiar's suspicions. He revealed that there were some who had spoken against Esfandiar and convinced the king that the crown prince was planning sedition against him.

Despite this intelligence, Esfandiar went to the capital, as it was not possible to ignore the royal summons. When he entered the palace, the king turned to his courtiers with this question: "What is the appropriate punishment for an ungrateful son who repays his father's kindness by plotting to depose him?"

They gasped: "Exalted king! How could a son dream of ascending the throne while his father lives? Such a thing would be inconceivable."

Goshtasp replied: "Ah, but Esfandiar is indeed such a son, and I intend to make an example of him. Soon he will find death preferable to his punishment."

Esfandiar spoke up: "I am innocent. I have not hatched any plots against you. But if you deem me guilty, do what you want. Kill me or bind me as you wish."

The king ordered Esfandiar bound and banished to a faraway fortress. There he was fitted with heavy iron chains pinned to four steel pillars. The courtiers and even most of Esfandiar's brothers and sisters kept silent as he was sent to exile as a prisoner. Only his brother Farshidvard spoke out against those who had propagated the calumnies against the brave crown prince.

Having thus lain to rest all the worries about having to live up to his promises, King Goshtasp traveled to the land of Zabol on a mission to spread the new religion. For two years Rostam and Zaul tended to every desire of their royal guest.

As word spread that Esfandiar was imprisoned and Goshtasp was distracted with the new religion, the king of Turan, Arjasp, attacked the Persian city of Balkh. The Turanians sacked the city, massacred eighty Zoroastrian priests, extinguished the holy fire of their temple, took the king's daughters captive, and killed his father, Lohrasp.

This new invasion forced Goshtasp to give up his religious retreat in Zabol and go to war. The Turanians appeared insurmountable as they once again defeated Goshtasp. The king lost thirty-eight sons to the battle, and Farshidvard was severely wounded. Goshtasp retreated to a mountaintop, hopeless and desperate for succor. He knew that there was only one person who could save him from imminent disaster, and that was his son Esfandiar. He sent his trusted adviser Jamasp across the siege lines to the fortress were Esfandiar was imprisoned.

Jamasp entered the prison, prostrated himself in front of Esfandiar, and conveyed the king's greetings to the shackled crown prince. He beseeched Esfandiar to once again rescue his father. The king had promised that he would give up his crown and retire, just as his father had done.

Esfandiar said, "Why would one prostrate oneself before a captive who is tied up like a beast and despised as a demon? You convey the king's greetings to me? You might as well have conveyed Arjasp's greeting as he roams the land, inundating it in a pool of blood. I shall never forget that the king put his faith in worthless rumors and sent me to this dungeon. Instead of rewarding my services with exquisite treasures of gold, he has bestowed on me these heavy chains of iron."

Jamasp implored Esfandiar to forget the resentments of the past and spring to action. After all, he was obligated to seek revenge for the martyrdom of his grandfather Lohrasp, and that of the eighty priests of the temple at Balkh. The blood of his thirty-eight brothers remained unavenged, and his sisters languished in captivity. Esfandiar was unmoved.

"You speak of Lohrasp's blood? Avenging his death is, first and foremost, the obligation of his son Goshtasp. As for my brothers and sisters, I am not stirred by their plight, either. My brothers are already dead and I can't bring them back. Nor do I recall either they or my sisters having cared one whit as I was sent in chains to this dungeon."

Jamasp said, "What of your brother Farshidvard, who is mortally wounded? You know that he cursed this calumny against you no matter where he was, at banquet or in battle."

Hearing Farshidvard's name caused Esfandiar great sorrow. He rose and cried in anguish. The fate of Farshidvard had changed his mind about staying away from Goshtasp's wars. Ironworkers were called to remove his chains. But the work was slow. Esfandiar scolded them for being unable to undo their own work. Then he broke the remainder of the chains using his own strength. The exertion was so great that he fainted after breaking out of his restraints. When he came to, he saw to his horse, which had been badly neglected during his imprisonment. Why, he thought, would they stoop to mistreating a horse for the alledged guilt of his master? Soon the preparations for battle were complete and the heroic crown prince was on his black steed riding out to rescue his father.

Once more, Esfandiar routed the enemy and won the battle. Arjasp fled and his soldiers asked for quarter. It was obvious that after his solemn and public promise, the king would have to surrender his crown and abdicate. But on the day of Esfandiar's victory, the king broke his promise again on the grounds that the battle was not really finished, as his daughters Homai and Behafarid were still in captivity. Esfandiar pledged to rescue his sisters from bondage at Arjasp's Invincible Castle.

Before embarking on his journey to liberate his sisters, Esfandiar picked a number of capable warriors and put them under his brother Pashutan's command to help him conquer Arjasp's stronghold. He also chose a high-ranking

Turanian captive as his scout. The scout revealed that there were three ways to the Invincible Castle. The easy road was lush with forests and meadows. This road could be traversed in three months. The middle road was harsher but could be crossed in one month. There was a shortcut that would take a traveler to the Invincible Castle in only one week. However, this path was fraught with difficult terrain, inclement weather, dangerous beasts, and menacing magical creatures.

The Invincible Castle, the scout said, was walled and guarded by dedicated soldiers. A turbulent river encircled it. Sufficient unto itself, the castle could withstand long sieges, as its inhabitants grew crops and made flour in their own mills. Esfandiar was not discouraged by his scout's descriptions of the difficult road and the impregnable fortress. Instead he swiftly set off to liberate his sisters, taking the shortest path.

Esfandiar went through seven labors on his way to the Invincible Castle. He killed ferocious wolves and lions, survived snowstorms, and overcame a sorceress. To contend with the teeth of a dragon and the powerful claws of an enchanted bird, Esfandiar fabricated and fought from within a wooden enclosure that had sharp spikes all around it.

The taking of the castle itself was the last and the most difficult of Esfandiar's labors. He accomplished it not by strength but by cunning: First, he disguised himself as a merchant to gain access to the fortress and win Arjasp's trust. Then he persuaded the king to allow him to host a banquet on the roof of the castle. The fires of the banquet were a cue to his brother Pashutan to rush the ramparts as Esfandiar took the castle from inside, beheaded Arjasp, and opened the castle to the forces of Pashutan and liberated his sisters.

Why does the nightingale alight
And sing such a sad song by a lovely
Narcissus on a stormy night?

It is for Esfandiar that the bird grieves
As Rostam roars in thunderclaps
Above the shaking wet leaves.

The Story of Rostam and Esfandiar

Having freed his sisters and killed the king of Turan, Esfandiar sent forth a train of camels to Goshtasp's palace carrying the endless treasures of Arjasp, including the Turanian king's own sisters and daughters. The Invincible Castle, thus conquered, was torched and destroyed. Its commanders, who had killed the sons of Goshtasp, were executed. With this triumph, Esfandiar took the leisurely road back to the royal court fully expecting to receive the long-promised crown of kingship.

Goshtasp came forward with a large entourage to welcome his triumphant son. He invited many people to the palace and arranged for lavish festivities. The king spoke about various subjects, but once again there was no hint, in words or deeds, of fulfilling his promise to abdicate in favor of Esfandiar. When he requested that the heroic crown prince relate the stories of his seven labors, Esfandiar refused. "This is not the time or the place for those stories. You shall hear the full account when you are sober."

The king was ominously silent. It was clear that Goshtasp had no intention of fulfilling his promises. More desperate and disappointed than ever, Esfandiar went to queen Katayun bitterly complaining of his father's faithlessness. He listed his victories against the enemies of the land and his brave service that had saved the crown several times. He had won two battles against Turan, killed the enemy king, liberated his sisters, and propagated the religion of righteousness. Goshtasp had promised to make him king in exchange for each one of these missions but denied him the prize every time. Esfandiar swore that he would ask the king one last time to fulfill his promise. If denied again, he would wrest the crown by force.

Katayun advised her son to bide his time and savor his position as the crown prince. One day Goshtasp would pass away and he would be king through natural succession. The impetuous Esfandiar rejected Katayun's counsel, blaming himself for having confided in a woman. "I ought to have heeded the ancient wisdom against consulting with women," he said to his mother, "for they betray your confidence and offer worthless advice."

Katayun fell silent, deeply wounded by these words.

Esfandiar did not go back to Goshtasp. Rather he retired to his own quarters and sought solace in wine and the embrace of one of his consorts.

The meaning of Esfandiar's absence was not lost on Goshtasp. Distressed over the growing strain with his son, the king called on his adviser Jamasp, the royal astrologer, to cast the horoscope of the crown prince and disclose when and by whose hands he would die, if indeed his lot were to be a violent death.

The answer stunned the king: Esfandiar was destined to die at the hands of Rostam in the land of Zabol. Goshtasp asked whether fate could be circumvented. Would, for instance, his son be saved if he were to abdicate? Jamasp answered that fate was ineluctable. The king brooded over this strange prediction. He inclined to wickedness and allowed iniquity and cravings for worldly things, including the crown, to guide his thoughts.

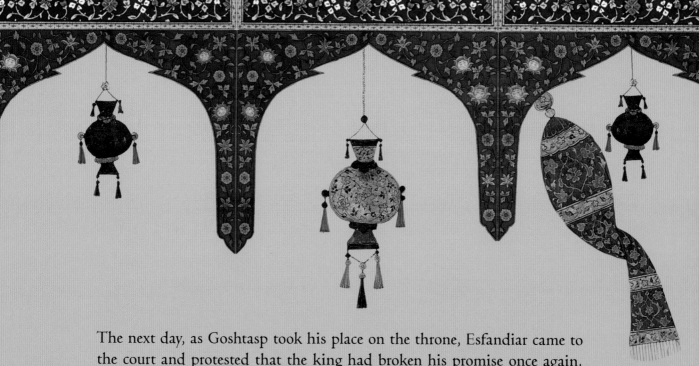

The next day, as Goshtasp took his place on the throne, Esfandiar came to the court and protested that the king had broken his promise once again. There were no enemies, no infidels, no captives, and no contenders. What possible excuse was left? What pretext could the king offer to deny him his rightful place on the throne?

King Goshtasp granted that Esfandiar had been unremitting in pursuit of his royal commands. But it was not true that there were no contenders left, for Rostam, the son of Zaul, would not bow to the king's authority. He claimed that Rostam had been heard saying: "Goshtasp has a new crown, but ours is older." So, although it was true that there were no external enemies, an internal enemy remained. Thus one last labor awaited Esfandiar: humbling the house of Saum. Goshtasp commanded Esfandiar to go to Zabol, bind Rostam's hands, and bring him as a captive to the court along with his father, brother, and son. The king swore a solemn oath to give up his throne once Rostam was chastened.

Esfandiar replied: "You have spurned the ways of the ancestors. It would behoove you to challenge such worthy opponents as the King of China. Why would you instead go after an old, honorable man who served the kings of yore, from Kay Qobad to Kay Khosrow? For his services he received such royal titles as the World Conqueror, the Crown Bestower, and the Lion Slayer.

The king reminded his son of the importance of obeying the directives of one's king as if they were commands from God.

Esfandiar said, "Don't stray from the path of righteousness. You don't care for humbling Rostam. You mean to find an excuse to get me out of your way, as you are loath to surrender your royal office. Keep your crown. An obscure corner of the world will suffice for me.

"And yet your wish remains my command. I will do your bidding, but I will not need an army for this task. A few of my own relatives will serve in this undertaking."

Esfandiar left the royal chamber in despair. Katayun had heard from her grandson Bahman that Esfandiar was given the impossible mission of humbling Rostam in exchange for the crown. She bitterly wept. "Surely you have heard of the great deeds of Rostam," she said to her son, "spilling rivers of blood to avenge Siavosh and subduing legendary heroes and fabulous beasts. Don't lose your head to gain a crown. I curse this crown and throne and all this butchery and plunder. Heed my advice. Don't lower me to the dust of mourning for you."

Esfandiar said that he was aware of the exalted station and nobility of Rostam and knew well that humbling him would not be an easy task. But he had no choice in the matter. It was not proper for him to disobey the king's command. Katayun begged him to at least leave his three sons, Bahman, Mehrnush, and Nushazar, behind. Esfandiar refused. Boys were meant to see the battlefield and endure the hardships of war. Remaining with women would corrode their character. With this, Esfandiar, his brother Pashutan, and his sons set off for the land of Zabol at the head of a small contingent of warriors.

Esfandiar Camps at the Hirmand River

When the supply caravan of the war party reached a fork in the road, the lead camel lay down and refused to move. Esfandiar took this as a bad omen and slew the beast to counteract the portentous omen. Later, the party set up camp at the bank of the river Hirmand, which marked Rostam's realm. Esfandiar sent forth his son Bahman along with ten prominent priests to deliver an extraordinary message to Rostam:

Anyone who is favored by heaven must know that our destiny is death and that we receive our just deserts in this world and the next. Now, we must judge your deeds according to the rules of reason. You have lived long and seen many kings. You have earned worldly goods and won honors from my ancestors. You have paid your respects at neither the court of King Lohrasp nor that of his son, my father, King Goshtasp. He has humbled the world from China to Rome, reduced the desert Arabs and Indian kings to obedient vassals, and killed Arjasp, the king of Turan. You have chosen the path of pride, drunk as you are on your own power and station. This behavior cannot be tolerated. The king has sworn an oath to bring you to his court with your hands bound. I have come to ensure that you act according to the royal summons.

If you choose the path of repentance and obedience, I swear by the sun, my father's life, and the divine spirit that I will intercede on your behalf. As my brother Pashutan is my witness, I have tried to dissuade the king from this path but my father is a king and I am his subject. I want you, your father, Zaul, your mother, Rudabeh, your brother Zavareh and your son Faramarz to hear my words of advice. This clan of yours must not be wiped out. This land that belongs to you must not be divided among the gallant knights of Iran. If you let me take you to the king in bondage, I swear to take your side and quell his anger. I pledge my honor and give you my word that I shall not allow even a cold breeze to chill your soul.

Bahman took up the royal standard and set off to discharge his mission. When Zaul heard that a daring knight with a golden helmet had crossed the Hirmand River on a black horse, he rode up to a vantage point. The old silver-haired knight of Zabol sported a lariat on his saddle and was wielding a mace as he rode up the slope. On the peak he looked down. The rider was from the royal clan of King Lohrasp. Zaul heaved a cold sigh as he sensed that this mission would not bode well for his clan. Bahman came forth, identified himself as the son and the emissary of Esfandiar, and asked the whereabouts of Rostam. Zaul dismounted and humbled himself before the prince. He said that Rostam was out hunting with Zavareh and invited Bahman to rest and partake of wine until their return. Bahman replied that he was not permitted rest before accomplishing his mission. Zaul bowed and sent a scout to point the way to Rostam's camp.

At the hunting grounds, Bahman climbed a mountain with a commanding view of the surrounding lands. From there he could see a colossal man who had uprooted a tree to use it as a spit for an onager that he had just hunted. Bahman's heart sank. It was evident that Esfandiar was no match for this giant. If only he could kill Rostam and save his father!

Bahman tore a boulder from the mountainside and rolled it down toward Rostam. As the boulder plunged downhill, raising a cloud of dust, Rostam stood his ground and kicked the rock off to one side with unbelievable ease. Full of foreboding for the impending confrontation of this hero with his father, Bahman rode down the slope. He introduced himself and announced that he was carrying a message from Esfandiar.

Rostam expressed his pleasure at meeting the young prince and invited him to share in a meal of fresh game and wine. A spread was prepared, and Rostam and Zavareh hosted Esfandiar's messenger. Rostam ate his customary huge portion of the meat and drank copious amounts of wine while teasing Bahman for how little he ate and drank. He replied, "It is at the battlefield that a man proves his mettle, not at the table. It is not fitting for a prince to speak or eat much in public."

After the meal Bahman conveyed his father's message in full. Rostam reflected on the graveness of the message and sent a reply to Esfandiar:

A man who is noble in birth and spirit and accomplished in arts of war and the practice of reason must avoid greed and vain speech. You have surpassed your ancestors in virtue and your name is known as far afield as India, Rome, and China. I have long wished to behold your countenance. Allow me to come and see you alone. We shall ponder my covenants with past kings and reflect on all that I have done for this land. I shall appoint you the judge. You decide if the reward of my long service to the kings of Iran is abject servitude. If you so judge me, then I will wear a packsaddle, put my own feet in shackles, and offer my neck to your sword.

Act as a prince and don't say what is unseemly. Banish wrath and the reckless judgments of youth from your heart. No one has ever seen me in chains. Come to my quarters instead and stay for a couple of months. Let this elder knight rejoice in hosting a gallant young prince like you. The hunting grounds are teeming with game and I am eager to see how you hunt lions and tigers. After this respite, you will receive my exquisite parting gifts and return to King Goshtasp. I shall ride along with you to the court and soften the king's heart. I will douse the fire of his royal anger with my kisses and apologies.

With these words Bahman took Rostam's message back to his father. Rostam sent his brother Zavareh back to Zaul with a command to prepare the palace for an honored guest in case Esfandiar accepted his invitation. Then he went to the shore of the river Hirmand and waited for Esfandiar's response.

Bahman carried Rostam's dispatch to his father and prefaced it with words of praise for the hero he had met. Esfandiar reprimanded his inexperienced son for flattering the foe in public and within earshot of the troops. But he confided in private to his brother Pashutan that Bahman's descriptions of Rostam indicated that the passage of years had not broken the old warrior.

The Crown Prince Meets the Old Knight

Esfandiar ordered his black stallion to be fitted with a golden saddle and rode to the banks of the Hirmand. Rostam crossed the river to Esfandiar and dismounted. He hailed the prince as a beloved friend whose arrival had made him as happy as seeing Siavosh alive. Esfandiar praised Rostam and said that he brought back fond memories of his uncle Zarir, who had been killed in the war against the Turanians. Rostam repeated his wish to host the worthy prince. Esfandiar said that he could not accept that invitation. "It would behoove you to submit to the king. If he wishes to see you in chains, you should put the shackles on your own hands and feet and present yourself at the royal court. If you come to court in humility, the blame would go to the king for mistreating you. My heart aches for you, and I wish to be your servant. I pledge that your confinement will not last past nightfall. When I wear the

crown, you will return to Zabol in the season of blossoms, unashamed before God and king."

Rostam replied: "I have long wished to see you, so how can I be disagreeable? Young or old, we are both proud warriors. I am afraid some demon has come between us. Your heart is obsessed with assuming royal office.

"It would be an indelible stain on my honor if a commander of your rank refused to be my guest in my land. If you banish the demon of hatred from your heart and come to my quarters, I will do anything you want. But I cannot accept the disgrace of bondage. No one shall see me in chains while I live. "

Esfandiar said, "You are the last of the race of heroes, and everything you have said is true. But I cannot come as a guest to your house, for that would be tantamount to disobeying my king, an act of impiety. Besides, should you refuse the royal command, I would have no choice but to fight you. I cannot shed the blood of one who has hosted me in his home. However, if you wish, we can eat and drink together tonight at my encampment. Who knows what tomorrow will bring?"

Rostam accepted the invitation. But as he had been hunting for a week, he asked leave to refresh himself and come back later. They agreed that a messenger would come calling on Rostam when the repast had been set at Esfandiar's camp. Rostam returned to his palace and sang the praises of the gallant prince of Iran to Zaul while expressing his grave anxiety over the outcome of their encounter.

On the other side of the Hirmand River, Esfandiar regretted the arrangement he had proposed. Of course, he had made the right decision when he had refused to go to Rostam's house. But for the same reasons it was wrong for Rostam to be his guest. Thus Esfandiar decided to renege on his promise and refrained from sending someone to escort Rostam to his camp. He confided in Pashutan that he had underestimated the difficulty of the task he had undertaken. Pashutan advised his brother to be more accommodating and to seek the path of peace with Rostam, as he was not likely to undergo the humiliation of bondage. Esfandiar replied that he could not compromise because disobeying the king was a sin. With this he called for the stewards to serve dinner and raised a chalice of wine to the glory of his adventures that had led to the conquest of Arjasp's Invincible Castle.

Meanwhile, it was becoming clear to Rostam that no one would come to collect him. He ordered his horse to be saddled and took Zavareh as witness to the appalling conduct of Esfandiar. He arrived at Esfandiar's camp and derided him for abandoning the manners of a host. Esfandiar laughed and said that he did not wish to trouble Rostam, as the trek was long and the evening hot. Instead, he had planned to go to Rostam in the morning, offer his apologies, and seek an audience with Zaul. He added, "Now that you have taken the trouble of coming here, pick up a chalice of wine and put aside your anger."

Esfandiar offered his guest a seat to his left. Rostam protested that he was a highborn knight descended from the lineage of Saum who traced his ancestors back to King Hushang. Only when a golden seat was set for him opposite his host did Rostam deign to sit down. In response to this outburst, Esfandiar made a biting remark about Rostam's father, Zaul, as an outcast abandoned by his father and brought up in the nest of a wild bird. Rostam replied that without his exploits, from saving King Kay Kavous to the conquest of Turan, there would be no Iran to speak of, and that Esfandiar should stop boasting of his upstart grandfather Lohrasp, or the new religion of his father, Goshtasp. He demanded: "Who told you, 'Go and tie Rostam's hands?' The high vault of the heavens is incapable of putting me in shackles."

Esfandiar advised Rostam to keep his peace, drink his wine, and await the events of the next day. "I will tie your hands and take you to the king. But I shall champion your cause and relieve you of all your sorrows."

Rostam laughed. "You are about to have your fill of fighting. You are yet to see how true champions fight. But do not worry. I will take you off the saddle and bring you in my embrace to the noble Zaul. I shall open up my treasure houses, enrich you with gifts, and make you king." There was nothing else to say. They drank wine and parted ways.

Rostam worried about the outcome of the affair. If captured alive and taken to the court tied up as a slave, he would be shamed forever. If he were killed in battle, his entire clan would be wiped out. And if he were to emerge victorious, people would curse him for shedding the blood of a noble prince. His only hope was to capture Esfandiar alive. He shared his plan with Zaul, saying, "I will not bare my blade or draw my heavy mace on him. Rather I shall lift him off his saddle in a friendly contest and carry him here. I will serve him as an honored guest and then take him to the capital and make him king just as I did with Kay Qobad."

Zaul laughed. "Don't speak like that if you don't want to be a laughingstock. The throne was empty then, and Iran was in disarray. You cannot go against a sitting king of Iran. Nor can you take Esfandiar off his saddle with the ease you describe. This is a man who has vanquished the kings of the world."

In utter desperation Zaul prostrated himself and fervently prayed that God turn the coming disaster away from his house. He did not rise from his position of supplication all night.

The First Day of Battle

The next day Rostam suited up for war. He donned his tiger skin over his armor, picked up his heavy lance, and set off for the shore of the Hirmand. Zavareh followed him, but Rostam instructed him to hang back with the troops—the contest was to be between the two champions. Esfandiar, too, asked his brother Pashutan and his sons to stay back with their troops. Rostam announced his readiness for battle while still beseeching his opponent to reconsider the matter. "If it is vengeance and bloodshed you desire," he said, "I will bring my armies from Zabol and Kabul to fight against your Iranian troops."

Esfandiar was offended. "How dare you suggest that I desire to shed innocent blood? If you wish to bring help, that is your choice. But I am sufficient unto myself. Let us see whose horse will return without a master at the end of this day."

With these words, a pitched battle between the two champions commenced. They fought with lances, javelins, swords, and maces until their weapons, shields, and armor were in tatters and their horses were exhausted. Then they engaged in a contest to lift each other from the saddle, but they were equally matched at this as well. Finally, caked in dirt and mud and drenched in sweat and blood, they separated to rest.

Farther from the scene of this contest, Rostam's and Esfandiar's troops faced each other. Zavareh grew impatient and used foul language to taunt Esfandiar's troops. He asked why they were standing idle instead of pursuing their mission to take Rostam alive. Esfandiar's son Nushazar replied in kind and added that they did not have permission to fight but that they would defend themselves if attacked. At this Zavareh led the charge and killed many of the opposing troops. Nushazar joined the fray and killed Rostam's lance holder in a swordfight. Moved to anger, Zavareh struck the young lad with a spear and killed him. Then Mehrnush went forth to avenge his brother's death, and he, too, was killed—by Faramarz.

Distraught, Bahman rode out to Esfandiar and told him of the calamity that had befallen the army. Esfandiar was livid. Turning to Rostam, he said, "Is that how you keep your promise, you dishonorable man? Did you not pledge to keep your troops at bay while we fought? Where is your shame before God and man? Now two worthless men from your side have slain my royal sons."

Rostam was dismayed. He swore by the sun, the sword, the battlefield, and the king's soul that he had not ordered his troops to fight and pledged to bind and surrender the culprits, even though they were his own brother and son. He gave Esfandiar the right to execute them in retribution. This did not seem a fair exchange to Esfandiar. "Kings act justly seeking revenge for their kin. They do not shed the blood of snakes to avenge the slaughter of peacocks. Now think of saving your own miserable life as I stitch you to your horse with my arrows. If you survive, I will drag you away like a base slave. This will teach you to rebel against your superiors."

Rostam sighed, realizing that talking no longer served a purpose. A shooting contest began and the mighty Esfandiar ran circles around Rostam, shooting at him with diamond-tipped arrows that easily pierced his and Rakhsh's armor. He galloped so fast that none of Rostam's arrows could find their target. Rostam was overwhelmed as Esfandiar's deadly missiles gravely wounded him and his steed. Visibly diminished and bleeding, Rostam dismounted. He allowed Rakhsh to walk back and sought refuge in higher ground. Esfandiar mocked him. "What happened to your legendary strength? Demons wept at your approach and terrible beasts were flayed alive at the glint of your sword. You were once a war elephant. But now you act the part of a scared fox."

Zavareh, who had traced Rakhsh's footprints back to Rostam, learned that the battle had gone badly for his brother. He took the bad news back to Zaul. They knew that their entire clan was in peril.

Esfandiar spoke to the wounded Rostam: "How long are you going to hide up there? Whom do you expect to come to your rescue? Put down your weapons and suffer me to tie your hands and spare your life. I shall have your sins forgiven in front of the king. But if you wish to fight, appoint someone in your stead and beg God to forgive your sins, as you are about to pass from this world."

Rostam, who was desperate to find a way out of his predicament, replied: "Darkness is falling, and no one fights at night. Return now to your camp and allow me to go back and dress my wounds before conveying your commands to Zavareh, Faramarz, and Zaul."

Esfandiar called Rostam a man of many wiles but added: "I accept your words, duplicitous as they are. I don't want to see you dishonored, and thus I offer you safe conduct this night. But be sure to live up to your word and stop your trickery."

Relieved, Rostam staggered back across the river, wading through the waves despite the arrows that were embedded in his flesh. Astonished at the strength of the old champion, Esfandiar praised him as a wonder of creation and went back to his own camp, where Pashutan was mourning the deaths of Mehrnush and Nushazar. He dismounted and briefly grieved over the bodies of his young sons. Then he commanded the company of mourners to moderate their lamentations. "I see no profit in shedding bloodstained tears or in clinging to life. Young or old, we are all destined to die. The point is to live in the light of reason while we are alive."

He ordered his sons' corpses to be placed in gold-encrusted teak coffins and sent them back to his father, Goshtasp, with a message: "You schemed to humiliate Rostam. The tree you planted has now borne fruit. Behold the coffins of Nushazar and Mehrnush and muzzle your greed. Their fate is sealed, but their father's destiny remains uncertain."

The Final Battle

When Rostam went back to his palace he found his father, mother, brother, and son in tears of sorrow and despair. He pleaded that they find some cure for Rakhsh's wounds before tending to him. Zaul lamented that he had lived to see his brave son in such a state. Rostam called on his kinsmen to be calm and submit to fate. About Esfandiar he said, "Nothing seems to mollify this impudent man. My humility inflames his pride. In a life of contending with demons, beasts, and champions of the world I have never seen the equal of Esfandiar. My arrows, which used to pierce even an anvil, are rendered harmless by his armor, and my blade, which caused tigers to hide under rocks, can't even tear his silken headband. My only stroke of good fortune came in the shape of the darkness that descended and saved me from the claws of that dragon. Now my only choice is to leave my horse behind and escape. Esfandiar is sure to sack our land. He will eventually tire of it, but perhaps it will be too late for us."

Rostam's family despaired of their impending fate. But Zaul had a plan. He went up a nearby hill with three braziers of glowing coals and singed a feather of the great bird that had reared him from a fondling and saved the life of Rostam at birth. He crouched by the ambers and waited for the Simorgh. Suddenly the night seemed to grow darker. The Simorgh found the silver-headed boy she had raised throwing incense and sandalwood in the fires to welcome her.

"What has driven you, my gallant champion, to call upon me?"

Zaul said, "This wretch of a lowborn man Esfandiar has brought us much suffering. Rostam's wounds are nearly fatal, and Rakhsh, with so many arrows in his flesh, is at death's door. Not satisfied with the fruit, Esfandiar wants to uproot the whole tree, root and branch. He wants to destroy our clan."

The Simorgh told Zaul not to torment himself and called for Rakhsh and Rostam. First she scolded Rostam for clashing with the invincible Esfandiar, who had been blessed by the prophet Zarathustra. Rostam explained that he had to fight because he preferred death to the dishonor of captivity. The Simorgh countered that captivity to Esfandiar would be no dishonor.

Using her healing powers, she extracted six arrowheads from Rakhsh's neck and healed his wounds. The injured horse neighed with the power of a healthy beast once again. Turning her eyes upon Rostam's body, she removed four arrowheads from his flesh and extracted the foul blood from him with her beak. Then she passed her feathers on his wounds to cure them until he felt the instant return of his vigor.

The Simorgh said to Rostam: "Pledge to repent from challenging Esfandiar and implore him for peace. He will refuse your overture if his time has come. For that occasion I shall provide you with a weapon to raise your head to the sun."

Rostam was relieved that the dreadful prospect of his captivity had been lifted. "But," the Simorgh continued, "it is written that the killer of Esfandiar will be harried by fate in this life and tormented in the hereafter. If you are reconciled to this, you shall be brave on the battlefield. Now take a glittering dagger and ride Rakhsh, following the path of my flight in the sky."

The marvelous bird led the son of Zaul to the edge of the Sea of China, where she landed, filling the air with the scent of musk. There she pointed at the shaft of a tamarisk tree and said, "The fate of Esfandiar shall be sealed by this shaft. Cut it down, straighten it with fire, marinate it in wine, arm it with an ancient arrowhead, and fasten feathers to its end. Use it only after you have pleaded for peace. Your words might kindle in him remembrances of your past service to Iran. But if he insists on despising you, then put this arrow in your bow. You must aim only at his eyes, for the rest of his body is invincible. Shoot the arrow and allow fate to guide it to its target."

With the completion of these instructions, the Simorgh bid farewell, took wing, and soared high into the sky. Rostam went to work, preparing the arrow as he had been instructed.

The next morning the hero returned to Esfandiar's camp and roared that it was time to rise to the challenge of the day. Esfandiar heard this and was astonished that Rostam had survived the night and come back as if he had not been grievously injured the previous day. He turned to Pashutan. "I did not expect this man to live through the night, covered as he was with my arrows, dragging behind his armor and helmet. I had heard that Zaul was a formidable sorcerer. Alas, I didn't believe it."

Rostam replied: "I have not come to fight you. I have come to ask for your indulgence and to beg your pardon. You have treated me with inequity and unreason. I beg you in the name of the sun, the moon, the holy fire, and the divine books of Zarathustra to turn this harm from me. Forget the past, and let me enrich you with the treasures of Saum and accompany you to the royal court. If the king wants to kill me or tie my hands, I will submit. I will do anything for peace."

Esfandiar said, "Stop your account of treasures and the stories of peacemaking, as the time for speeches has passed. If you want to stay alive, prepare the chains of your captivity."

Rostam renewed his entreaties, but Esfandiar said that nothing would tempt him away from the command of his king. War or bondage were Rostam's only choices. At long last the old hero saw that supplication was useless. He pulled the shaft of the tamarisk arrow from his quiver and looked toward the heavens, asking for forgiveness. Esfandiar took Rostam's delay as a sign of hesitation. "It seems you have not had your fill of arrows, you worthless man. Behold the arrow of the house of Goshtasp and Lohrasp."

Rostam pulled at the string of his bow, training his choice arrow at Esfandiar's eyes. The tamarisk shaft flew in the air and found its target. Esfandiar lurched in the saddle and dropped his bow. His tall torso bent forward until his forehead touched his saddle. He clutched the mane of his horse as blood streamed from his eyes.

Rostam taunted him: "The sapling of your pride has borne fruit. You boasted of being invincible. I did not cry in pain once when I was wounded by scores of your arrows yesterday. Now you slump over your horse and turn away from battle because of one arrow! Soon your head will be lowered to the ground and your gentle mother will mourn you."

Esfandiar's world grew dark and his awareness waned. He fell off his horse and lay still. With the return of consciousness he sat up and pulled out the bloody arrow. Bahman saw his father on the ground in a pool of blood holding the arrow that had ended his domination on the battlefield. He ran to camp and told his uncle of what had happed. Pashutan came to Esfandiar's side and lamented his demise. "Providence and the evil eye conspired to lower our flawless prince in the dust. My curses on the crown and the throne of Goshtasp and on that sycophant Jamasp."

Esfandiar muttered: "Don't grieve for me, as this was the result of my own lust for the crown. Death is written for us all. Glorious kings like Hushang, Feraydun, and Jamshid also died. This is my fate. I have done good deeds, and it is my hope that I shall be rewarded in paradise. Rostam did not kill me in honest combat, either. Look at this shaft that I hold in my grasp. It is from the Simorgh. It is proof of Zaul's sorcery."

Rostam arrived on the scene and confessed. "I have seen many champions in my time but none as worthy as Esfandiar. I was unable to match him, so I looked for help in the shaft of the tamarisk. We are all destined to die.

Although I stand here laden with the guilt of killing the prince, it was destiny that spelled his doom. The tamarisk shaft and I were mere instruments of fate."

Esfandiar said, "My days are at an end, and my views have changed. You were not the one who killed me. You were the tool, as were the Simorgh, the bow, and the arrow. It was my father, Goshtasp, who killed me. He commanded me to lay waste to your land. He abandoned me to sorrow so that he could keep his crown and treasures.

"It causes me pain that your good name is stained because of this affair, Rostam. All your good deeds for the previous kings are smeared. But this was the will of the heavens. Now I leave my last remaining son, Bahman, to your care. Keep him in the land of Zabol, and be his benefactor in my absence. Teach him the arts of war, hunting, and courtly conduct. Jamasp, that accursed diviner, has foreseen that he will inherit the crown."

Rostam stood, held his hand on his heart, and swore an oath to instruct Bahman as if he were his own son. Zavareh advised him against accepting the charge. Bahman, he contended, would one day seek to avenge the death of his father on the clan of Saum. But Rostam was honor-bound to take the son of the man he had slain under his wing.

Zaul came on the scene crying for Esfandiar as much as he was grieving for his own son. He, too, had heard from soothsayers that misfortune and disasters would hound the slayer of Esfandiar and that torments would await him in the hereafter.

Esfandiar turned to Pashutan and said that he no longer desired anything from the world except the shroud he would take to the grave. He charged Pashutan to relay a message to his father:

Don't look for alibis when all this is due to your plans. The world is to your liking, all royal seals are still in your name. Your share is the throne, the crown, and the army. Mine is the shroud and the casket. I did not expect this from you, and yet I should have expected nothing but this. I cleansed the world of your enemies and spread the religion of the righteous path by my sword. In public you advised me with lofty words but in secret you plotted my demise. Now you will rightly take the blame for my death. Don't look at my face in the coffin, for this will increase your torment. Don't gloat in your victory either, for soon you will join me on my eternal journey. There I will bring you to the presence of the Almighty and let Him judge between us.

Then the fallen prince asked Pashutan to convey his message to his sisters and wife: "Fare you well, my dear ones. It was the desire for the crown that brought me low."

He inhaled one last time and uttered his final words: "Goshtasp was unjust to me."

Rostam tore at his clothes in mourning. He wished his victim an abode in paradise and echoed him: "Goshtasp has sullied my good name."

Four black horses carried Esfandiar's iron casket. Pashutan led the procession as it moved back to the capital. Esfandiar's mother, wife, and daughters surrounded his horse, which carried his weapons. Its tail and mane had been cropped as a sign of mourning. They stroked the horse and asked him why he had forsaken his gallant master.

Back at the capital, Goshtasp, too, tore his cloths in mourning and wept for his righteous son. But the noblemen of Iran questioned his sincerity and accused him of intentionally sending the crown prince to his death. Pashutan did not mince words with Goshtasp. Nor did Esfandiar's sisters. One of them addressed the king with these words: "Esfandiar avenged your brother Zarir, your father, Lohrasp, and all of your sons. He twice routed Arjasp when you could not. He liberated us from captivity at Arjasp's Invincible Castle and killed him. He was the protector of your crown. But it was you who sent him to his death in the land of Zabol. Rostam and Zaul were not the culprits in this affair. You killed your own son for the love of your office. Shame on you and your white beard."

The king was roundly denounced for his faithlessness and his murderous greed.

> Thereafter an annual mournful wail would arise
> From the squares and alleys of the land of Iran
> As people gathered to mourn Esfandiar's demise.

> They sang of a king who wished to put his knight in chains
> And spoke of a tamarisk shaft that flew that day
> In the air and found its target, causing so much pain.

بلند آسمان بر زمین برزنم	توای نگ گفتی کو روم تنم	که آوردی آن تخم زمین بکار	جین تک رستم تا سفند یار
نخستی برین بار ناندار	یک تیر برکشتی از کار زار	جز او دم نمایدم از بام و نگ	سر از دست تو مشت پی جدگ
به زرد دل احمد یان دست	هم اکنون بخاک اندر آمدت	زدی بر بلب بره جدگ	یک تیر سپه یا کرفتی زجنگ

The Demise of the Knightly House:
Death of Rostam

I heard this tale from a man who could recite
The ancient lore by heart and was wise and strong
Descended as he was from Saum the legendary knight.

The Ill-Starred Child

In the good years prior to the calamity of Esfandiar, Zaul had a beautiful concubine skilled in the arts of singing and playing the lute. She gave birth to a boy who was lovelier than the moon upon the sky. The clan of Saum was pleased, as the infant resembled their founder in stature and appearance. Astrologers and diviners of many religions were called upon to cast the horoscope of the newborn. Bewildered at the disastrous future that awaited the infant, they went to Zaul and declared their shared judgment: "The verdict of the heavens on your son is severe. He will destroy the house of Saum and bring about the ruin of this realm. Then he will perish in a calamity of his own making."

Zaul was sad to hear the fate of the infant, but he sought solace in God and prayed for divine protection. He called his son Shaghad.

When the boy had grown into a winsome young man, he was sent to the court of the vassal king of Kabul for further education and refinement. It was in Kabul that he matured into a lethal warrior skilled in the use of the lariat and the mace. The king was so charmed by Shaghad that he gave his daughter to him in marriage, along with a treasure trove of gifts as dowry.

According to custom, every year vassal kings gave a cowhide full of gold pieces as tax to Rostam, the reigning knight of Zabol. The king of Kabul presumed that taking Shaghad as his son-in-law would exempt him from the annual tribute. To his surprise, however, the tax collectors arrived as usual and collected the gold without much ceremony. Shaghad was shocked and offended. He kept his peace at first, but when the emissaries of Zabol left, he confided in his father-in-law, the king of Kabul: "I am weary of the affairs of this world. Rostam dishonors me. He treats me more as a stranger than a brother. This business we just witnessed is but one example of his poor treatment of me. Let us lay a trap for him. We shall gain repute in the world if we succeed in bringing low the Champion of the World." They conspired through the night to slay Rostam and bring grief to his father, the old Zaul, and disregarded the wisdom of the sages:

> He who sows evil, said the man of reason,
> Shall reap evil aplenty when the time
> Is ripe and in the right season.

Shaghad and the vassal king of Kabul agreed to stage a public dispute whereby the king would heap insults on Shaghad, causing him to go to the court of Zabol and seek redress. Rostam was sure to come out to help his brother, making him easy prey in their treacherous plot.

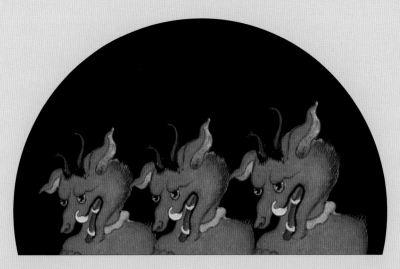

The Plot

The king called the dignitaries of Kabul to a feast and they came in droves. First they ate, and then copious amounts of wine were served to the sounds of the lute and pleasant song. Shaghad drank to excess and started to boast of his grand lineage. "Who can surpass my nobility in this gathering? I am from the house of Saum. My father is Zaul and my brother is the world-renowned Rostam!"

The king of Kabul sneered: "Truth be known, you are not from the seed of Saum. Zaul never mentions you by name. Nor does his wife, Rudabeh, recognize you as a brother to Rostam. At best, you are a lowly servant at Rostam's gate."

Shaghad sulked and left the court in protest. He rode out with a contingent of his close allies and officers of the army. In the eyes of the dignitaries present at the banquet, the king's son-in-law left the gathering because he had lost face. But the king knew that he was performing his part in their scheme. Leaving nothing to chance, Shaghad conveyed secret instructions to the king about the execution of their plan: "Dig deep pits in the hunting ground and plant them with sharp blades and lances. Make sure that they are large enough to swallow both Rostam and his horse. Cover them with branches and straw and keep the affair in strict secrecy. Err on the side of caution. Dig a hundred pits if you reckon that five will suffice."

After Shaghad's departure the king brought skilled ditch diggers to the hunting grounds and had them hollow it out with hidden pits whose bottoms bristled with javelins, swords, and lances.

When Shaghad arrived in Zabol he was greeted by Zaul. Happy and proud to see his young and handsome brother, Rostam gushed: "The progeny of the noble Saum are indeed mighty and brave. How is Kabul, and what does its king say of Rostam?"

Shaghad replied: "Don't mention the name of that vile man to me. At first he treated me with respect, but now he holds me in disdain. He resents his obligation to pay tribute to you and considers himself your equal in lineage and power. He says I am no son of Zaul and that if I am it is of no consequence. I have turned my back on Kabul with a broken heart and sallow cheeks."

Rostam was furious: "Such talk from that man will not remain hidden. And for that reason he has forfeited his crown and his life. I shall bestow his crown upon you."

Shaghad was quartered in luxury as a guest of honor while Rostam gathered an army to invade Kabul. When all was ready, Shaghad went to him and said, "There is no need to invade Kabul with an army. I am certain that the king has sobered up by now and that he is terrified of confronting you. He would never lock horns with you. And I am convinced that he regrets the insulting words he uttered at that banquet. Once we appear in Kabul, he is sure to humble himself before us and beg our pardon for his past behavior."

Rostam agreed that the affair was not worth deploying the army. Instead they set off on the road to Kabul ahead of a hundred equestrian warriors and as many infantrymen under the command of Zavareh. Shaghad dispatched a secret runner to the king of Kabul informing him of Rostam's imminent arrival. When they reached the vicinity of Kabul, the king came out, displaying signs of public contrition. He approached Rostam's horse bareheaded and barefoot. Prostrating himself and crying tears of regret, he appealed for forgiveness. He tearfully implored: "If a slave gets drunk and speaks unwisely, is it not fitting for the master to forgive his folly?"

Rostam took pity on the king, restored his royal garments, and confirmed him as the ruler of Kabul. Grateful for this apparent kindness, the king invited Rostam to a feast. As the matter of the king's insolence appeared to have been resolved, Rostam accepted the invitation. The company retired to a pleasant meadow outside Kabul, where delectable food and wines were set in front of decorated daises. The company partook of food and drank their fill of wine to the melodies of skilled musicians. Then the king volunteered that the grounds were teeming with mountain sheep, deer, and onager. Rostam was lured by the pleasures of a hunt. Eagerly he picked up his bow and ordered his horse to be saddled.

The fate of Rostam must have been sealed for he received
All that hospitality without once suspecting
Foul play or that he was being deceived.

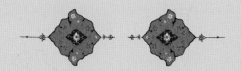

The Death of Rostam

The hunting party took to the plains as trained hawks and falcons flew above. The men spread out over the hunting grounds, and many of them, including Zavareh and Rostam, rode in the direction of the hidden pits. Shaghad anxiously trailed behind.

Rakhsh approached one of the ditches, smelled the freshly overturned dirt, and reared up, stomping the ground. Rostam urged him forward with irritation. Rakhsh found a narrow passage of firm ground between two pits and gingerly ambled on. Furious with the unruliness of his steed, Rostam cracked his whip. As Rakhsh tried to jump over the ditch, the ground gave way and his hind legs sank into the edge of one of the ditches. In vain did he try to hold on to the brink with his front legs. Horse and rider crashed through the false cover of the pit. Thus Rostam and Rakhsh came to lie there, mortally impaled and gashed by the weapons that had been planted at the bottom of the ditch.

Zavareh perished in an adjacent pit, another victim of Shaghad's treachery. The rest of the men accompanying Rostam also died, with the exception of one who made his way back to Zabol with the dreadful news of the death of the hero and his men.

Despite his grave wounds, Rostam made a heroic effort and pulled himself up to the edge of the pit. He now realized that he was the object of a dastardly plot carried out by his brother. When he saw Shaghad coming to inspect the scene, he said, "You have ruined our ancestral home, you wretch of an ill-starred man. You shall regret this evil deed before your impending death."

The conniving Shaghad replied: "You have finally received your just deserts. For how long did you think you could shed blood, plunder, and murder? You have preened yourself as the first knight of Iran for long enough. Now taste death at the hands of the demons."

At this point, the king of Kabul arrived at the pit. Pretending to be surprised, he feigned concern for Rostam and offered to bring a healer to tend to his injuries. It was a cowardly lie, and Rostam knew it. "Give up the pretense. Shed no false tears for me, you wretch of a lowborn man. No physician can help me now. Your time will come soon enough. I am dying before you, and in this I am joining the kings and heroes of yore. I am surely not more exalted than Jamshid, whose body was cleaved in two by Zahhak's henchmen. Nor am I better than the late kings Feraydun and Kay Qobad. Prince Siavosh's neck was slashed by Goruy when his time came as well. They all departed and left us behind. But rest assured that my son Faramarz shall come to avenge me."

He turned to Shaghad with these words: "Now that it has come to this,
at least bring me my bow and arrow so I can defend myself against the
scavenging lions that might want to attack me while I am still alive."

Glad that the death of his famed brother was imminent, Shaghad came
forward carrying Rostam's bow and two arrows. He put them by the side
of the pit and snickered, gloating over his own success. Rostam picked an
arrow, notched it in the bow, and pulled the string. Shaghad panicked and
ran to seek the cover of an old plane tree. The tree bore green leaves but its
trunk was hollowed out by the passage of time. Rostam gathered all his
strength and, despite the pain that rankled him, pulled the bowstring
tighter. Then he loosed a mighty shaft that pierced both the tree and the man
who was hiding behind it. Pinned to the ancient trunk by Rostam's arrow,
Shaghad heaved a sigh and died. Rostam's last words were the prayers of
thanks offered to God for having allowed him to avenge his own death before
the sun could set on his demise.

Back in Zabol, Zaul was beside himself with grief. He wallowed in the dirt and lacerated his face, saying: "From now on I shall wear a shroud and spend my time in mourning for my sons Rostam and Zavareh. The accursed Shaghad has uprooted this majestic tree. How could an ill-omened fox ensnare these elephants in that faraway land? Who has heard of such a thing? What reason do I have to live after this day? What comforts can life and its joys offer me now? Alas, my valiant, world-conquering son who contended with lions is no more!"

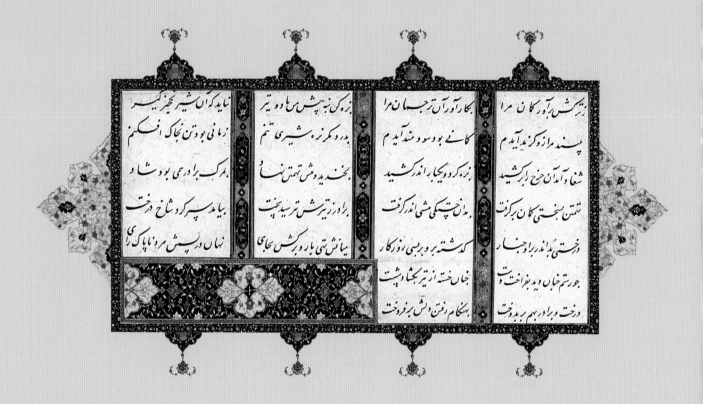

Avenging Rostam's Death

Zaul sent his grandson Faramarz with an army to retrieve the bodies of the dead heroes. Faramarz found the city of Kabul deserted of its leaders. The noblemen had fled, and the ordinary people appeared stricken with bewilderment and grief over the disaster that had befallen the guests of their king. Faramarz went to the hunting grounds, threw himself on the earth and cried for his father and uncle. "I curse the wretched man who did this to you and swear by the soul of our ancestor Saum I shall avenge you. I shall not take off my armor until I have brought low everyone who was connected to this vile plot."

Then he ordered his men to attend to the corpse of Rostam.

They brought the body out and laid it on two bejeweled slabs, as one was not enough for his mammoth size. They sutured his wounds with golden thread and gently washed the blood off his body, hair, and beard. While a mixture of saffron and gray amber burned close by, they rubbed the body with camphor and rosewater and combed Rostam's white beard. Finally, they draped his body in perfumed silk and put it in a coffin that was fashioned out of ivory inlaid teak planks joined together with golden pegs. The coffin was sealed with pitch infused with the essence of musk and rosewater.

The body of Zavareh was pulled out of another pit, similarly prepared for entombment, and placed in a coffin made of the root of an elm tree. At last, the corpse of Rakhsh was hauled out of the pit, restored, washed, draped in silk, and put on the back of an elephant, a labor that lasted two days.

The funerary procession from Kabul traveled for two days and one night to reach the land of Zabol. Crowds of people thronged the procession and helped carry the coffins. Not once were the caskets put down until they reached Zabol. Nor did anyone hear a voice unless it was a wail of lamentation. In Zabol the bodies were taken to a garden and put on two golden platforms for display. The people of the city, both freeborn and slave, brought flowers and musk and mourned their fallen hero:

"What has befallen you? Why, of all the perfumes of the world, do you require only musk and gray amber? Why are you no longer shining on the battlefield and at the center of the banquet? Why don't you generously give a treasure of worldly goods as you used to do? Alas, you are gone from among us. Live forever in paradise, for your soul was the essence of justice and valor."

Once Rostam and Zavareh were consigned to the darkness of the luxurious crypt that was prepared for them, Faramarz gathered a great avenging army. At dawn the army left the gates of Zabol to the sound of trumpets and drums. The king of Kabul also gathered a massive army to engage the forces of Faramarz. A dark wind rose as the two ironclad armies clashed on the battlefield. The jangling of steel and the throbbing of drums deafened the ear. Faramarz penetrated the heart of the enemy with a small contingent of brave warriors and captured the king of Kabul alive. The king's army panicked and ran away, but the army of Zabol gave chase and set upon them like wolves, turning the dirt into a reddish mud with the blood of the fleeing enemy. Those who were not killed escaped without a care for the families and homes they left behind.

The king of Kabul was brought to the hunting ground in a trunk hoisted on an elephant. He was tied up and suspended over one of the pits as blood streamed from his mouth. Later he and forty of his relatives were executed. Firewood was piled on the plane tree where Shaghad remained pinned by Rostam's arrow. The man and the tree burned in the flames.

Faramarz appointed a king for Kabul as the entire clan of the old one had been annihilated. He went back to Zabol, but there was no joy in this victory. The public lamentation for Rostam lasted a whole year. No one was as stricken by the death of Rostam as Rudabeh. In her grief one day, she told Zaul: "Let us weep for the loss of Rostam. No one has ever suffered a darker day than this since the world began."

Zaul reproached his wife, saying that extreme hunger alone was harder to bear. Rudabeh was offended and swore an oath to abstain from food. For a week she mournfully communed with her departed son. As Rudabeh's eyes grew dim and her body became feeble, her attendants followed her around, afraid that she would harm herself. In her grief and hunger she was beset by delusions. As night fell, she found a dead snake in a stream and attempted to bite off its poisonous head. An attendant caught her in time and led her away to her quarters to be nursed back to health. Later, when she had recovered, Rudabeh agreed with Zaul that in extreme hunger, sorrow and happiness become indistinguishable. She had grown wiser about the tragedy of losing her heroic son. "Rostam is gone," she said, "and we, too, shall join him. We shall all be one with the creator of the universe. Oh God, forgive the sins of my son, admit him to paradise, and reward him for his good deeds."

The Reign of Bahman

When King Goshtasp knew his time of departure from this world was nigh, he called his adviser Jamasp and confided in him: "I was so heartbroken by the death of Esfandiar that I have not had one good day since his death. Now I pass from this world entrusting the crown to his son Bahman. Let him reign and let my brother Pashutan serve as his royal adviser."

Rostam had groomed Bahman for the royal arts, according to the pledge he had made to Esfandiar. When his training was complete, Bahman had returned to his grandfather's court on the condition that the old animosities be set aside. The crown prince came to his grandfather's deathbed and received the keys to the royal treasury. Goshtasp reflected on his own shortcomings and advised Bahman in the art of ruling as a righteous king: "Keep the wise close at hand and eschew the wicked. I give you my throne and my treasures, as a dying king who dominated the world for one hundred and twenty years."

After a royal funeral, the king was consigned to a magnificent crypt in a coffin made of ivory and ebony.

Bahman sat on the throne and generously endowed the army with worldly goods. He addressed the assembly of knights and noblemen with words that expressed his desire for avenging his father's death: "You all remember what Rostam and that old sorcerer Zaul did in the course of the terrible events that led to the martyrdom of my father. Now his son Faramarz continues to disrespect us. I can't entertain any thoughts but that of avenging my father, Esfandiar, and my brothers Nushazar and Mehrnush. They were all murdered by the lowly men of Zabol.

"Honor demands that I even the score and slay those who killed my father. Manuchehr exacted revenge for the murder of his father, Iraj, on his dastardly uncles Tur and Salm. Kay Khosrow killed Afrasiab and extinguished his hearth as punishment for the murder of his father, Prince Siavosh. My own

grandfather Goshtasp sought justice for the death of his father, Lohrasp, when he went to war with the king of Turan. Even Rostam's son Faramarz killed his father's murderers and desecrated their bodies on the plains of Kabul. I, too, deserve to exact revenge for the peerless Esfandiar. Now advise me. What is your counsel?"

The knights and noblemen pledged their obedience to Bahman's commands. One of those assembled said, "When it comes to the affairs of the past you are more knowledgeable. But this much we know: We are all your servants. Do what you wish to win fame and glory in the world. None of us will disobey your commands."

These words inflamed Bahman's desire for revenge. Soon the drums of war were sounding and the air was thick with the dust kicked up by an army of one hundred thousand soldiers leaving the capital for the banks of the river Hirmand. A messenger from Bahman went across the river and into the realm of the clan of Saum with this message for Zaul: "The yearning to avenge the death of Esfandiar and my brothers is within me. My life is bitter. I have come for revenge and I shall dye the river Hirmand with the blood of the wrongdoers."

Pain and sorrow filled the heart of Zaul when he heard this message. He responded with these words: "The affair of your father was a matter of preordained fate. Not even dragons and lions can escape the verdict of destiny. I grieved for Esfandiar. And when your father entrusted your care to Rostam, you did not suffer harm at our hands.

"Besides, you ought to remember the services Saum and Rostam rendered to the kings of Iran. Your own ancestors owe a debt of gratitude to our heroes. Come now and let us assuage your rage. I will give you all the riches of Rostam and all the treasures of Saum. We will turn a new page; you will be our shepherd and we will be your docile flock."

Zaul enriched the messenger with a horse and gifts and sent him back with his plea of reconciliation. But Bahman was not mollified. He rode into the city of Zabol and looked down on Zaul, who had come out to plead with him again: "This is the time for forgiveness, the time of cleansing the heart of the resentments of the past," Zaul said. "You grew up among us. Pardon us our sins in exchange for the services we have rendered you. Leave the past behind and don't seek to punish the dead. Humbled and leaning on a cane, this is, I, Zaul, the son of Saum. I implore you for mercy."

Ignoring the advice of his counselors, Bahman rejected this gesture of extreme humility from the elder knight and ordered that his feet be placed in shackles. Then he ransacked the treasury of the house of Saum, sending back caravans loaded with gold and silver, Arabian horses with golden bridles, jewel-encrusted weapons, sacks of rare spices, and many slaves. Whatever Rostam had gathered over the years was carried off. The treasury of Zabol was plundered while the lords of Iran received heaps of gold and lavish crowns.

Faramarz was in Bost when he heard of Bahman's sack of Zabol and the mistreatment of his grandfather Zaul. Outraged, he gathered his generals and said, "Zavareh told my father more than once that Bahman would one day seek vengeance for his father's death. At his own peril did Rostam ignore this advice. Now Bahman's army has come upon us like a rising black cloud. He has put my grandfather in bondage and plundered our treasury. Advise me, my lords: What is your counsel?"

The leaders of the army pledged their obedience to Faramarz as they had obeyed his forefathers. His head full of memories of Rostam's exploits, Faramarz donned his armor and led his men into combat against the enemy. Bahman, too, brought an army forward. The two sides lined up on the plain of Gourabad. The dust of their horses formed a thick cloud. The trumpets sounded and the drums rolled. Arrows poured from the sky like raindrops from black clouds. Maces and blades grew out of thin air.

The battle raged for three days and three nights. On the fourth day a wind blew against the forces of Faramarz. Bahman saw his opportunity in the change of the wind and took to the field. With the wind at his back, the young king drew his sword and led an attack, routing the armies of Zabol and Kabul until none was left on the battlefield. They either died or ran away, leaving their leaders behind. So many had been killed on both sides that their tangled corpses resembled a range of hills.

A brave lion descended from a line of brave lions, Faramarz fought along
with a small band of his followers until he was injured and captured. He
was brought to the king in chains. Bahman took no pity on his captive.
He had Faramarz suspended upside down from the gallows and killed in a
torrent of arrows.

The Epic Ends

Appalled by the cruelty of Bahman, Pashutan rose to speak: "King of truth and justice, if it was vengeance you sought, now you have it. Don't command or consent to further carnage and plunder. Fear God and have shame before us. Beware of the play of fate. It wantonly raises some high or lowers others to the dust. Didn't your own father come to his final rest in a casket? Didn't the legendary Rostam meet his end at the bottom of a pit in some hunting ground? Keep your hand from harassing noble souls while you are king. Free Zaul from captivity. The stars have favored you, but the old knight's sigh could incur the wrath of the heavens and reverse your fortunes. And don't forget that you, like the line of kings starting from Kay Qobad, owe your crown to the labors of Rostam. Indeed, you are more indebted to him than to your own father and grandfather."

Regretting his excesses, Bahman issued orders for the disbanding of the camp and a return to the capital. He also released Zaul from captivity and arranged for a proper funeral for Faramarz. When Rudabeh was reunited with Zaul, she raised a cry of lamentation for her dead son: "Woe is me, my brave, departed Rostam. You were descended from a line of exalted knights. You outshined Goshtasp on his throne. Now your treasure houses are robbed, your son is murdered in a shower of arrows, and your old father is made a slave. May no one share your fate. May the land be cleansed from the seed of Esfandiar."

The sound of weeping rose from the clan of Saum as the tragedy of Rostam was always fresh in their minds. Bahman was frightened by the curse of Rudabeh and made haste to depart. As the mountains were painted red with the setting sun that evening, the army of Bahman left the land of Zabol.

Pashutan urged his king to make haste
And leave the plain of Zabol as Rudabeh
Started to curse Bahman and lambast

Him and lament that he had razed
The city of Zabol and enslaved
The benefactors by whom he was raised.

Magnificent buildings decay by the dint of time
And exposure to the elements wrecks even a house of flint
But the poetic edifice I have erected in rhyme

Shall endure the contagion of the rain and the sun.
For three decades have I thus suffered to restore
This Persian tongue and now my work is done.

تاریخ انجام شاهنامه

August 2008 – October 2012

Genealogy of the Main Characters

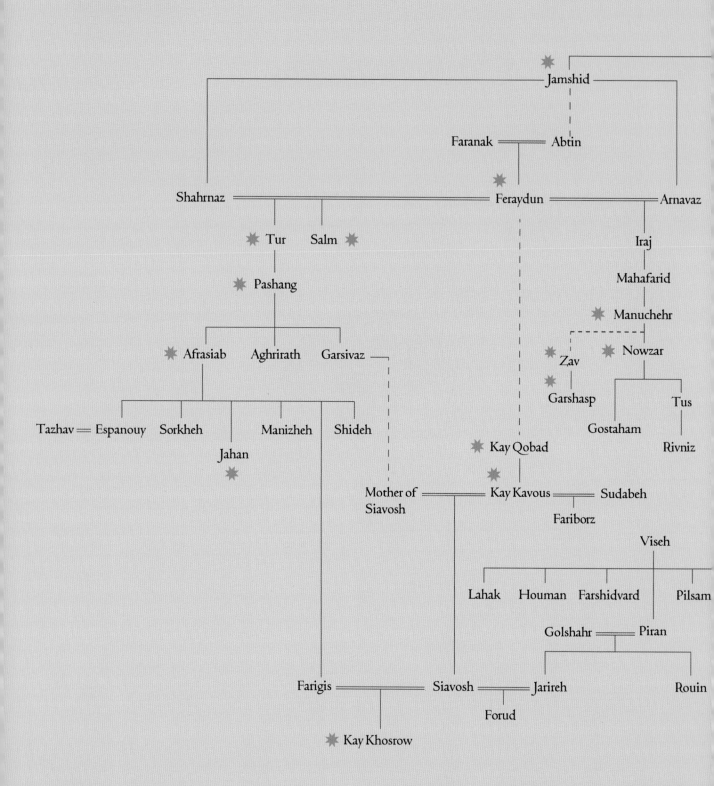

Circa 2nd millennium BCE   ZARATHUSTRA BEGINS HIS TEACHINGS

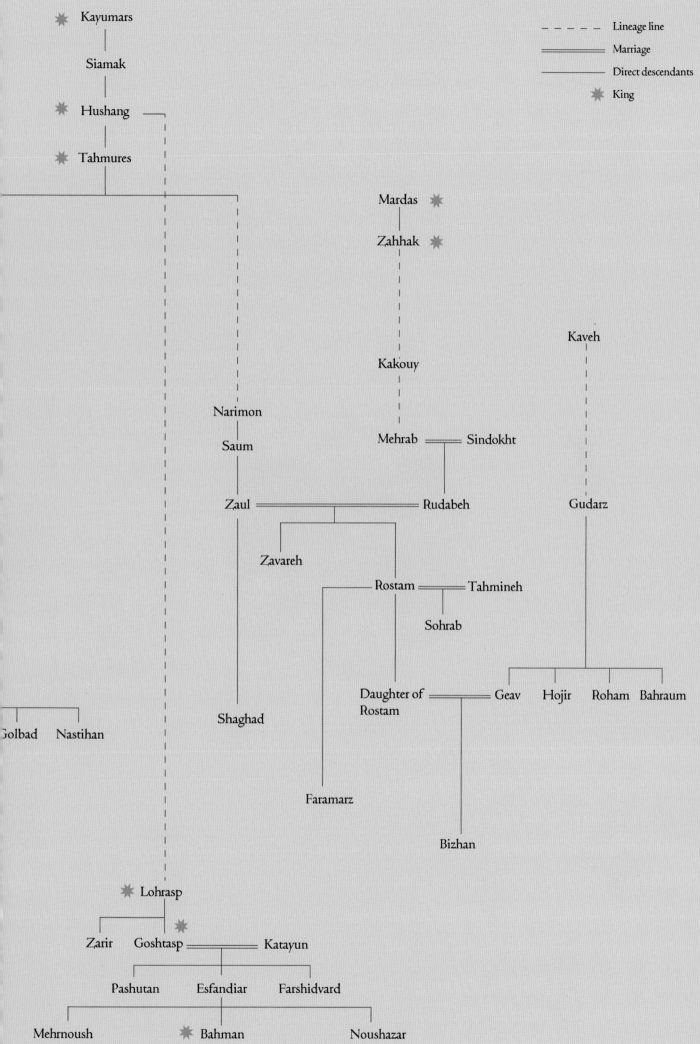

Kayumars

Siamak

Hushang

Tahmures

Mardas

Zahhak

Kaveh

Kakouy

Narimon

Saum

Mehrab — Sindokht

Gudarz

Zaul = Rudabeh

Zavareh

Rostam = Tahmineh

Sohrab

Golbad   Nastihan

Shaghad

Daughter of Rostam = Geav   Hojir   Roham   Bahraum

Faramarz

Bizhan

Lohrasp

Zarir   Goshtasp = Katayun

Pashutan   Esfandiar   Farshidvard

Mehrnoush   Bahman   Noushazar

Unraveling the Visual Culture of *Shahnameh*

Making of the Panels

The following pages will give the reader a glimpse into the pleasurable yet painstaking process of creating the new illustrations in this book. There are thousands of single elements taken from hundreds of miniatures, illuminations, and lithographs, all culled and put together to create this new edition of *Shahnameh*.

The visual elements used in this book were collected from the region heavily influenced by classical Persian painting: Iran, Mughal India, and the Ottoman Empire from the fifteenth to the mid-nineteenth centuries. My sources include a vast array of folios, not only from the *Shahnameh* but from other tales as well.

Introduction to the Illustrations

I created the panels in this edition much like a film editor or a deejay weaves together different components to create a new work of art. Instead of sampling sounds or frames, I used bits and pieces from miniatures and lithographs. Every panel contains upwards of one hundred and twenty elements that were digitally collaged into new illustrations. In many of the panels, elements from different eras, schools, and stories were seamlessly mixed together.

Each detail on the page went through a laborious process of research, scanning, cutting, composing, and retouching. In general, except for natural elements such as clouds, rocks, flowers, and cliffs, there are few elements that repeat. Although the panels were heavily manipulated, there is little that had been drawn from scratch. The only new elements are stars in the night skies and the halos (*farr*) of the kings. This patchwork of ingredients was sedulously unraveled from the original works and weaved back together into new compositions.

A technique I often used was blurring the foreground or background to create a depth of field, giving readers the feeling that they are looking through a camera lens (e.g., pages 306, 350).

In the example on the facing page, you can see the process of creating the character Sohrab. In this panel, he is sitting with his mother, Tahmineh (page 220). First I examined my source materials for a sitting character that represented Sohrab in my mind's eye. I found a late-fifteenth-century painting from an unknown artist (no. 1) sitting with a hawk. I liked the pose and basic structure but the face and clothing had severely deteriorated. I needed a face that I could establish as Sohrab for the whole chapter. It was much like auditioning actors for a film, searching for the perfect face to fit a scene. I was drawn to a face from a seventeenth-century painting by Moin Mosavvar from the school of Esfahan (nos. 2 and 3). However, the face did not have an ear. I found the right ear in another painting from the early seventeenth century by Reza Abassi (nos. 4 and 5). The next step was to carefully emulate the brush strokes of the original masters and put my Sohrab together. Finally I cleaned and restored the dress, hands, and hawk (nos. 6 and 7). Later, as I continued to create panels for Sohrab, I used the same face on different bodies to fit the action.

Creating New Characters

Creating consistent and recognizable main characters was important to me. Often I used portrayals of existing figures and only enhanced them. Other times I recast random figures, so to speak, into new roles. Some characters grow old with time, such as in the cases of Rostam and Afrasiab. Rostam, for example, grows from a young boy into an old man (see above).

In some panels, finding the perfect pose to fit a particular action from my source materials was almost impossible. I needed to manipulate body parts of existing characters to fit the action described in the text. In the example below, I used the body of an existing depiction of Kaveh from the sixteenth-century *Shahnameh Shah Tahmasp* (pages 40–41) and a face from a different source. I used the existing pose for one scene then changed his stance for a different action later in the text. For instance, the figure of Kaveh holding the standard of Kaveh was built from fifteen different pieces.

In this scene, the Simorgh heals Rakhsh, Rostam's horse. I combined two different birds from different schools of painting, creating a dramatic new Simorgh. The first (no. 1) came from the school of Tabriz from the mid-sixteenth century. The other

was extracted from a miniature of the late-sixteenth-century Shiraz school. The arrows were taken from an eighteenth-century Indian miniature.

Making New Patterns

Sometimes stories unfold at specific locations that play important roles, for example, the Sepand fortress (page 223) and the Kalat fortress (page 364).

The Kalat fortress (no. 2) from chapter nine was built entirely from a small section of a single miniature (no. 1). Since the location in this story is key, I wanted to illustrate the castle in a way that would give readers the sense that they are witnessing the action from different perspectives. Even the inside of the castle uses the same elements, giving the impression that the walls have opened up to reveal the intimate scenes between mother and son (pages 359, 374).

While illustrating Jarireh's nightmare, (pages 370–71), I looked everywhere in my source materials for a lone sleeping woman. When I could not find one, I decided to create the scene, borrowing from an Iranian miniature (*Shahnameh Shah Tahmasp*) of a young couple sleeping together (no. 3). I moved the female character to the center of the mattress and completely eliminated the male character, retouching the pattern on the blanket and pillow so that it looked seamless. Since Jarireh is a recurring character, I copied her face from a previous panel and, to complete my new composition, closed her eyes to give the impression that she is dreaming.

3

4

In the case of the Sepand fortress, I found a sixteenth-century Indian painting (no. 1) by Jekchehoon. I dismantled the original painting and rebuilt the fortress, then retouched it to fit the scene. Because this fortress was used on every page, I reconfigured it differently to give readers the feeling that they were looking at it from various vantage points.

Examples 5 and 6 show the process of building and coloring the additional characters that were inserted into the fortress. The original was a nineteenth-century lithograph.

Repetition

The use of repetition has been a common theme in Iranian art for the past seven centuries, particularly in ceramics and illuminations. I have continued in this tradition, using repetition with small variations to create a sense of drama and pageantry (see pages 192, 205, 386). In this next example one can see how I have created an army out of only three elements.

On page 30 (no. 4) I created an army constructed solely of two small portions of two different lithographs from the mid-nineteenth century: one by Aligholi Khuie (no. 1) and the other by Ostad Sattar (no. 2). The banners in the background were added as a final touch and taken from a scene from *Shah Juki's Shahnameh* from the fifteenth century (no. 3).

On the facing page, one can see another example of how repetition was used to create a massive army.

My access to lithographs depicting large armies was limited. Or maybe there were not many in the first place. I decided to create a background army from the only source I had, a mid-nineteenth-century lithograph by Ostad Sattar (no. 1). Each color (no. 2) indicates a different layer. By carefully extracting the mountains from the original and repeating the heads of the troops into the horizon, I created the illusion of an enormous army. This illustration is composed of eleven background layers and thirty-six foreground layers.

Stitching

A technique that I used a few times to create a sense of drama was the stitching of larger elements together. In this example (no. 3), Manuchehr chases after Tur (page 74). For this chase scene I created an illustration that graphically rises to a crescendo with the action described in the text. I stitched together four different lithographs. Below, each color represents a different element. Another example of this technique can be viewed on page 378. The miniature in the background for "The Night Attack" consists of nine different elements woven together to create a sense of mayhem.

Retouching

The final step in the construction of a panel was retouching. After a panel had been composed, every individual element went through the time-consuming and meticulous process of cleanup, restoration, and enhancement. The example below and on the facing page reveals the labor involved in this process. On the facing page, one can see the progress, starting with an original folio (nos. 1–3) and ending with the finished element for the illustration on page 283.

A Final Word

Creating the illustrations for this book has taken close to ten thousand hours of research and dedication. This endeavor was possible only because of the passion I have for the visual traditions of my culture and my desire to share them with a new generation of art lovers, regardless of their origins or traditions.

This book is a project of

**Fictionville
Studio**

www.theepicofthepersiankings.com

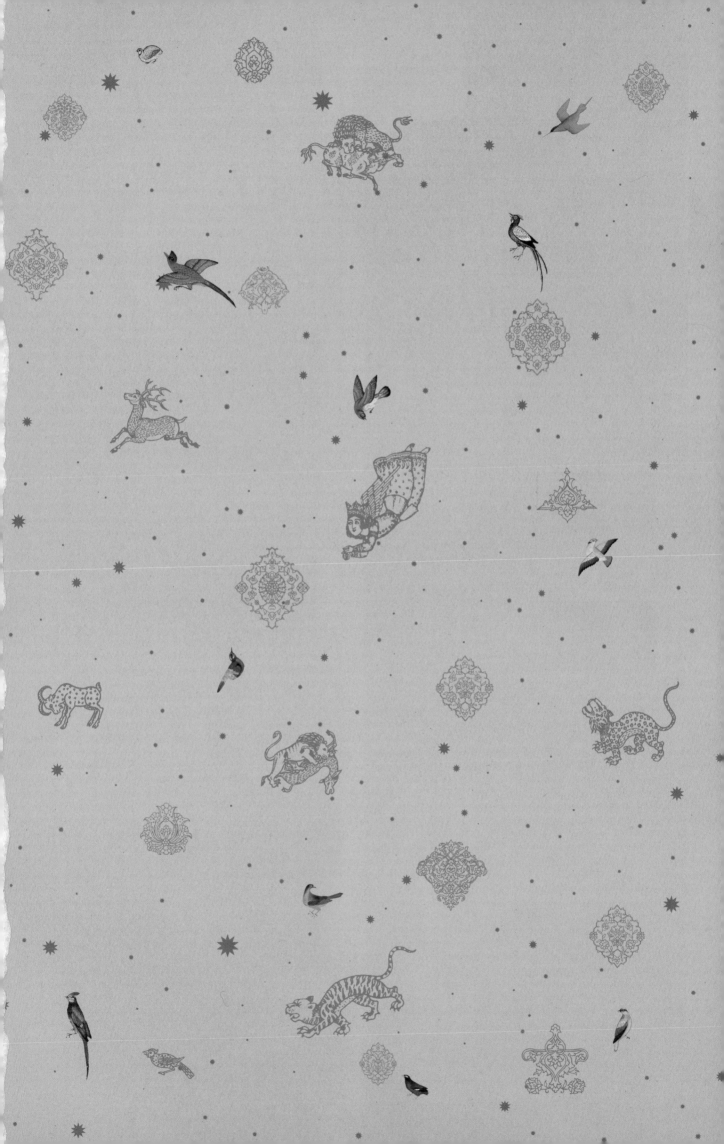

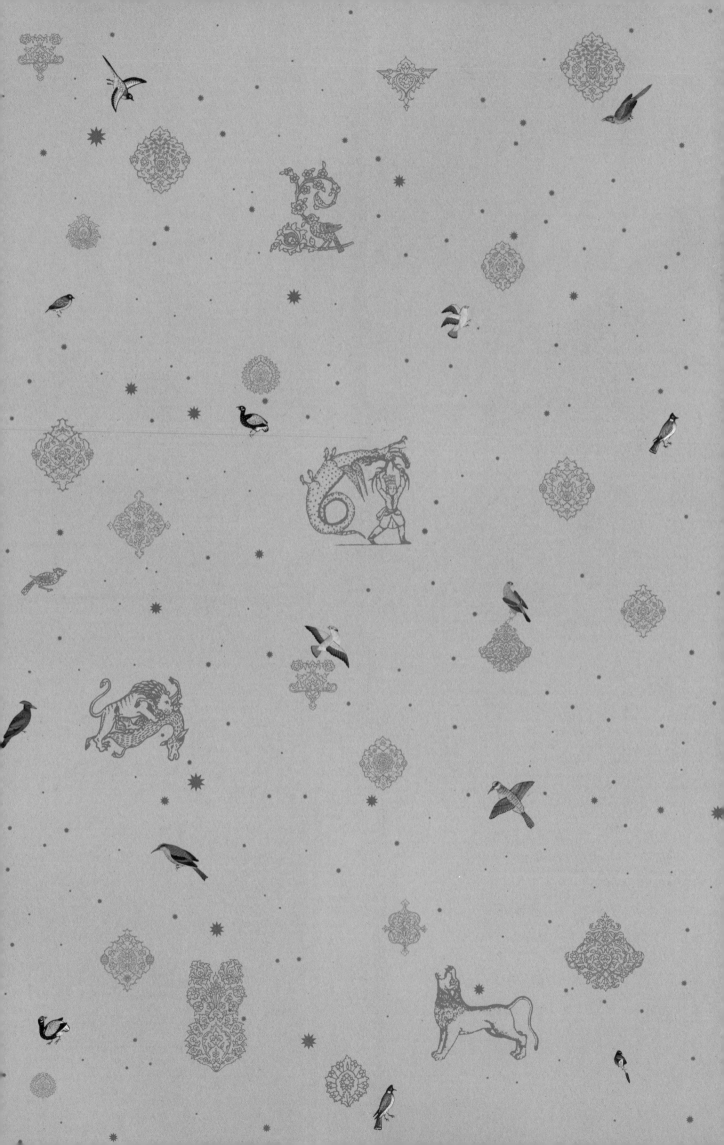